SALADS

Lobster, Papaya & Avocado Salad (page 14)

CRAB, AVOCADO & DRIED TOMATO LOUIS

THIS STYLISH MAIN DISH OFFERS AN UPDATE OF THE TRADITIONAL LOUIS DRESSING, WITH DRIED TOMATOES TAKING THE PLACE OF THE USUAL TOMATO-BASED CHILI SAUCE. TO ADJUST THE SALAD'S RICHNESS, SERVE THE DRESSING ON THE SIDE AND SPOON ON JUST THE AMOUNT YOU LIKE. SERVE WITH A CHILLED CHARDONNAY AND PLENTY OF CRUSTY SOURDOUGH BREAD.

20 MINUTES

Dried Tomato Louis Dressing (below)

4 ounces thin green beans (ends removed)

4 cups lightly packed finely shredded iceberg lettuce, rinsed and crisped

6 to 8 ounces cooked crabmeat

1 medium-size tomato (about 6 oz.), cut into wedges

1 hard-cooked large egg, cut into wedges

1 medium-size firm-ripe avocado (about 6 oz.), pitted, peeled, and sliced

Lemon wedges

DRIED TOMATO LOUIS DRESSING

2 tablespoons whipping cream

¼ cup mayonnaise

2 to 3 tablespoons oil-packed dried tomatoes, drained well and minced

2 tablespoons minced green onion

2 tablespoons lemon juice

2 teaspoons tomato paste

Ground red pepper (cayenne)

1. Prepare Dried Tomato Louis Dressing.

2. In a 1- to 1½-quart pan, bring about 2 inches of water to a boil over high heat. Drop beans into boiling water; return to a boil and cook, uncovered, until beans are just tender-crisp when pierced (3 to 5 minutes). Drain beans and immerse in ice water until cool; then drain well again.

3. Divide lettuce between 2 dinner plates. Mound crab in center of lettuce. Decoratively arrange tomato and egg wedges, beans, and avocado around crab. Garnish with lemon wedges. Offer dressing to add to taste.

PER SERVING WITHOUT DRESSING: 288 calories, 15 g total fat, 3 g saturated fat, 202 mg cholesterol, 323 mg sodium, 16 g carbohydrates, 4 g fiber, 27 g protein, 217 mg calcium, 4 mg iron

DRIED TOMATO LOUIS DRESSING

In a chilled small, deep bowl, beat cream with an electric mixer on high speed until it holds soft peaks. Gently stir in mayonnaise, dried tomatoes, onion, lemon juice, and tomato paste. Season to taste with red pepper. Cover and refrigerate until ready to serve. Makes about ¾ cup.

PER TABLESPOON: 49 calories, 5 g total fat, 1 g saturated fat, 5 mg cholesterol, 47 mg sodium, 1 g carbohydrates, 0 g fiber, 0 g protein, 4 mg calcium, 0 mg iron

SEARED SEA SCALLOPS ON WARM CHANTERELLE, CORN & BACON SALAD

IMPRESS SOMEONE SPECIAL WITH THIS SOPHISTICATED FIRST COURSE. LARGE WHOLE SEA SCALLOPS ARE SEARED ON BOTH SIDES AND SERVED ATOP A WARM MIXTURE OF SAUTÉED FRESH CHANTERELLES, CRISP BACON, RED BELL PEPPER, AND CORN. TARRAGON LENDS ITS BOLD, DISTINCTIVE FLAVOR TO BOTH THE SHELLFISH AND THE VEGETABLE MÉLANGE.

25 MINUTES

To Have on Hand for Vegetarian Cooking

Canned vegetable broth

Canned beans, such as black, red kidney, and cannellini (white kidney) or other white beans

Fresh garlic

Onions

Fresh lemons (for peel and juice)

Olive oil

Vegetable oil, such as canola, corn, or safflower

Soy sauce

Eggs

Quick-cooking brown rice

Polenta

Quinoa

Dried lentils

Packaged baked pizza crusts

To Have on Hand for Desserts

Brown and granulated sugar

Chocolate (semisweet or bittersweet chocolate chips and bars; milk chocolate bars)

Unsweetened cocoa

Nuts, such as pecans, macadamias, walnuts, and almonds

Dried and candied fruits

Ice cream, sorbet, and sherbet

Ice cream toppings, such as chocolate and caramel sauce

Amaretti cookies

Brandy and favorite liqueurs (orange-flavored, amaretto)

VEGETARIAN ENTRÉES

Main dishes that depend for their flavor and substance on generous amounts of vegetables require good technique with kitchen knives. Practice with your chef's knife until you can chop onions and other vegetables with an efficient rocking motion. Garlic is a popular seasoning for vegetarian entrées, so it's useful to be able to peel it quickly. Learn the trick of flattening a clove of garlic with the side of your knife so that you can then remove the papery peel with minimum effort.

Grains such as rice, couscous, barley, and bulgur are popular components of the vegetarian pantry; look for quick-cooking varieties of those that take longer than 30 minutes to cook in their usual forms. Although they're low in fat, some whole grains do contain oils that can become rancid in hot climates. If you plan to store them for long, keep them in the refrigerator or freezer.

DESSERTS

You may not always serve dessert, but when you do, it ought to be special. Keep an eye out for seasonal fruits when they're at their best—berries in spring and summer; apricots, peaches, and plums at the peak of summer; grapes and melons in early autumn; and pears, apples, and citrus fruits as fall slips into winter.

A noted restaurant pastry chef says that people eat the main course for nourishment, but dessert satisfies a need for emotional fulfillment. Fixing a fancy dessert can be a tall order when time is tight, though! Still, you can accomplish a lot with a good supply of chocolate and some favorite flavors of ice cream tucked away in the freezer.

Ready-baked cakes and cookies are another good start for appealing desserts. Use your imagination as you embellish them with fresh fruit, whipped cream or prepared lemon curd, and toasted nuts. Keep nuts in sturdy plastic bags in the freezer to prevent them from developing off-flavors.

ABOUT OUR NUTRITIONAL DATA

For each recipe in this book, we provide a nutritional analysis prepared by Hill Nutrition Associates, Inc., of Florida. The analysis states calorie count; grams of total fat and saturated fat; milligrams of cholesterol and sodium; grams of carbohydrates, fiber, and protein; and milligrams of calcium and iron. Generally, the analysis applies to a single serving, based on two servings per recipe and the amount of each ingredient. If a range is given for the amount of an ingredient, the analysis is based on the average of the figures given.

The nutritional analysis does not include optional ingredients or those for which no specific amount is stated. If an ingredient is listed with a substitution, the information was calculated using the first choice.

2 ounces fresh chanterelles or regular mushrooms

2 slices thick-cut bacon (about 3 oz. *total*), cut crosswise into ¼-inch-wide strips

6 large sea scallops (about 8 oz. *total*), *each* 1½ to 2 inches in diameter

3 tablespoons tarragon wine vinegar

1 tablespoon olive oil

1 clove garlic, minced or pressed

1 large shallot, thinly sliced

½ cup diced red bell pepper

1 cup fresh yellow corn kernels

1 tablespoon chopped fresh tarragon or ½ teaspoon dried tarragon

Salt and freshly ground pepper

2 cups lightly packed frisée, rinsed and crisped

Tarragon sprigs

1. Place mushrooms in a plastic food bag. Fill bag with water; then seal bag and shake to wash mushrooms. Drain mushrooms well; if they are still gritty, repeat rinsing. Trim and discard stem ends. Cut larger mushrooms lengthwise into ¼-inch-thick slices; leave small ones whole. Set mushrooms aside.

2. Cook bacon in a wide frying pan over medium-high heat, stirring often, until brown and crisp (4 to 5 minutes). Remove bacon from pan with a slotted spoon and drain on paper towels. Set aside.

3. Rinse scallops, pat dry, and add to pan, flat side down. Cook for 2 minutes. Then sprinkle scallops with 1 tablespoon of the vinegar, turn over with a spatula, and continue to cook until well browned on bottom and just opaque but still moist in center; cut to test (about 2 more minutes). Transfer to a plate; cover and keep warm.

4. To pan, add mushrooms, oil, garlic, shallot, and bell pepper. Cook, stirring often, until vegetables begin to brown (about 5 minutes). Add corn, remaining 2 tablespoons vinegar, and any scallop juices that have accumulated on plate. Cook, stirring often, until almost all liquid has evaporated (1 to 2 minutes). Add bacon and chopped tarragon; season to taste with salt and pepper.

5. Line 2 dinner plates with frisée. Mound mushroom mixture atop frisée. Place 3 scallops on each salad alongside mushroom mixture; garnish with tarragon sprigs.

PER SERVING: 545 calories, 34 g total fat, 10 g saturated fat, 66 mg cholesterol, 573 mg sodium, 36 g carbohydrates, 6 g fiber, 30 g protein, 240 mg calcium, 4 mg iron

Seared Sea Scallops on Warm Chanterelle, Corn & Bacon Salad

LOBSTER, PAPAYA & AVOCADO SALAD

Pictured on page 11

SIT DOWN TO DINNER AND PREPARE TO BE DAZZLED! THIS SALAD IS A TREAT FOR THE EYES. COMBINED WITH FRUIT AND TINY SWEET TOMATOES, JUST ONE LOBSTER TAIL IS ENOUGH FOR TWO SERVINGS. USUALLY SOLD FROZEN, LOBSTER TAILS ARE EASIER TO HANDLE THAN THE WHOLE SHELLFISH. IF YOU'RE REALLY PRESSED FOR TIME, PURCHASE A COOKED LOBSTER FROM YOUR FISH MARKET AND HAVE THE MEAT REMOVED FROM THE SHELL.

30 MINUTES

Champagne-Citrus Dressing (below)

1 spiny or rock lobster tail (8 to 9 oz.), thawed if frozen

4 large butter lettuce leaves, rinsed and crisped

½ small papaya, peeled, seeded, and sliced crosswise

1 small avocado (about 5 oz.), pitted, peeled, and sliced

½ cup whole tiny cherry tomatoes; or ½ cup halved regular-size cherry tomatoes

2 tablespoons chopped cilantro

Lime wedges

CHAMPAGNE-CITRUS DRESSING

1 tablespoon champagne vinegar or white wine vinegar

1 teaspoon shredded orange peel

½ teaspoon shredded lime peel

1 tablespoon orange juice

1 tablespoon lime juice

2 tablespoons olive oil

2 teaspoons Dijon mustard

2 teaspoons honey

⅛ teaspoon crushed red pepper flakes

1. In a 4- to 5-quart pan, bring about 2 quarts water to a boil over high heat. While water is heating, prepare Champagne-Citrus Dressing and set aside.

2. When water comes to a boil, add lobster and cook until meat is just opaque but still moist in thickest part; cut to test (about 10 minutes). Drain lobster and immerse in ice water until cool; then drain well again. With scissors, clip fins from sides of soft undershell of lobster tail; then snip along edges. Lift off and discard undershell. Working from body end, use a fork to remove meat from shell in one piece. Thinly slice meat crosswise.

3. Line 2 dinner plates with lettuce. Decoratively arrange lobster, papaya, avocado, and tomatoes atop lettuce; sprinkle with cilantro. Spoon dressing over salads and garnish with lime wedges.

CHAMPAGNE-CITRUS DRESSING

In a small bowl, whisk together vinegar, orange peel, lime peel, orange juice, lime juice, oil, mustard, honey, and red pepper flakes to blend.

PER SERVING: 337 calories, 22 g total fat, 3 g saturated fat, 50 mg cholesterol, 395 mg sodium, 20 g carbohydrates, 2 g fiber, 16 g protein, 68 mg calcium, 1 mg iron

QUICK NIÇOISE SALAD WITH LEMON-CAPER AÏOLI

WHEN THE WEATHER HEATS UP, A CHILLED MAIN-DISH SALAD IS A WELCOME CHOICE FOR LUNCH OR SUPPER. CANNED TUNA, RED POTATOES, SLENDER GREEN BEANS, HARD-COOKED EGGS, AND RIPE TOMATOES ARE THE KEY INGREDIENTS IN THIS CLASSIC DISH; A LEMON-CAPER AÏOLI IS SPOONED OVER INDIVIDUAL SERVINGS.

25 MINUTES

Quick Niçoise Salad with Lemon-Caper Aïoli

3 small red thin-skinned potatoes (*each* 1½ to 2 inches in diameter), scrubbed and cut into quarters

4 ounces thin green beans (ends removed)

Lemon-Caper Aïoli (below)

6 large butter lettuce leaves, rinsed and crisped

1 can (about 6 oz.) oil-packed solid white tuna, drained

1 medium-size firm-ripe tomato (about 6 oz.), cut into wedges

2 hard-cooked large eggs, cut into quarters

¼ cup Niçoise olives

¼ cup thinly sliced mild red onion, separated into rings

Canned anchovy fillets (optional)

LEMON-CAPER AÏOLI

⅓ cup mayonnaise

1 large clove garlic, minced or pressed

½ teaspoon shredded lemon peel

2 teaspoons lemon juice

2 teaspoons chopped drained capers

Dash of liquid hot pepper seasoning

1. Place potatoes in a 2- to 3-quart pan and add enough water to cover. Cover and bring to a boil over high heat; then reduce heat and simmer, covered, until potatoes are tender when pierced (7 to 9 minutes). About 3 minutes before potatoes are done, drop beans into pan. Continue to cook until beans are just tender-crisp when pierced. Drain potatoes and beans and immerse in ice water until cool; then drain well again.

2. While vegetables are cooking, prepare Lemon-Caper Aïoli.

3. Line 2 dinner plates with lettuce. Arrange tuna, tomato, eggs, potatoes, and beans in separate mounds on lettuce; place olives in center. Scatter onion rings over salads. If using anchovies, drain well; then arrange in a crisscross pattern atop salads. Offer Lemon-Caper Aïoli to spoon over salads to taste.

PER SERVING WITHOUT DRESSING: 355 calories, 13 g total fat, 3 g saturated fat, 246 mg cholesterol, 597 mg sodium, 27 g carbohydrates, 5 g fiber, 32 g protein, 76 mg calcium, 3 mg iron

LEMON-CAPER AÏOLI

In a bowl, stir together mayonnaise, garlic, lemon peel, lemon juice, capers, and hot pepper seasoning. Makes about ½ cup.

PER TABLESPOON: 67 calories, 7 g total fat, 1 g saturated fat, 5 mg cholesterol, 86 mg sodium, 1 g carbohydrates, 0 g fiber, 0 g protein, 3 mg calcium, 0 mg iron

THAI PORK, MINT & PEANUT SALAD
MANY TRADITIONAL THAI DISHES ARE FIERY HOT, BUT THIS MAIN-DISH SALAD IS RELATIVELY TAME—BY COMPARISON, AT ANY RATE. PORK TENDERLOIN IS BRUSHED WITH A GINGER-AND-LIME DRESSING, THEN GRILLED, THINLY SLICED, AND SERVED ON A BED OF GREENS WITH COOL CUCUMBERS, CARROTS, AND AROMATIC MINT. ALONGSIDE, SERVE GLASSES OF COLD BEER AND MANGOES WITH A SQUEEZE OF FRESH LIME.

25 MINUTES

Ginger-Lime Dressing (below)

8 ounces pork tenderloin

3 cups lightly packed bite-size pieces red leaf lettuce, rinsed and crisped

½ cup thinly sliced cucumber

⅓ cup matchstick-size carrot sticks

2 tablespoons chopped fresh mint

¼ cup chopped roasted salted peanuts

GINGER-LIME DRESSING

1 tablespoon seasoned rice vinegar

1 tablespoon hoisin sauce

2 tablespoons lime juice

2 teaspoons minced fresh ginger

¼ teaspoon chili oil or crushed red pepper flakes

1 teaspoon Asian fish sauce (*nuoc mam* or *nam pla*), optional

1. Prepare Ginger-Lime Dressing and set aside.

2. Brush pork all over with 1 tablespoon of the dressing. Place on a lightly oiled grill 4 to 6 inches above a solid bed of medium coals (you can hold your hand at grill level for 4 to 5 seconds) or over medium heat on a gas grill. Close lid on gas grill. Cook, turning often, until pork is evenly browned on outside and no longer pink in thickest part (cut to test; about 15 minutes) or until a meat thermometer inserted in thickest part registers 155°F. Transfer pork to a board and cut across the grain into thin slanting slices.

3. Divide lettuce between 2 dinner plates. Arrange pork over lettuce; then top with cucumber, carrot, and mint. Drizzle Ginger-Lime Dressing and any meat juices that have accumulated on board over salads; sprinkle with peanuts.

GINGER-LIME DRESSING

In a small bowl, whisk together vinegar, hoisin sauce, lime juice, ginger, oil, and fish sauce (if used) to blend. Stir before using.

PER SERVING: 335 calories, 16 g total fat, 4 g saturated fat, 73 mg cholesterol, 553 mg sodium, 18 g carbohydrates, 4 g fiber, 30 g protein, 99 mg calcium, 3 mg iron

PEPPERED STEAK SALAD WITH RED ONIONS & ROQUEFORT CROUTONS
A THICK STEAK SERVED WITH ONIONS AND BLUE CHEESE IS A POPULAR CHOICE FOR A HEARTY MAIN COURSE. HERE, THE SAME INGREDIENTS STAR IN A WARM ENTRÉE SALAD. THIN SLICES OF GRILLED BEEF FILLET AND RED ONIONS COOKED IN BALSAMIC VINEGAR UNTIL SWEET AND GLAZED ARE SERVED OVER PEPPERY ARUGULA, WITH CRISP BAGUETTE CROUTONS TOPPED WITH ROQUEFORT CHEESE ALONGSIDE. ADD A GLASS OF CABERNET SAUVIGNON AND ENJOY!

30 MINUTES

---

2 tablespoons olive oil

1 large red onion (about 10 oz.),
cut into ¼-inch-thick slices

1 teaspoon sugar

¼ cup balsamic vinegar

1 beef fillet steak (about 8 oz.),
about 1½ inches thick

¼ teaspoon coarsely ground pepper

¼ teaspoon garlic salt

4 slices sourdough French bread
baguette (*each* about ¼ inch thick)

2 ounces Roquefort cheese
or other blue-veined cheese

4 cups lightly packed arugula or
watercress sprigs, rinsed and
crisped

Salt

1. Heat 1 tablespoon of the oil in a wide frying pan over medium-high heat. Add onion slices and cook, stirring occasionally, until soft and beginning to brown (about 10 minutes). Add sugar and 2 tablespoons of the vinegar; continue to cook, stirring more often, until onion is richly browned and almost all liquid has evaporated (8 to 10 more minutes). Remove from heat and set aside.

2. While onion is cooking, sprinkle steak all over with pepper and garlic salt. Place steak on a rack in a broiler pan and broil 4 to 6 inches below heat until browned (6 to 7 minutes). Turn steak over and continue to broil until browned on other side and done to your liking; cut to test (7 to 8 more minutes for medium-rare). Transfer steak to a board and slice thinly across the grain. Reserve any juices that accumulate on board.

3. Using 2 teaspoons of the oil, brush both sides of each baguette slice with oil. Arrange on a baking sheet and broil 4 to 6 inches below heat, turning once, until lightly browned on both sides (1 to 2 minutes). Spread toast evenly with cheese and broil just until cheese is melted (about 30 seconds). Set aside.

4. Divide arugula between 2 dinner plates. Top with steak, then onion. To pan used for onion, add remaining 2 tablespoons vinegar, remaining 1 teaspoon oil, and any accumulated meat juices. Stir often over medium heat until mixture begins to bubble. Pour evenly over salads. Serve salads with croutons; season to taste with salt.

PER SERVING: 609 calories, 39 g total fat, 14 g saturated fat, 91 mg cholesterol, 941 mg sodium, 34 g carbohydrates, 4 g fiber, 32 g protein, 353 mg calcium, 5 mg iron

Peppered Steak Salad with Red Onions & Roquefort Croutons

Kung Pao Shrimp Risotto (page 145)

Fresh garlic

Onions and shallots

Fresh parsley

Fresh lemons (for peel and juice)

Olive oil

Vegetable oil, such as canola, corn, or safflower

Vegetable oil cooking spray

Butter or margarine

Asian sesame oil

Soy sauce

Dijon mustard

Major Grey's chutney

Bottled capers

All-purpose flour

To Have on Hand for Pasta

Favorite pasta shapes: long, bite-size, and filled (such as ravioli and tortellini)

Pasta sauces in jars or cans

Tomato paste in a tube

Canned tomatoes and tomato sauce

Olive oil

Fresh garlic or bottled garlic cloves

Parmesan cheese, in a wedge (to grate as needed); or packaged grated or shredded

Meats, Poultry & Seafood

When you choose these main-course basics, look for cuts that can be cooked in a jiffy and are available in convenient amounts. With meats, this means learning to identify tender cuts such as beef steaks, pork tenderloin and chops, lamb from the loin or leg, veal chops and cutlets, ground meats, and sausages (both raw and fully cooked).

Much poultry is quick and easy to cook. You have a choice of chicken breasts, thighs, and drummettes, and turkey breast tenderloins and cutlets. Ground chicken or turkey and poultry sausage offer variety.

Just about any fish or shellfish can (and should) be cooked in minimum time. Because raw seafood doesn't keep well, it's best to buy on the day you plan to cook it so that flavors will be fresh.

For pounding meats and poultry so they'll cook faster, invest in a heavy, flat-sided mallet. If time or weather considerations prevent you from grilling outdoors, consider acquiring a cast-iron range-top grill. The ridged surface lets fat drain away from the food and produces convincing grill marks.

Pasta

When you cook pasta, always heat the water at the same time you're preparing the sauce. Even if you're cooking only enough for two, you'll still need an ample quantity of rapidly boiling water—at least 2 quarts—so that the pasta can cook without sticking together. If the water boils before you need it, reduce the heat to keep it at a simmer; then increase the heat again just before cooking the pasta.

Both dried and fresh pasta are sold in such a variety of forms today that you can eat it often without getting bored. Keep it in stock on your pantry shelf or in the refrigerator or freezer, ready to serve at a moment's notice with a sauce featuring your favorite cheeses, vegetables, meats, poultry, or seafood.

Assemble the ingredients and utensils you'll need. French chefs call this process the *mise en place,* and it puts everything involved in preparing the recipe right at your fingertips.

Many of our recipes are so satisfying that you'll need only a good loaf of bread and a favorite beverage to complete the repast. But if you're putting together a more conventional meat-potatoes-and-vegetable meal, you'll need to think about when you'll prepare and cook the accompaniments to the entrée. Try to fit them smoothly into the time frame of the recipe you're following.

COOKING EFFICIENTLY

For every recipe category in this book, we've collected a few tips for making preparation as efficient as possible. Check the "to have on hand" lists, too, for ingredients used so frequently that we think of them as staples.

SALADS

As soon as you bring salad greens home from the market, rinse and crisp them so they'll be ready to use on the spur of the moment. For iceberg lettuce as well as looseleaf types such as romaine, red and green leaf lettuce, and butter lettuce, this involves cutting out and discarding the core, then immersing the leaves in cold water. Drain the leaves and shake off excess moisture; or whirl them in a salad spinner (a tool many hurried cooks wouldn't be without). Then wrap the leaves loosely in paper towels or a big, clean kitchen towel and refrigerate in a plastic bag until crisp (30 to 45 minutes is usually enough).

Crisped iceberg and romaine lettuce will keep in the refrigerator for up to 5 days. Other salad greens, including spring mix and other lettuce mixes you buy loose or packaged at the supermarket or farmers' market, will last for about 2 days after rinsing and crisping.

If you prefer homemade salad dressings to bottled ones, prepare a double or triple recipe of a favorite and keep it on hand in a covered container in the refrigerator. All it needs is a quick shake, and it's ready to drizzle over crisp greens.

SOUPS

With a few well-chosen and convenient ingredients, you can produce quick soups that taste as if they've simmered for hours. Some are light enough to be sipped from a mug, accompanied by crackers or a sandwich; others are so robust you'll want to ladle them into big, wide bowls—and maybe set the table with knives and forks as well as soup spoons.

To cook soups from scratch, you'll need a heavy pan that distributes heat efficiently and evenly. A blender or food processor is useful for making puréed soups (choose the blender for the smoothest purée).

To Have on Hand for Salads

Olive oil

Vegetable oil, such as canola, corn, or safflower

Vinegars, such as red wine, white wine, seasoned rice, and balsamic

Fresh garlic

Fresh lemons (for peel and juice)

Dijon mustard

Mayonnaise

To Have on Hand for Soups

Canned chicken broth (we recommend fat-free reduced-sodium broth)

Canned beef broth

Canned vegetable broth

Canned beans, such as black, red kidney, and cannellini (white kidney) or other white beans

Thin noodles and small pasta shapes, such as orzo or pastina

Frozen tiny peas

Fresh garlic

Onions

Fresh celery and carrots

CONTENTS

Enjoying Cooking for Two

When it comes to cooking, cooking for two may be the best of all possible culinary worlds. Think about it: recipes for two take much less time to prepare. When dinner is ready, you have someone with whom to share your accomplishments. And maybe best of all, there are seldom (if ever) any leftovers.

This book is for those who, for whatever reason, are serving meals to a cozy twosome—and who don't have much time to spend in the kitchen. Each recipe can be completed in a tidy 30 minutes or less: the time stated for each is an overall time, including both the time needed to prepare the ingredients and the time the dish takes to cook. *And each recipe makes just two servings.* Occasionally you'll find an accompaniment that makes more than that, such as Pronto Apricot Chutney (page 116) and Dried Tomato Louis Dressing (page 12). But even these recipes are quick to prepare, and they can be refrigerated or frozen to enjoy another time.

Whereas food shopping once took place in a family-size world, today there's much more freedom to buy in just the quantity you need. Fresh foods, even produce, are increasingly available in convenient, ready-to-use forms: think of sliced mushrooms, baby-cut carrots, peeled pineapple, and prewashed spinach and salad greens.

While a microwave oven might seem to be requisite for an efficient kitchen, our recipes demonstrate that it's rarely necessary. Nor will you need a food processor to put a meal together swiftly, though it does come in handy for puréeing soups and sauces. Keep in mind, though, that a standard food processor is not at its most effective for scaled-down dishes: it works best for larger quantities of food. If you want a processor for small tasks such as making pesto or grinding nuts, look into the smaller models with a work-bowl capacity of 3 cups or less.

Quick start-ups

It may seem almost too obvious to state, but the first step in preparing a new dish successfully is to *read the recipe*— thoroughly. Take a moment to imagine carrying out each step. You'll work more efficiently if you know in advance what's required of you. It's important, too, to dovetail tasks; you can slice vegetables for a salad while croutons toast in the oven, for example, or simmer a pasta sauce at the same time water is coming to a boil for linguine.

If you'll be using the oven—especially if it's at a temperature of 400° or hotter—*turn it on right away.* Even with state-of-the-art ranges, preheating takes time. If you're barbecuing food on a charcoal grill, start the fire first so that the coals have time to ignite and reach the required heat level. (This is a good chore for the other diner in your household if you have your hands full.)

EQUIPPING YOUR KITCHEN FOR QUICK COOKING FOR TWO IS A PARED-DOWN PROCESS. HAVE A LOOK AT OUR RECIPES AND NOTE THE BASIC UTENSILS AND SMALL APPLIANCES SPECIFIED. COOKWARE ON THE MOST-FREQUENTLY-USED LIST INCLUDES:

• A wide frying pan (a 10- to 12-inch pan is the most useful size). A durable, heavyweight pan is a good investment, because you'll use it nearly every day. Choose one with a nonstick coating if you prefer to cook with little if any fat. A pan with a heatproof handle can go into the oven when need be.

• You'll need one or more covered saucepans for making sauces, cooking rice or vegetables, and preparing soups. A 1½- to 2-quart pan is a versatile size. A larger pan, such as a 3- to 4-quart size, is useful for cooking pasta.

• Though you may not be baking many desserts when time is short, you'll find an 8- or 9-inch-square baking pan a good choice for toasting bread crumbs and nuts and for baking pieces of chicken or fish.

• Find a set of mixing bowls that pleases you. You'll use the large or medium-size one for salads; the medium-size and small ones are useful for mixing salad dressings and sauces.

• Remember measuring equipment: glass measuring cups for liquid ingredients, nested metal or plastic cups for dry ones. A set of measuring spoons lets you manage fractions of teaspoons accurately.

• Handy tools include a sturdy wooden or heat-resistant plastic spoon for stirring hot foods; a flexible yet strong, wide spatula for lifting and turning (if your frying pan has a nonstick coating, select a heat-resistant nylon or plastic spatula); a rubber or heatproof silicone spatula for scraping mixtures from one container to another; and a wire whisk for beating eggs and smoothing sauces.

• Good cutlery is essential. If you buy only two really fine kitchen knives, make them a basic chef's knife for chopping and slicing and a versatile paring knife. A familiar vegetable peeler makes quick work of peeling potatoes, carrots, and apples.

SUNSET BOOKS
Vice President, General Manager: Richard A. Smeby
Vice President, Editorial Director: Bob Doyle
Production Director: Lory Day
Art Director: Vasken Guiragossian

STAFF FOR THIS BOOK
Developmental Editor: Linda J. Selden
Recipe Development and Text: Sandra Bakko Cameron,
Paula M. Freschet, and Cynthia Scheer
Copy Editor: Rebecca LaBrum
Design: Robin Weiss
Photographer: Noel Barnhurst
Food and Set Direction: George Dolese
Associate Food Stylist: Leslie Busch
Food Stylist Assistant: Elisabet der Nederlander
Prop Stylist: Jeff Finney
Photographer's Assistant: Noriko Akiyama
Production Coordinator: Patricia S. Williams

For additional copies of *Quick Cooking for Two* or any other
Sunset book, call 1-800-526-5111. Or see our web site at
www.sunsetbooks.com

FRONT COVER: Sesame Noodles with Gingered Pork &
Vegetables (page 169). Cover design by Robin Weiss.
Photograph by Noel Barnhurst. Food styling by George
Dolese. Art direction by Vasken Guiragossian.
FRONTISPIECE: Lobster, Papaya & Avocado Salad (page 14).
Photography by Noel Barnhurst.
ENDSHEETS: Photography by Richard Jung.

Quick
COOKING *for* TWO

By the Editors of Sunset Books

SUNSET BOOKS • MENLO PARK, CALIFORNIA

Quick Cooking for Two

PEAR, CANDIED WALNUTS, BACON & GORGONZOLA ON MIXED GREENS

THIS SALAD IS FULL OF GOOD THINGS, WITH SWEET FRESH PEAR AND CANDIED WALNUTS CONTRASTING NICELY WITH SALTY BACON AND TANGY BLUE CHEESE. IT'S AN APPETIZING FIRST COURSE FOR A SPECIAL OCCASION; TRY IT AS A LEAD-IN TO AN AUTUMN FEAST OF MARINATED GRILLED PORK TENDERLOIN OR CENTER-CUT PORK CHOPS, GARLIC MASHED POTATOES, WILTED GREENS, AND WARM HOMEMADE APPLESAUCE.

20 MINUTES

Shallot Vinaigrette (below)

2 tablespoons sugar

¼ cup walnut pieces or halves

2 slices thick-cut bacon (about 3 oz. *total*), cut crosswise into ¼-inch-wide strips

4 cups lightly packed mixed salad greens, rinsed and crisped

1 small firm-ripe red-skinned pear (4 to 5 oz.), halved, cored, and thinly sliced

1 small wedge (about 3 oz.) Gorgonzola cheese, cut into 2 thin wedges

Freshly ground pepper

SHALLOT VINAIGRETTE

1 tablespoon minced shallots

2 tablespoons sherry vinegar

1 tablespoon walnut oil

2 teaspoons coarse-grained mustard

2 teaspoons sugar

1. Prepare Shallot Vinaigrette and set aside.

2. Pour the 2 tablespoons sugar into a small frying pan. Set pan over medium-high heat and shake often until almost all sugar is melted (2 to 3 minutes). Reduce heat to medium and continue to heat, tilting pan to mix melted and any remaining dry sugar, until syrup is amber colored (about 1 more minute). Quickly stir walnuts into melted sugar, then immediately pour into a foil-lined pan. Working fast, use 2 forks to separate nuts. Let cool.

3. In another small frying pan, cook bacon over medium-high heat, stirring often, until brown and crisp (4 to 5 minutes). Remove from pan with a slotted spoon and drain on paper towels; set aside.

4. Divide greens between 2 salad plates; top with pear slices. Scatter candied walnuts and bacon over pear. Set a wedge of cheese on one side of each salad. Spoon Shallot Vinaigrette over salads; season to taste with pepper.

SHALLOT VINAIGRETTE

In a small bowl, whisk together shallots, vinegar, oil, mustard, and the 2 teaspoons sugar to blend.

PER SERVING: 519 calories, 36 g total fat, 13 g saturated fat, 48 mg cholesterol, 864 mg sodium, 35 g carbohydrates, 3 g fiber, 16 g protein, 303 mg calcium, 1 mg iron

BABY SPINACH & FRISÉE WITH MARINATED PEPPERS & CROUTONS

ROASTED RED PEPPERS AND OLIVES MARINATED IN EXTRA-VIRGIN OLIVE OIL AND BALSAMIC VINEGAR ARE TOSSED WITH BABY SPINACH, FRISÉE, AND CRUNCHY OVEN-TOASTED BAGUETTE SLICES IN THIS PRETTY GREEN-AND-RED SALAD. PAIR IT WITH A CHUNK OF FONTINA CHEESE AND A GLASS OF PINOT NOIR FOR A LIGHT SUPPER. TO FINISH THE MEAL, DRIZZLE ORANGE LIQUEUR OVER YOUR CHOICE OF FRESH FRUIT.

25 MINUTES

About 4 teaspoons extra-virgin olive oil

6 slices slender French bread baguette (*each* about 2 inches in diameter and ¼ inch thick)

⅓ cup canned or bottled roasted red peppers, drained

About 1 tablespoon balsamic vinegar

1 clove garlic, minced or pressed

8 to 10 Niçoise or calamata olives

¼ cup thinly sliced mild red onion

3 cups lightly packed packaged triple-washed baby spinach, rinsed and crisped

1 cup lightly packed frisée or curly endive, rinsed and crisped

Salt

2 tablespoons freshly grated Parmesan cheese

1. Using about 1½ teaspoons of the oil, brush baguette slices lightly on one side with oil. Arrange bread, oiled side up, in a 9-inch baking pan. Bake in a 375° oven until lightly toasted (10 to 12 minutes). Let croutons cool in pan.

2. Meanwhile, cut peppers into ¼-inch-wide strips and place in a wide salad bowl. Add 1 teaspoon of the oil, 1 tablespoon of the vinegar, garlic, and olives; mix well. Then add onion, spinach, and frisée; mix well. Season to taste with salt and, if desired, more vinegar.

3. Heat remaining 1½ teaspoons oil in a small frying pan over high heat for about 30 seconds. Pour oil over salad and mix. Sprinkle with cheese and croutons; mix again. Serve at once.

PER SERVING: 258 calories, 14 g total fat, 3 g saturated fat, 5 mg cholesterol, 483 mg sodium, 27 g carbohydrates, 3 g fiber, 8 g protein, 176 mg calcium, 2 mg iron

BLUSH WINE–MARINATED CHICKEN & NECTARINE SALAD

COMBINING SLICED GRILLED CHICKEN BREASTS AND JUICY NECTARINES, THIS ATTRACTIVE MAIN-DISH SALAD IS DELIGHTFUL FOR ALFRESCO DINING ON A WARM EVENING. A WHITE ZINFANDEL–BASED DRESSING SWEETENED WITH A TOUCH OF HONEY DOUBLES AS A MARINADE FOR THE CHICKEN. IF NECTARINES AREN'T AVAILABLE, USE DRAINED CANNED MANDARIN ORANGE SEGMENTS IN THEIR PLACE.

30 MINUTES

Blush Wine–marinated Chicken & Nectarine Salad

Blush Wine Dressing (below)

2 small boneless, skinless chicken
    breast halves (about 4 oz. *each*)

2 tablespoons slivered almonds

4 cups lightly packed torn romaine
    lettuce, rinsed and crisped

1 large nectarine (about 6 oz.), pitted
    and sliced

2 tablespoons thinly sliced green
    onion

Salt and freshly ground pepper

BLUSH WINE DRESSING

2 tablespoons white Zinfandel

2 tablespoons red wine vinegar

2 tablespoons vegetable oil

1 clove garlic, minced or pressed

2 teaspoons minced shallot

1 tablespoon honey

2 teaspoons Dijon mustard

½ teaspoon crumbled dried rosemary

1. Prepare Blush Wine Dressing. Rinse chicken, pat dry, and place in a small heavy-duty plastic food bag. Pour 2 tablespoons of the dressing over chicken; then seal bag and turn it several times to distribute marinade. Set bag in a bowl and let stand for 5 minutes.

2. Meanwhile, pour almonds into a small frying pan. Toast over medium heat, shaking pan often, until almonds are golden (3 to 4 minutes). Pour out of pan and set aside.

3. Lift chicken from marinade, drain briefly, and place on a grill 4 to 6 inches above a solid bed of hot coals (you can hold your hand at grill level for only 2 to 3 seconds) or over high heat on a gas grill. Close lid on gas grill. Cook chicken for 5 minutes, then turn over and brush with any dressing remaining in bag; close lid on gas grill again. Continue to cook until meat in thickest part is no longer pink; cut to test (about 5 more minutes). Remove from grill and cut diagonally across the grain into ½-inch-wide strips.

4. Divide lettuce between 2 dinner plates. Arrange chicken and nectarine slices over lettuce; sprinkle with onion. Spoon remaining dressing over salads and sprinkle with almonds. Season to taste with salt and pepper.

BLUSH WINE DRESSING

In a small bowl, whisk together Zinfandel, vinegar, oil, garlic, shallot, honey, mustard, and rosemary to blend.

PER SERVING: 408 calories, 20 g total fat, 3 g saturated fat, 66 mg cholesterol, 207 mg sodium, 24 g carbohydrates, 4 g fiber, 31 g protein, 93 mg calcium, 3 mg iron

ROASTED ASPARAGUS WITH CRISPY PROSCIUTTO-TANGERINE DRESSING

SIMPLE BUT ELEGANT, THIS FIRST COURSE IS A LOVELY CHOICE DURING THE WINTER HOLIDAYS, WHEN TANGERINES HIT THEIR PEAK. THE VIBRANT SHADES OF ORANGE, GREEN, AND RED LIGHT UP YOUR TABLE. TO ENJOY THE SALAD AT OTHER TIMES OF YEAR, SUBSTITUTE AN ORANGE FOR THE TANGERINE.

20 MINUTES

---

8 ounces asparagus, tough ends snapped off

2 tablespoons olive oil

2 large tangerines (about 6 oz. *each*) or medium-size oranges

1 clove garlic, minced or pressed

2 ounces thinly sliced prosciutto, cut into thin strips

4 large radicchio leaves, rinsed and crisped

1. Arrange asparagus in a 9- by 13-inch baking pan and brush with 2 teaspoons of the oil. Bake in a 450° oven until tender-crisp when pierced (about 10 minutes). Remove from oven; set aside.

2. While asparagus is roasting, grate ½ teaspoon peel (colored part only) from one of the tangerines; set aside. From same tangerine, squeeze enough juice to make 2 tablespoons; set aside. Cut peel and all white membrane from remaining tangerine; then cut fruit crosswise into 6 equal slices and set aside.

3. Heat remaining 4 teaspoons oil in a small frying pan over medium-high heat. Add garlic and prosciutto; stir often until prosciutto is brown and crisp (4 to 5 minutes). Remove pan from heat and stir in tangerine peel and juice.

4. Divide asparagus between 2 salad plates. Tuck radicchio partially beneath asparagus to one side of each plate. Lay tangerine slices over asparagus; spoon prosciutto dressing over all.

PER SERVING: 261 calories, 18 g total fat, 3 g saturated fat, 23 mg cholesterol, 530 mg sodium, 17 g carbohydrates, 3 g fiber, 12 g protein, 43 mg calcium, 1 mg iron

Roasted Asparagus with Crispy Prosciutto-Tangerine Dressing

WILD MUSHROOMS
& PANCETTA ON ARUGULA
A WARM ARRAY OF FRESH WILD MUSHROOMS SEASONED WITH PANCETTA, SHERRY VINEGAR, AND TARRAGON IS QUICKLY TOSSED WITH COOL, CRISP ARUGULA AND MIXED GREENS FOR AN ENTICING FIRST COURSE. TOASTED BAGUETTE SLICES SPREAD WITH SOFT FRESH GOAT CHEESE MAKE A PERFECT GARNISH.

25 MINUTES

---

8 ounces assorted fresh mushrooms, such as chanterelle, crimini, morel, oyster, pompon, porcini, portabella, shiitake, and button (choose 3 or 4 kinds)

About 2 tablespoons walnut or olive oil

1½ ounces pancetta or bacon, cut into thin strips

1 tablespoon pine nuts

1 tablespoon minced shallots

1 clove garlic, minced or pressed

4 slices slender French bread baguette (*each* about 2 inches in diameter and ¼ inch thick)

1 ounce soft fresh chèvre

2 tablespoons sherry wine vinegar

1 teaspoon minced fresh tarragon or ¼ teaspoon dried tarragon

Salt and freshly ground pepper

2 cups lightly packed arugula or watercress sprigs, rinsed and crisped

2 cups lightly packed mixed salad greens, rinsed and crisped

1. Place mushrooms in a plastic food bag. Fill bag with water; then seal bag and shake to wash mushrooms. Drain mushrooms well; if they are still gritty, repeat rinsing. Trim and discard bruised stem ends. Cut larger mushrooms lengthwise into ¼-inch-thick slices; leave small ones whole.

2. Combine oil and pancetta in a wide frying pan. Cook over medium-high heat for 1 minute, then add pine nuts. Continue to cook, stirring often, until pancetta is brown and crisp and nuts are pale gold (about 2 more minutes). Remove from pan with a slotted spoon and transfer to a large bowl; set aside.

3. To pan, add shallots and garlic; cook, stirring often, for 1 minute. Add mushrooms. Cook, stirring often, until liquid has evaporated and mushrooms are beginning to brown (about 8 minutes).

4. Meanwhile, arrange baguette slices in a small baking pan and broil 4 to 6 inches below heat until golden (about 1 minute). Turn bread over, spread with chèvre, and broil until cheese is melted (about 30 seconds). Keep warm.

5. When mushrooms are cooked, remove pan from heat and stir in vinegar and tarragon. Season to taste with salt and pepper. Transfer mushroom mixture to bowl with pancetta and pine nuts. Add arugula and salad greens; toss to mix well. Divide mixture between 2 salad plates. Serve at once, accompanied with warm croutons.

PER SERVING: 382 calories, 32 g total fat, 8 g saturated fat, 21 mg cholesterol, 269 mg sodium, 16 g carbohydrates, 4 g fiber, 11 g protein, 115 mg calcium, 3 mg iron

Spinach, Pancetta & Pine Nut Salad

IN THIS VERSION OF POPULAR WILTED SPINACH SALAD, RASPBERRY VINEGAR LENDS A SWEET, FRUITY ACCENT TO THE DRESSING, OFFERING A NICE CONTRAST TO THE SALTINESS OF THE PANCETTA. SERVE WITH ASSORTED GRILLED SAUSAGES AND SOFT POLENTA; PURCHASED POUND CAKE TOPPED WITH SWEETENED FRESH BERRIES MAKES A NICE DESSERT.

20 MINUTES

2 tablespoons pine nuts

2 ounces sliced pancetta or bacon, coarsely chopped

2 teaspoons olive oil (if using pancetta)

2 teaspoons minced shallot

2 tablespoons raspberry vinegar

1 teaspoon coarse-grained mustard

4 cups lightly packed packaged triple-washed baby spinach, rinsed and crisped

2 tablespoons thinly sliced green onion

1 hard-cooked large egg, finely chopped

Freshly ground pepper

1. Pour pine nuts into a small nonstick frying pan. Toast over medium heat, shaking pan often, until nuts are pale gold (2 to 3 minutes). Pour out of pan and set aside.

2. Increase heat to medium-high. To pan, add pancetta and oil (omit oil if using bacon). Cook, stirring often, until pancetta is brown and crisp (about 3 minutes). Remove from pan with a slotted spoon and drain on paper towels; set aside.

3. Add shallot to pan and cook for 1 minute; then stir in vinegar and mustard. Remove pan from heat and set aside.

4. Place spinach, onion, egg, and pancetta in a medium-size bowl; pour hot dressing over all and toss to coat evenly. Divide salad between 2 salad plates; sprinkle with pine nuts and serve immediately. Offer pepper to add to taste.

PER SERVING: 289 calories, 24 g total fat, 8 g saturated fat, 125 mg cholesterol, 390 mg sodium, 9 g carbohydrates, 6 g fiber, 13 g protein, 189 mg calcium, 6 mg iron

Autumn Fruit Salad with Pomegranate

THE WARM COLORS OF AUTUMN GIVE THIS FRUIT SALAD ITS HANDSOME LOOKS. SERVE IT AS AN ELEGANT STARTER, OR PAIR IT WITH BUTTERED TOAST AND A WEDGE OF CHEESE FOR A SATISFYING LUNCH OR LIGHT SUPPER. THE FRISÉE'S MILD BITTERNESS NICELY BALANCES THE SWEETNESS OF THE FRUIT, BUT YOU CAN OMIT THE GREENS IF YOU LIKE.

20 MINUTES

Autumn Fruit Salad with Pomegranate

1 tablespoon pine nuts

1 small firm-ripe Fuyu persimmon
(about 6 oz.)

1 small ruby grapefruit (12 to 14 oz.)

1 very small Asian pear (about 4 oz.)

1 tablespoon lime juice

1 tablespoon unseasoned rice vinegar

2 teaspoons honey

1½ cups lightly packed frisée, rinsed
and crisped

¼ cup pomegranate seeds

Salt

1. Pour pine nuts into a small frying pan. Toast over medium heat, shaking pan often, until nuts are pale gold (2 to 3 minutes). Pour out of pan and set aside.

2. Trim and discard leafy top from persimmon; slice fruit crosswise into thin rounds. Cut peel and all white membrane from grapefruit; then, holding fruit over a bowl to catch juice, cut between segments and inner membrane to release fruit into bowl. Squeeze juice from membrane into bowl; discard membrane.

3. Cut pear crosswise (right through core) into thin rounds. Dip pear slices into grapefruit juice to coat.

4. Measure 1 tablespoon grapefruit juice (from bowl with grapefruit segments) into a cup and stir in lime juice, vinegar, and honey. Set aside.

5. Line 2 salad plates with frisée. Lift grapefruit segments from bowl; reserve juice left in bowl for other uses. Arrange grapefruit, persimmon, and pear atop greens. Sprinkle fruit with pomegranate seeds and pine nuts; moisten with grapefruit juice mixture. Season to taste with salt.

PER SERVING: 226 calories, 3 g total fat, 0 g saturated fat, 0 mg cholesterol, 64 mg sodium, 52 g carbohydrates, 5 g fiber, 5 g protein, 69 mg calcium, 4 mg iron

TRICOLOR TOMATO SALAD WITH FRESH MOZZARELLA

THIS SALAD IS ESPECIALLY DELIGHTFUL MADE WITH VINE-RIPENED TOMATOES; BUY THE BEST YOU CAN FIND, TRYING FOR SEVERAL DIFFERENT COLORS. FRESH COW'S MILK MOZZARELLA IS SOLD IN YOUR MARKET'S GOURMET CHEESE CASE. SERVE THE SALAD WITH CRUSTY BREAD DRIZZLED WITH A LITTLE OF THE BASIL OIL.

10 TO 15 MINUTES

¼ cup lightly packed fresh basil leaves

2 tablespoons extra-virgin olive oil

1 *each* medium-small firm-ripe red, yellow, and orange tomato (about 5 oz. *each*); or use all of one color

4 ounces fresh whole-milk mozzarella, thinly sliced

6 canned anchovy fillets, drained well

Basil sprigs

Coarse sea salt

Freshly ground pepper

1. In a 1-quart pan, bring about 2 cups water to a boil over high heat. Immerse basil leaves in boiling water; then immediately drain and immerse in ice water to cover. Drain well on towels.

2. Transfer drained basil to a blender or food processor and whirl until puréed; add oil and whirl until blended. Pour oil mixture through a fine wire strainer into a small bowl, using a spoon to press oil from basil residue. Discard residue and set basil oil aside.

3. Cut tomatoes into ¼-inch-thick slices. Alternate tomato and cheese slices on 2 salad plates; top with anchovies. Drizzle each salad with basil oil; garnish with basil sprigs. Season with a light sprinkling of sea salt and pepper.

PER SERVING: 370 calories, 30 g total fat, 11 g saturated fat, 57 mg cholesterol, 688 mg sodium, 10 g carbohydrates, 3 g fiber, 17 g protein, 362 mg calcium, 3 mg iron

MOROCCAN CARROT SALAD

THINLY SLICED, LIGHTLY COOKED CARROTS SEASONED WITH TOASTED SPICES, LEMON JUICE, AND OLIVE OIL MAKE A RUSTIC SALAD THAT'S DELICIOUS WITH PAN-SAUTÉED LEMON-HERB CHICKEN BREASTS AND STEAMED ARTICHOKES. FINISH THE MEAL WITH DATES, TANGERINES, AND HOT MINT TEA.

20 MINUTES

3 cups thinly sliced carrots

¼ teaspoon ground coriander

¼ teaspoon ground cumin

¼ teaspoon ground red pepper (cayenne)

1 tablespoon lemon juice

About 1 tablespoon extra-virgin olive oil

1 tablespoon minced parsley

1 small clove garlic, minced or pressed

Salt

1. Place carrots in a 1½- to 2-quart pan and add enough water to cover. Bring to a boil over high heat; then reduce heat, cover, and simmer until just tender to bite (about 5 minutes). Drain.

2. While carrots are cooking, stir coriander and cumin in a small frying pan over medium-high heat until fragrant (about 45 seconds). Remove from heat and pour into a medium-size bowl.

3. To spices in bowl, add red pepper, lemon juice, 1 tablespoon of the oil, parsley, garlic, and carrots; mix well, then season to taste with salt. If desired, moisten salad with a little more oil. Serve at room temperature.

PER SERVING: 157 calories, 8 g total fat, 1 g saturated fat, 0 mg cholesterol, 77 mg sodium, 23 g carbohydrates, 7 g fiber, 2 g protein, 66 mg calcium, 1 mg iron

CAESAR SALAD FOUR WAYS

A RESTAURANT CLASSIC FOR DECADES, CAESAR SALAD HAS BECOME A FAVORITE FOR SERVING AT HOME AS WELL. HERE ARE FOUR VARIATIONS ON THE THEME. OUR SOUTH-OF-THE-BORDER CAESAR FEATURES A CREAMY AVOCADO DRESSING AND CRISP TORTILLA "CROUTONS"; THE RED-AND-GREEN RENDITION IS MADE WITH RADICCHIO IN ADDITION TO THE USUAL ROMAINE. IF YOU'RE LOOKING FOR ENTRÉE SALADS, TRY THE SHELLFISH AND GRILLED CHICKEN CAESARS. FOR ANY OF THESE SALADS, USE AN IMPORTED PARMESAN CHEESE (LABELED PARMIGIANO-REGGIANO) RATHER THAN A DOMESTIC VARIETY; ITS SHARPER, MORE COMPLEX FLAVOR WILL MAKE A DIFFERENCE.

NOTE: THE ORIGINAL CAESAR SALAD CALLS FOR A RAW OR VERY LIGHTLY COOKED EGG IN THE DRESSING, BUT WE'VE OMITTED IT DUE TO CURRENT CONCERNS ABOUT SALMONELLA. WE THINK YOU'LL AGREE, THOUGH, THAT THE OMISSION DOESN'T DETRACT FROM THE FLAVOR.

SOUTH-OF-THE-BORDER CAESAR SALAD
20 MINUTES

- ½ large tomato- or chili-flavored flour tortilla (about 10 inches in diameter)
- 1 very small firm-ripe avocado (about 4 oz.), pitted, peeled, and cut into chunks
- 2 teaspoons lemon juice
- 1 clove garlic, minced or pressed
- 1 teaspoon Dijon mustard
- 1 teaspoon white wine vinegar
- 1 tablespoon cilantro leaves
- ½ small fresh jalapeño chile, seeded and minced
- 1 tablespoon avocado or olive oil
- Salt and freshly ground pepper
- 4 cups lightly packed bite-size pieces romaine lettuce, rinsed and crisped
- 1 tablespoon roasted shelled pumpkin seeds
- 1 tablespoon crumbled cotija or feta cheese
- Cilantro sprigs

1. Cut tortilla into ¼- by 2-inch strips. Arrange in a single layer in a 9- by 13-inch baking pan. Bake in a 400° oven until crisp (about 5 minutes). Set aside.

2. While tortilla strips are baking, combine avocado, lemon juice, garlic, mustard, vinegar, cilantro leaves, and chile in a blender or food processor. Whirl until mixture is smooth and cilantro is finely chopped. With motor running, slowly add oil. Season dressing to taste with salt and pepper.

3. Place lettuce in a wide salad bowl. Add dressing and mix well. Divide salad between 2 salad plates. Top with tortilla strips, pumpkin seeds, and cheese; garnish with cilantro sprigs.

PER SERVING: 233 calories, 17 g total fat, 3 g saturated fat, 2 mg cholesterol, 244 mg sodium, 15 g carbohydrates, 4 g fiber, 5 g protein, 84 mg calcium, 3 mg iron

SHELLFISH CAESAR WITH SPICY ROUILLE DRESSING & GARLIC-CAYENNE CROUTON STICKS
25 MINUTES

- 1 clove garlic, minced or pressed
- 1½ tablespoons extra-virgin olive oil
- 2 slices sourdough bread (*each* about 4 by 4 inches and ½ inch thick)
- Ground red pepper (cayenne)
- 1 to 2 tablespoons canned or bottled roasted red peppers, drained and finely minced
- 2 tablespoons mayonnaise
- 1 tablespoon lemon juice
- 1 tablespoon red wine vinegar
- Salt
- 4 cups lightly packed shredded romaine lettuce, rinsed and crisped
- 1 tablespoon freshly grated imported Parmesan cheese
- 4 ounces cooked crabmeat
- 4 ounces small cooked shrimp
- Lemon wedges

1. In a small microwave-safe bowl, combine garlic and oil. Microwave on high (100%), uncovered, for about 30 seconds or until oil is very warm and garlic is fragrant.

2. Cut bread into ½- by 4-inch sticks. Brush all over with 1 tablespoon of the garlic oil. Arrange in a single layer in a 9- by 13-inch baking pan. Bake in a 375° oven until crisp and golden (about 15 minutes). Sprinkle lightly with ground red pepper and set aside.

3. While croutons are baking, combine roasted red peppers, mayonnaise, lemon juice, and vinegar in a small bowl. Whisk together to blend. Season dressing to taste with salt and ground red pepper.

4. Place lettuce in a wide salad bowl. Pour remaining garlic oil over lettuce and sprinkle with cheese; toss until lettuce is coated. Divide between 2 dinner plates and top equally with crab and shrimp. Arrange croutons atop salads, stacking them one on top of the other. Offer dressing and lemon wedges to season salads to taste.

PER SERVING: 419 calories, 25 g total fat, 4 g saturated fat, 178 mg cholesterol, 616 mg sodium, 20 g carbohydrates, 3 g fiber, 29 g protein, 191 mg calcium, 4 mg iron

GRILLED CHICKEN CAESAR WITH HERBED PARMESAN CRISPS
30 MINUTES

2 tablespoons extra-virgin olive oil

1 clove garlic, minced or pressed

1 tablespoon lemon juice

¼ teaspoon anchovy paste

¼ teaspoon Worcestershire

2 small boneless, skinless chicken breast halves (about 4 oz. *each*)

Garlic salt and freshly ground pepper

¾ cup finely shredded imported Parmesan cheese

¼ teaspoon dried basil

¼ teaspoon dried oregano

10 inner romaine lettuce leaves, rinsed and crisped

1. In a small bowl, whisk together oil, garlic, lemon juice, anchovy paste, and Worcestershire to blend. Set aside.

2. Rinse chicken and pat dry. Sprinkle generously with garlic salt and pepper. Place in a small heavy-duty plastic food bag. Pour 1 tablespoon of the dressing over chicken; then seal bag and turn it several times to distribute marinade. Set bag in a bowl and let stand for 5 minutes.

3. Meanwhile, in a wide nonstick frying pan, combine cheese, basil, and oregano; spread out in an even layer. Cook over medium heat, uncovered and without stirring, until cheese is

melted and pale golden brown in color (5 to 7 minutes). Remove pan from heat and let cool for 2 minutes; then slide cheese crisp onto a plate and let cool completely.

4. Lift chicken from marinade, drain briefly, and place on a grill 4 to 6 inches above a solid bed of hot coals (you can hold your hand at grill level for only 2 to 3 seconds) or over high heat on a gas grill. Close lid on gas grill. Cook chicken for 5 minutes, then turn over and brush with any dressing remaining in bag; close lid on gas grill again. Continue to cook until meat in thickest part is no longer pink; cut to test (about 5 more minutes). Remove chicken from grill and cut diagonally across the grain into ½-inch-wide strips.

5. Arrange 5 lettuce leaves on each of 2 dinner plates. Arrange chicken over lettuce. Break cheese crisp into irregular pieces and set on salads (some pieces should be standing up). Spoon remaining dressing over salads.

PER SERVING: 426 calories, 27 g total fat, 9 g saturated fat, 95 mg cholesterol, 802 mg sodium, 4 g carbohydrates, 1 g fiber, 42 g protein, 544 mg calcium, 2 mg iron

RED & GREEN CAESAR SALAD WITH ROASTED GARLIC–ANCHOVY CROSTINI
20 MINUTES

1 or 2 canned anchovy fillets, drained well and minced

2 tablespoons minced prepared roasted garlic cloves

3 tablespoons freshly grated Asiago cheese

1 tablespoon roasted garlic oil or extra-virgin olive oil

6 slices French bread baguette (*each* about ¼ inch thick)

1½ tablespoons extra-virgin olive oil

1 tablespoon lemon juice

1 teaspoon balsamic vinegar

2 cups lightly packed bite-size pieces romaine lettuce, rinsed and crisped

2 cups lightly packed bite-size pieces radicchio, rinsed and crisped

Salt and freshly ground pepper

1. In a small bowl, combine anchovies, 1 tablespoon of the roasted garlic cloves, and 1 tablespoon of the cheese. Set aside.

2. Using 1½ teaspoons of the roasted garlic oil, brush baguette slices lightly on one side with oil. Place slices, oiled side up, in a 9-inch baking pan. Bake in a 375° oven until crisp and golden (about 15 minutes). Remove from oven and spread with anchovy mixture. Turn off oven; return crostini to oven to keep warm.

3. While crostini are baking, combine remaining 1½ teaspoons roasted garlic oil, olive oil, remaining 1 tablespoon roasted garlic cloves, lemon juice, and vinegar in a large bowl. Whisk together to blend. Add lettuce, radicchio, and remaining 2 tablespoons cheese; toss until greens are coated. Season to taste with salt and pepper.

4. Divide salad between 2 salad plates. Serve with warm crostini.

PER SERVING: 339 calories, 22 g total fat, 5 g saturated fat, 9 mg cholesterol, 475 mg sodium, 26 g carbohydrates, 3 g fiber, 9 g protein, 172 mg calcium, 2 mg iron

MINTED CUCUMBER, TOMATO & RED ONION SALAD WITH FETA

COLORFUL AND FRESH, THIS GREEK-STYLE SALAD TAKES ONLY MINUTES TO PREPARE. SERVE IT SOON AFTER YOU MIX IT; IF IT'S LEFT TO STAND TOO LONG, THE TOMATOES TEND TO JUICE UP AND MAKE THE DRESSING WATERY. ACCOMPANY WITH GRILLED LAMB OR BEEF BURGERS AND A SAVORY MIXED-GRAIN PILAF. TRY PURCHASED BAKLAVA FOR DESSERT.

10 MINUTES

2 tablespoons red wine vinegar

1 teaspoon sugar

¼ teaspoon salt

1 small English cucumber (about 6 oz.), halved lengthwise, each half cut crosswise into ½-inch-thick slices (or use a regular cucumber, halved lengthwise, seeded, and sliced crosswise)

⅓ cup coarsely chopped mild red onion

1 large firm-ripe tomato (about 8 oz.), coarsely chopped and drained well

3 tablespoons chopped fresh mint

¼ cup crumbled feta cheese

Mint sprigs

Freshly ground pepper

1. In a bowl, stir together vinegar, sugar, and salt until sugar is dissolved. Stir in cucumber and onion; let stand for 5 minutes.

2. Add tomato and chopped mint; stir gently to coat with dressing. Sprinkle with cheese and garnish with mint sprigs. Serve at once; offer pepper to add to taste.

PER SERVING: 103 calories, 4 g total fat, 3 g saturated fat, 15 mg cholesterol, 490 mg sodium, 14 g carbohydrates, 3 g fiber, 5 g protein, 114 mg calcium, 2 mg iron

Minted Cucumber, Tomato & Red Onion Salad with Feta

MARINATED FENNEL & OIL-CURED OLIVES WITH ORANGES

THE SUN-DRENCHED FLAVORS OF THE MEDITERRANEAN COME THROUGH IN THIS REFRESHING SALAD, A COMBINATION OF SLIVERED FENNEL AND OIL-CURED OLIVES IN A ROSEMARY-SCENTED ORANGE JUICE VINAIGRETTE. SERVE THE COLORFUL SIDE DISH WITH BROILED OR GRILLED LAMB CHOPS (PRESS FRESH BAY LEAVES ONTO THE MEAT BEFORE COOKING) AND LIGHTLY BUTTERED COUSCOUS.

20 MINUTES

2 tablespoons pine nuts or slivered almonds

2 medium-size oranges (about 6 oz. *each*)

1 tablespoon olive oil

2 tablespoons white wine vinegar

½ teaspoon minced fresh rosemary or ¼ teaspoon crumbled dried rosemary

¼ cup oil-cured black ripe olives (pitted, if desired)

1 medium-size head fennel (about 3½ inches in diameter)

2 large butter lettuce leaves, rinsed and crisped

Salt and freshly ground pepper

1. Pour pine nuts into a small frying pan. Toast over medium heat, shaking pan often, until nuts are pale gold (2 to 3 minutes). Pour out of pan and set aside.

2. Finely shred ½ teaspoon peel (colored part only) from one of the oranges; set aside. From same orange, squeeze enough juice to make 3 tablespoons; set aside. Cut peel and all white membrane from remaining orange, then thinly slice fruit crosswise and set aside.

3. In a medium-size bowl, stir together shredded orange peel, orange juice, oil, vinegar, rosemary, and olives. Set aside.

4. Rinse fennel and cut off coarse stalks, reserving some of the feathery leaves. Trim and discard base and any discolored or bruised parts from fennel bulb; quarter bulb lengthwise, then sliver each quarter crosswise. Add fennel to olives and dressing in bowl; stir gently and let stand for 5 minutes.

5. Place a lettuce leaf on each of 2 salad plates. Top lettuce with fennel mixture and orange slices; sprinkle with pine nuts and garnish with reserved fennel leaves. Season to taste with salt and pepper.

PER SERVING: 242 calories, 18 g total fat, 2 g saturated fat, 0 mg cholesterol, 746 mg sodium, 19 g carbohydrates, 4 g fiber, 5 g protein, 129 mg calcium, 3 mg iron

MELON & FIG ANTIPASTO

FIND A SHADY SPOT ON THE PATIO AND RELAX WITH THIS LIGHT ANTIPASTO LUNCH. CHOOSE TWO OR THREE KINDS OF ITALIAN CURED MEATS, THEN SERVE THEM WITH PISTACHIOS, MELON, AND FRESH FIGS INSTEAD OF THE MORE TRADITIONAL ROASTED PEPPERS, ARTICHOKES, OLIVES, AND CHEESE. ACCOMPANY WITH BREADSTICKS AND A CRISP WHITE WINE; FINISH THE MEAL WITH A SCOOP OF GELATO.

15 MINUTES

2 tablespoons roasted salted pistachio nuts

6 thin slices cantaloupe

6 thin slices honeydew melon

3 medium-size fresh ripe figs (stems trimmed, if desired), cut into halves

3 to 4 ounces thinly sliced cold meats, such as prosciutto, coppa, and salami (choose 2 or 3 kinds)

Lime wedges

Coarsely ground pepper

1. Place pistachios in a small frying pan. Toast over medium heat, shaking pan often, until nuts are lightly toasted (3 to 5 minutes). Pour out of pan and let cool.

2. Decoratively arrange cantaloupe, honeydew melon, figs, meats, and pistachios on 2 dinner plates. Offer lime wedges to squeeze over fruit; season salads to taste with pepper.

PER SERVING: 292 calories, 16 g total fat, 4 g saturated fat, 40 mg cholesterol, 963 mg sodium, 24 g carbohydrates, 3 g fiber, 15 g protein, 46 mg calcium, 2 mg iron

ITALIAN BREAD SALAD

THOUGH IT'S SIMILAR TO THE CLASSIC TUSCAN PANZANELLA, THIS SATISFYING SALAD DOES NOT CALL FOR TOMATOES. FOR BEST RESULTS, USE A CRUSTY, COARSE-TEXTURED ITALIAN BREAD (SUCH AS CIABATTA, FRANCESE, OR PANE PUGLIESE) AND A FRUITY EXTRA-VIRGIN OLIVE OIL. SERVE WITH HERB-BASTED GRILLED CHICKEN AND A SEMIDRY TO DRY WHITE WINE SUCH AS PINOT GRIGIO.

20 TO 25 MINUTES

1 coarse-textured Italian white roll (about 3 oz. and 6 inches long), cut into 1-inch cubes (about 3½ cups cubes)

2 tablespoons extra-virgin olive oil

1 small head fennel (about 3 inches in diameter)

1½ tablespoons balsamic vinegar

1 teaspoon anchovy paste

⅓ cup thinly sliced mild red onion

⅓ cup canned or bottled roasted red peppers, drained and cut into very thin strips

⅓ cup pitted Niçoise olives

¼ cup firmly packed fresh basil leaves, cut into thin slivers

Freshly ground pepper

1. In a 9- by 13-inch baking pan, mix roll cubes with 2 teaspoons of the oil. Bake in a 375° oven until crisp and golden (about 15 minutes), shaking pan occasionally. Let cool in pan.

2. Meanwhile, rinse fennel and cut off coarse stalks, reserving some of the feathery leaves. Trim and discard base and any discolored or bruised parts from fennel bulb; quarter bulb lengthwise and sliver each quarter crosswise. Set aside.

3. In a medium-size bowl, whisk together vinegar, remaining 4 teaspoons oil, and anchovy paste. Add slivered fennel, onion, red peppers, olives, and basil; mix gently but thoroughly. Stir in croutons. Season to taste with pepper and garnish with reserved fennel leaves. For best flavor and appearance, serve at once.

PER SERVING: 362 calories, 24 g total fat, 3 g saturated fat, 1 mg cholesterol, 811 mg sodium, 32 g carbohydrates, 6 g fiber, 8 g protein, 170 mg calcium, 4 mg iron

Italian Bread Salad

Asian Slaw with Coconut-Peanut Topping

ASIAN SLAW WITH COCONUT-PEANUT TOPPING

ASIAN SEASONINGS OF SOY, RICE VINEGAR, AND GINGER LEND A NEW DIMENSION TO AN OLD FAVORITE. THE CRUNCHY COCONUT-PEANUT TOPPING IS ADDICTIVE! ANOTHER TIME, TRY IT SPRINKLED OVER STEAMED WHITE RICE.

20 TO 25 MINUTES

Coconut-Peanut Topping (below)
2 tablespoons seasoned rice vinegar
2 teaspoons soy sauce
¼ teaspoon chili oil
1 clove garlic, minced or pressed
2 teaspoons minced fresh ginger
1½ cups finely shredded red cabbage
1½ cups finely shredded napa cabbage
½ cup shredded carrot
¼ cup chopped cilantro
2 tablespoons chopped green onion

COCONUT-PEANUT TOPPING

1 teaspoon vegetable oil
¼ cup shredded sweetened coconut
2 tablespoons roasted salted peanuts
2 teaspoons lime juice
½ teaspoon ground coriander

1. Prepare Coconut-Peanut Topping and set aside.

2. In a medium-size bowl, stir together vinegar, soy sauce, chili oil, garlic, and ginger. Add red cabbage, napa cabbage, carrot, cilantro, and onion; mix well. Offer Coconut-Peanut Topping to add to taste.

COCONUT-PEANUT TOPPING

Heat vegetable oil in a small frying pan over medium heat. Add coconut, peanuts, lime juice, and coriander. Toast, stirring often, until coconut is lightly browned (8 to 10 minutes). Remove from heat.

PER SERVING: 179 calories, 11 g total fat, 4 g saturated fat, 0 mg cholesterol, 727 mg sodium, 19 g carbohydrates, 4 g fiber, 5 g protein, 99 mg calcium, 1 mg iron

Jicama, Grapefruit & Avocado Salad

Blending the margaritas while you prepare this colorful south-of-the-border salad. With a fat-free dressing of fresh pink grapefruit juice, rice vinegar, and basil, it's definitely on the light side. Try it with fish tacos (see pages 130–131) or burritos and canned refried black beans.

20 MINUTES

4 ounces jicama

1 small ruby or pink grapefruit (12 to 14 oz.)

1 tablespoon seasoned rice vinegar

2 teaspoons slivered fresh basil or ¼ teaspoon dried basil

1 small clove garlic, minced or pressed

2 tablespoons thinly sliced mild red onion

2 tablespoons thinly sliced radishes

1 small firm-ripe avocado (about 5 oz.)

Salt and freshly ground pepper

1. Cut off and discard peel and any tough fibers from jicama; then cut jicama into 2- to 3-inch-long matchstick pieces. Set aside.

2. Cut off and discard peel and all white membrane from grapefruit. Holding fruit over a wide serving bowl to catch juice, cut between segments and inner membrane to release fruit into bowl. Squeeze juice from membrane into bowl; discard membrane. Drain juice from grapefruit segments; measure 2 tablespoons of the juice into a cup and reserve remainder for other uses.

3. To the 2 tablespoons grapefruit juice, add vinegar, basil, and garlic; stir to combine, then pour over grapefruit in bowl. Add jicama, onion, and radishes; mix gently.

4. Pit and peel avocado, then thinly slice onto salad. Mix gently and season to taste with salt and pepper.

PER SERVING: 145 calories, 8 g total fat, 1 g saturated fat, 0 mg cholesterol, 159 mg sodium, 18 g carbohydrates, 5 g fiber, 2 g protein, 31 mg calcium, 1 mg iron

Artichoke & Dried Tomato Mélange on Greens

A STUDY IN CONTRASTING FLAVORS AND TEXTURES, THIS SALAD FEATURES A WARM BLEND OF DRIED TOMATOES AND ARTICHOKE HEARTS TOSSED WITH COOL, PEPPERY WATERCRESS AND BITTER ENDIVE. CRISP GOLDEN POLENTA CROUTONS AND A FEW SHAVINGS OF DRY JACK CHEESE COMPLETE A STYLISH FIRST COURSE.

15 MINUTES

2 tablespoons oil-packed dried tomatoes

Half of 1 (9-oz.) package frozen artichoke hearts, thawed and drained

1 clove garlic, minced or pressed

1 tablespoon slivered fresh basil or ½ teaspoon dried basil

1 tablespoon balsamic vinegar

4 ounces prepared plain polenta roll, cut into 1-inch cubes

1 head Belgian endive (3 to 4 oz.), rinsed and crisped

2 cups lightly packed watercress sprigs, rinsed and crisped

¼ cup thinly shaved dry jack cheese

1. Drain tomatoes, reserving oil; measure oil, then add enough additional oil from jar to make 2 tablespoons total. Set aside. Cut tomatoes into thin slivers. Cut artichokes into quarters.

2. Heat 1 tablespoon of the tomato oil in a wide nonstick frying pan over medium-high heat. Add tomatoes, artichokes, and garlic; cook, stirring often, for 1 minute. Then cover and continue to cook until artichokes are tender to bite (3 to 4 more minutes). Stir in basil and vinegar; transfer to a bowl and set aside.

3. Heat remaining 1 tablespoon tomato oil in pan. Add polenta cubes and cook, turning as needed, until well browned on all sides (5 to 7 minutes).

4. Meanwhile, trim discolored stems from endive. Break off 6 outer leaves; arrange 3 leaves on each of 2 salad plates. Cut remaining endive crosswise into ¼-inch-wide strips. Add to artichoke mixture along with watercress; toss gently to mix. Divide mixture between plates.

5. To serve, sprinkle salads with croutons and cheese.

PER SERVING: 298 calories, 21 g total fat, 5 g saturated fat, 19 mg cholesterol, 321 mg sodium, 21 g carbohydrates, 8 g fiber, 10 g protein, 205 mg calcium, 2 mg iron

GRILLED ZUCCHINI RIBBONS WITH PARSLEY-OREGANO DRESSING

HERE'S AN IDEAL USE FOR THE PROLIFIC ZUCCHINI CROP FROM YOUR HOME GARDEN. SLICE THE SQUASH LENGTHWISE INTO LONG STRIPS AND BRUSH THEM WITH A FRUITY EXTRA-VIRGIN OLIVE OIL; THEN GRILL JUST UNTIL TENDER-CRISP AND SEASON WITH A SIMPLE DRESSING OF PARSLEY, OREGANO, AND LEMON. FOR BEST FLAVOR, SERVE AT ROOM TEMPERATURE.

15 MINUTES

4 teaspoons extra-virgin olive oil

2 teaspoons lemon juice

1 teaspoon minced parsley

1 teaspoon minced fresh oregano or ¼ teaspoon dried oregano

3 small zucchini (about 4 oz. *each*)
Salt and freshly ground pepper
Oregano sprigs

1. In a bowl, combine 2 teaspoons of the oil, lemon juice, parsley, and minced oregano; set aside.

2. With a sharp knife, cut zucchini lengthwise into ¼-inch-thick strips. Using remaining 2 teaspoons oil, brush both sides of each strip with oil. Sprinkle lightly with salt and pepper. Arrange zucchini on a grill 4 to 6 inches above a solid bed of medium coals (you can hold your hand at grill level for 4 to 5 seconds) or over medium heat on a gas grill. Close lid on gas grill. Cook for 4 to 5 minutes; then turn over and continue to cook until streaked with brown and tender-crisp when pierced (4 to 5 more minutes).

3. Transfer zucchini to bowl with dressing. Toss lightly to coat. If desired, season with additional salt and pepper. Serve at room temperature, garnished with oregano sprigs.

PER SERVING: 106 calories, 10 g total fat, 1 g saturated fat, 0 mg cholesterol, 6 mg sodium, 5 g carbohydrates, 1 g fiber, 2 g protein, 30 mg calcium, 1 mg iron

CLASSIC COLESLAW

THIS LOW-FAT VERSION OF AN ALL-TIME FAVORITE SIDE DISH GOES TOGETHER IN MERE MINUTES WHEN YOU USE THE PACKAGED COLESLAW MIX SOLD IN YOUR SUPERMARKET'S PRODUCE DEPARTMENT. SERVE WITH GRILLED TURKEY BURGERS ON FRESH ONION BUNS; OFFER MELON WEDGES FOR DESSERT.

5 MINUTES

¼ cup plain nonfat yogurt or nonfat mayonnaise

1 tablespoon Dijon mustard

1 tablespoon cider vinegar

3 cups packaged coleslaw mix

2 tablespoons thinly sliced green onion (including some of green top)

2 teaspoons minced parsley
Salt and freshly ground pepper

1. In a medium-size bowl, stir together yogurt, mustard, and vinegar.

2. Add coleslaw mix, onion, and parsley; stir to combine well. Season to taste with salt and pepper.

PER SERVING: 95 calories, 1 g total fat, 0 g saturated fat, 1 mg cholesterol, 253 mg sodium, 18 g carbohydrates, 1 g fiber, 5 g protein, 178 mg calcium, 2 mg iron

SOUPS

Winter Vegetable Soup with Parsley Pesto (page 48)

THAI SHRIMP BROTH WITH LEMON GRASS & GINGER

LEMON GRASS, FRESH GINGER, AND GARLIC GIVE THIS LIGHT BROTH ITS FRAGRANCE AND LIVELY FLAVOR. JULIENNE-CUT GREEN BEANS, SHRIMP, AND A MIX OF CHOPPED HERBS—MINT, BASIL, AND CILANTRO—FILL EACH BOWLFUL; A DASH OF LIME JUICE ADDS THE FINISHING TOUCH.

30 MINUTES

---

4 cups fat-free reduced-sodium chicken broth

⅓ cup chopped carrot

2 tablespoons thinly sliced fresh lemon grass

1 tablespoon minced fresh ginger

2 cloves garlic, thinly sliced

2 ounces green beans (ends removed), cut into julienne strips

6 ounces raw shrimp (16 to 20 per lb.), shelled and deveined

1 tablespoon finely chopped fresh mint

2 teaspoons finely chopped fresh basil

2 teaspoons finely chopped cilantro

⅛ teaspoon crushed red pepper flakes

1½ teaspoons lime juice

Thin lime slices

1. In a 2- to 3-quart pan, combine broth, carrot, lemon grass, ginger, and garlic. Bring to a boil over high heat; then reduce heat and simmer, uncovered, for 15 minutes. Pour broth through a fine wire strainer into a 1½- to 2-quart pan.

2. Return strained broth to a boil over high heat. Add beans, reduce heat, and simmer, uncovered, just until tender to bite (about 3 minutes). Rinse and drain shrimp; add to pan along with mint, basil, cilantro, and red pepper flakes. Continue to simmer until shrimp are just opaque but still moist in center; cut to test (1 to 2 more minutes).

3. Stir lime juice into soup. Ladle into 2 warm soup bowls; garnish with lime slices.

PER SERVING: 137 calories, 1 g total fat, 0 g saturated fat, 105 mg cholesterol, 1,354 mg sodium, 11 g carbohydrates, 2 g fiber, 21 g protein, 73 mg calcium, 3 mg iron

Thai Shrimp Broth with Lemon Grass & Ginger

PEANUT-COCONUT SOUP WITH SHRIMP

ASIAN FLAVORS STAR IN THIS SIMPLE-TO-PREPARE SHRIMP SOUP. COCONUT MILK LENDS SWEETNESS AND A RICH, SILKEN TEXTURE; PREPARED PEANUT SAUCE FLAVORS THE BROTH. THE SAUCE—A BLEND OF GROUND PEANUTS, SOY SAUCE, CHILES, GINGER, AND GARLIC—IS SOLD BOTTLED IN THE ASIAN FOODS SECTION OF MOST SUPERMARKETS; IT'S GREAT TO KEEP ON HAND FOR SPICING UP QUICK ENTRÉES SUCH AS GRILLED MEATS, SALADS, AND PASTAS.

10 MINUTES

1¼ cups fat-free reduced-sodium chicken broth

1¼ cups canned reduced-fat coconut milk

3 tablespoons prepared Asian peanut sauce

⅔ cup frozen tiny peas

6 ounces raw shrimp (26 to 30 per lb.), shelled and deveined

1 tablespoon chopped green onion

Lime wedges

1. In a 1½- to 2-quart pan, combine broth, coconut milk, peanut sauce, and peas. Stir frequently over high heat until mixture comes to a simmer (about 5 minutes).

2. Rinse and drain shrimp; then stir into soup, cover, and remove from heat. Let stand until shrimp are just opaque but still moist in center; cut to test (3 to 4 minutes).

3. Ladle soup into 2 warm soup bowls and sprinkle with onion. Offer lime wedges to squeeze into soup to taste.

PER SERVING: 278 calories, 13 g total fat, 6 g saturated fat, 105 mg cholesterol, 972 mg sodium, 21 g carbohydrates, 4 g fiber, 22 g protein, 50 mg calcium, 3 mg iron

ROASTED RED PEPPER CHOWDER WITH CRAB

TREAT YOUR DINNER PARTNER TO A DELICIOUS SHELLFISH CHOWDER, AN ELEGANT PALE PINK STARTER MADE WITH CANNED ROASTED RED PEPPERS. START BY SIMMERING BROTH, CLAM JUICE, WINE, AND VEGETABLES TO MAKE A FLAVORFUL STOCK; THEN THICKEN THE MIXTURE WITH A BUTTER-AND-FLOUR ROUX AND STIR IN THE PURÉED PEPPERS, FRESH COOKED CRAB, AND, IF YOU LIKE, A HANDFUL OF SWEET CORN KERNELS.

30 MINUTES

About 2 cups fat-free reduced-sodium chicken broth

1 bottle (about 8 oz.) clam juice

½ cup dry white wine

½ cup coarsely chopped onion

½ cup coarsely chopped carrot

½ cup coarsely chopped celery

5 parsley sprigs

1 thyme sprig or ¼ teaspoon dried thyme

½ teaspoon whole black peppercorns

½ cup canned or bottled roasted red peppers, drained

1 tablespoon butter or margarine

1½ tablespoons all-purpose flour

¼ cup half-and-half

4 ounces cooked crabmeat

½ cup fresh or frozen corn kernels (optional)

Salt and freshly ground pepper

1. In a 2- to 3-quart pan, combine 2 cups of the broth, clam juice, wine, onion, carrot, celery, 3 of the parsley sprigs, thyme sprig, and peppercorns. Bring to a boil over high heat; then reduce heat and simmer rapidly, uncovered, for 15 minutes. Pour through a fine wire strainer into a 1-quart glass measure or bowl. You need 2½ cups stock; if necessary, add more chicken broth to make this amount.

2. While stock is simmering, whirl red peppers in a blender or food processor until smoothly puréed.

3. In pan used for stock, melt butter over medium heat. Add flour and stir until a thick paste forms and begins to brown. Remove from heat and whisk strained stock, half-and-half, and puréed peppers into flour mixture. Return to medium-high heat and bring to a boil; then boil and stir until slightly thickened (about 2 minutes). Stir in crab and corn (if used). Season to taste with salt and pepper.

4. Ladle into 2 warm soup bowls and garnish each serving with a parsley sprig.

PER SERVING: 257 calories, 10 g total fat, 6 g saturated fat, 83 mg cholesterol, 1,196 mg sodium, 15 g carbohydrates, 2 g fiber, 17 g protein, 134 mg calcium, 1 mg iron

30-MINUTE LOBSTER BISQUE

WHEN YOU WANT TO PULL OUT ALL THE STOPS—FOR A BIRTHDAY, ANNIVERSARY, HOLIDAY, OR "JUST BECAUSE"—THIS FIRST COURSE PROMISES TO START THINGS OFF WITH A SPLASH. TO SAVE TIME, BUY A COOKED WHOLE LOBSTER FROM THE FISH MARKET; HAVE IT CRACKED AND CLEANED, WITH MEAT REMOVED. (IF YOU HAVE AN EXTRA 15 OR 20 MINUTES, WAIT TO PREPARE THE STOCK—STEP 2 IN OUR RECIPE—UNTIL AFTER YOU'VE REMOVED THE MEAT FROM THE COOKED LOBSTER; THEN SIMMER THE LOBSTER SHELLS ALONG WITH THE BROTH AND VEGETABLES. THEY'LL GIVE THE FINISHED SOUP A RICHER FLAVOR.)

30 MINUTES

30-minute Lobster Bisque

1 live American lobster (about 1½ lbs.)

About 3 cups fat-free reduced-sodium chicken broth

½ cup dry white wine

1 small onion (about 4 oz.), coarsely chopped

1 small carrot (about 4 oz.), peeled and coarsely chopped

1 stalk celery, coarsely chopped

½ teaspoon whole black peppercorns

1 small dried bay leaf

4 chervil sprigs or ½ teaspoon dried chervil

1½ tablespoons butter or margarine

2 tablespoons all-purpose flour

½ cup half-and-half

1 tablespoon tomato paste

1 tablespoon cognac (optional)

Salt and white pepper

Chervil sprigs

1. In a covered 6- to 8-quart pan, bring 4 quarts water to a rapid boil over high heat. Pick up lobster and, holding body from top, plunge headfirst into water. Cover pan and return water to a boil; boil for 10 minutes. Using tongs, lift lobster from pan and drain briefly; then place in a colander and rinse with cold water until cool. Drain well. Twist off tail and claws; use a fork to remove meat. Discard head and body. Coarsely chop lobster meat and set aside.

2. While lobster is cooking, in a 2- to 3-quart pan, combine 3 cups of the broth, wine, onion, carrot, celery, peppercorns, bay leaf, and the 4 chervil sprigs. Bring to a boil over high heat; then reduce heat and simmer rapidly, uncovered, for 15 minutes. Pour broth through a fine wire strainer into a 1-quart glass measure or bowl. You need 2¼ cups stock; if necessary, add more chicken broth to make this amount.

3. Melt butter in same pan over medium heat. Add flour; stir until a thick paste forms. Remove from heat and whisk in strained stock, half-and-half, tomato paste, and cognac (if used). Return to medium-high heat and bring to a boil; then boil and stir until slightly thickened (about 2 minutes). Stir in lobster meat and season to taste with salt and white pepper.

4. Ladle into 2 warm soup bowls; garnish with chervil sprigs.

PER SERVING: 347 calories, 16 g total fat, 10 g saturated fat, 99 mg cholesterol, 1,412 mg sodium, 18 g carbohydrates, 2 g fiber, 23 g protein, 137 mg calcium, 1 mg iron

FISH SOUP WITH YUKON GOLD POTATOES & FENNEL

SERVED WITH A SALAD, PLENTY OF FRENCH BREAD, AND DESSERT, THIS HANDSOME SEAFOOD SOUP IS A FINE MEAL FOR WEEKNIGHTS AND SPECIAL OCCASIONS ALIKE. THE POTATOES AND FENNEL ABSORB THE OCEAN FLAVOR OF FISH AND SHELLFISH SIMMERED IN A BASE OF BROTH, WINE, AND CREAM. FOR A DRAMATIC PRESENTATION, USE WHOLE SHRIMP WITH HEADS; THEY'RE SOLD IN ASIAN FISH MARKETS AND, OFTEN, IN OTHER FISH MARKETS AS WELL.

25 TO 30 MINUTES

Fish Soup with Yukon Gold Potatoes & Fennel

1 can (about 14½ oz.) fat-free reduced-sodium chicken broth

¼ cup Sauvignon Blanc or other dry white wine

3 tablespoons whipping cream

¼ teaspoon fennel seeds

¼ teaspoon fresh thyme leaves or dried thyme

8 ounces Yukon Gold or other thin-skinned potatoes, peeled and cut into ¼-inch-thick slices

1 small head fennel (about 3 inches in diameter)

8 to 10 mussels in shells

8 raw shrimp (16 to 20 per lb.)

4 ounces Chilean sea bass

1. In a 2- to 3-quart pan, combine broth, wine, cream, fennel seeds, thyme, and potatoes. Cover pan and place over high heat.

2. Rinse fennel and cut off coarse stalks, reserving some of the feathery leaves. Trim and discard base and any discolored or bruised parts from fennel bulb; then thinly slice bulb crosswise and add to broth.

3. When broth boils, reduce heat and simmer, covered, until potatoes are very tender when pierced (about 15 minutes). Meanwhile, prepare seafood: scrub mussels and pull off beards. Shell, devein, and rinse shrimp. Rinse sea bass, pat dry, and cut into 1-inch chunks. Set all seafood aside.

4. When potatoes are tender, add mussels to soup. Cover and simmer for 3 minutes. Add shrimp and sea bass and continue to simmer until mussels pop open (3 to 4 more minutes). Ladle soup into 2 warm wide, shallow soup bowls, discarding any unopened mussels; garnish with fennel leaves.

PER SERVING: 301 calories, 9 g total fat, 5 g saturated fat, 104 mg cholesterol, 775 mg sodium, 24 g carbohydrates, 3 g fiber, 25 g protein, 98 mg calcium, 3 mg iron

CLAMS IN TOMATO-FENNEL BROTH

HARD-SHELL CLAMS ARE STEAMED IN A FRAGRANT TOMATO-WINE BROTH THAT TAKES ON A SUBTLE LICORICE FLAVOR FROM THE ADDITION OF FRESH FENNEL. OFFER PLENTY OF FRENCH BREAD TO DIP INTO THE BROTH. THE CLAMS COOK VERY QUICKLY; WATCH CAREFULLY TO KEEP THEM FROM BECOMING OVERDONE.

25 MINUTES

1 small head fennel (about 3 inches in diameter)

2 cloves garlic, minced or pressed

1 bottle (about 8 oz.) clam juice

1 cup fat-free reduced-sodium chicken broth

½ cup dry white wine

1 cup canned no-salt-added sliced tomatoes (about half of a 1-lb. can)

2 pounds small hard-shell clams in shells, suitable for steaming, scrubbed

Freshly ground pepper

1. Rinse fennel and cut off coarse stalks, reserving some of the feathery leaves. Trim and discard base and any discolored or bruised parts from fennel bulb; then thinly slice bulb crosswise.

2. In a 2- to 3-quart pan, combine sliced fennel, garlic, clam juice, broth, and wine; cover and bring to a boil over high heat. Then reduce heat and simmer, covered, until fennel is tender when pierced (about 10 minutes).

3. Stir in tomatoes and clams. Cover and return to a simmer over high heat; then reduce heat and continue to simmer, stirring occasionally, until clams pop open (3 to 4 minutes). Meanwhile, mince enough of the reserved fennel leaves to make about 2 teaspoons.

4. Ladle soup into 2 warm soup bowls, discarding any unopened clams. Sprinkle soup with minced fennel leaves and garnish with a few whole fennel sprigs. Offer pepper to season soup to taste.

PER SERVING: 144 calories, 1 g total fat, 0 g saturated fat, 23 mg cholesterol, 717 mg sodium, 12 g carbohydrates, 2 g fiber, 13 g protein, 134 mg calcium, 11 mg iron

Yellow Tomato Gazpacho with Seared Bay Scallops

Often described as a salad in a soup bowl, cool and refreshing gazpacho easily ranks high on the list of healthful supper choices. This version gets added nutrition from tiny, tender quick-cooked bay scallops. For best flavor, select ripe tomatoes in season; we use yellow tomatoes, but any other color—red, orange, burgundy, striped—works just as well. For a nice presentation, garnish each serving with yellow cherry tomatoes and thin cucumber slices.

20 MINUTES

1½ pounds ripe yellow tomatoes, cut into chunks

⅓ cup tomato juice

2 tablespoons red wine vinegar

1½ tablespoons lemon juice

1 teaspoon Worcestershire

½ teaspoon liquid hot pepper seasoning

½ cup diced red bell pepper

½ cup peeled, seeded, diced cucumber

1 small clove garlic, minced or pressed

2 teaspoons chopped cilantro

1 teaspoon olive oil

4 ounces bay scallops

Salt and freshly ground pepper

Cilantro sprigs

1. In a food processor or blender, whirl tomatoes, a portion at a time, until coarsely puréed.

2. Pour tomatoes into a large bowl and stir in tomato juice, 1½ tablespoons of the vinegar, lemon juice, Worcestershire, hot pepper seasoning, bell pepper, cucumber, garlic, and chopped cilantro. Set aside.

3. Heat oil in a small nonstick frying pan over high heat. Rinse scallops, pat dry, and sprinkle all over with salt and pepper. Add scallops to pan and cook (do not stir) for 1½ minutes. Then turn scallops over and continue to cook until well browned on bottom and just opaque but still moist in center; cut to test (about 1½ more minutes). Sprinkle with remaining 1½ teaspoons vinegar and remove from heat.

4. Ladle soup into 2 bowls; gently place half the scallops in center of each bowl of soup. Garnish with cilantro sprigs.

PER SERVING: 160 calories, 4 g total fat, 0 g saturated fat, 19 mg cholesterol, 329 mg sodium, 22 g carbohydrates, 5 g fiber, 13 g protein, 41 mg calcium, 2 mg iron

Garlicky Lentil-Kielbasa Soup

To cut the cooking time of this hearty soup, we used hulled (decorticated) Red Chief lentils—they simmer to tenderness in just 10 minutes or so. And unlike hulled imported varieties, which fall apart by the time the liquid is boiling, Red Chiefs hold their shape. Look for them in supermarkets, natural food stores, and gourmet shops. Serve the soup with a salad; sip the unused Riesling alongside.

30 MINUTES

1 tablespoon olive oil

1 small onion (about 5 oz.), chopped

⅔ cup Red Chief or regular brown lentils

4 cups fat-free reduced-sodium chicken broth

½ cup semidry Riesling or other fruity white wine

6 large cloves garlic, minced or pressed

¼ teaspoon dried thyme

½ dried bay leaf

4 ounces kielbasa (Polish sausage), thinly sliced, slices cut crosswise into halves

1½ tablespoons minced parsley

About 2 teaspoons red wine vinegar

Salt

1. Heat oil in a 2- to 3-quart pan over medium-high heat. Add onion and cook, stirring occasionally, until it begins to brown (about 5 minutes). Meanwhile, sort lentils, discarding any debris; then rinse and drain lentils.

2. To onion, add lentils, broth, wine, garlic, thyme, and bay leaf. Bring to a boil; then reduce heat and simmer, uncovered, until lentils are tender to bite (8 to 10 minutes for Red Chiefs, 20 to 25 minutes for regular lentils).

3. About 5 minutes before lentils are done, add sausage, 1 tablespoon of the parsley, and 2 teaspoons of the vinegar.

4. Season soup to taste with salt and ladle into 2 warm soup bowls. Sprinkle with remaining 1½ teaspoons parsley; add more vinegar to taste, if desired.

PER SERVING: 571 calories, 23 g total fat, 7 g saturated fat, 38 mg cholesterol, 1,866 mg sodium, 51 g carbohydrates, 9 g fiber, 33 g protein, 108 mg calcium, 8 mg iron

Garlicky Lentil-Kielbasa Soup

WINTER VEGETABLE SOUP WITH PARSLEY PESTO

Pictured on page 39

ON COLD, RAW DAYS, A STEAMING BOWL OF SOUP IS THE PERFECT ANTIDOTE TO THE WEATHER. THIS ONE IS FULL OF VEGETABLES IN A FLAVORFUL BEEF BROTH; A SPOONFUL OF GARLICKY PARSLEY PESTO IS STIRRED IN BEFORE SERVING TO ADD COLOR AND FRESHNESS. FOR EXTRA-RICH FLAVOR WITHOUT HOURS OF SIMMERING, USE PURCHASED BEEF DEMI-GLACE; YOU'LL FIND IT IN THE SOUPS AISLE OR FREEZER CASE OF WELL-STOCKED SUPERMARKETS AND GOURMET FOOD SHOPS.

25 TO 30 MINUTES

---

1 tablespoon butter or olive oil

½ cup chopped carrot

½ cup thinly sliced leek

½ cup chopped celery

3 cups fat-free beef broth

1 tablespoon prepared beef demi-glace (beef stock reduction)

1 medium-size ripe tomato (about 6 oz.), chopped

½ cup chopped turnip

½ cup diagonally sliced green beans (1-inch lengths)

Parsley Pesto (below)

Salt and freshly ground pepper

PARSLEY PESTO

⅓ cup lightly packed Italian parsley leaves

1 large clove garlic

2 tablespoons olive oil

3 tablespoons grated Parmesan cheese

1. Melt butter in a 2- to 3-quart pan over medium-high heat. Add carrot, leek, and celery. Cook, stirring occasionally, until vegetables begin to brown and stick to pan bottom (7 to 10 minutes).

2. Add broth, demi-glace, tomato, turnip, and beans. Bring to a boil; then reduce heat, cover, and simmer until beans and turnip are tender when pierced (8 to 10 minutes). Meanwhile, prepare Parsley Pesto.

3. Season soup to taste with salt and pepper, then stir in 1 tablespoon of the pesto. Ladle soup into 2 warm soup bowls and offer remaining pesto to add to taste.

PARSLEY PESTO

In a blender or food processor, whirl parsley, garlic, and oil until puréed. Add cheese and whirl until blended, scraping sides of container often.

PER SERVING: 307 calories, 22 g total fat, 7 g saturated fat, 21 mg cholesterol, 1,257 mg sodium, 19 g carbohydrates, 4 g fiber, 11 g protein, 187 mg calcium, 3 mg iron

Golden Spiced Butternut Squash & Apple Soup

GOLDEN SPICED BUTTERNUT SQUASH & APPLE SOUP

WHEN THE LEAVES BEGIN TO CHANGE AND THE AIR TURNS CRISP, THE TIME IS RIGHT FOR THIS SMOOTH, GOLDEN SOUP. PIPPIN APPLE AND A BLEND OF THREE WARM SPICES—ALLSPICE, CINNAMON, AND NUTMEG—LEND SWEET AND TART ACCENTS TO THE MELLOWNESS OF THE BUTTERNUT SQUASH. FOR A SATISFYING SUPPER, SERVE WITH A SALAD SUCH AS PEAR, CANDIED WALNUTS, BACON & GORGONZOLA ON MIXED GREENS (PAGE 19).

30 MINUTES

1 tablespoon butter or margarine

1 small onion (about 5 oz.), chopped

1 small Newtown Pippin or Granny Smith apple (4 to 5 oz.), peeled, cored, and chopped

1 very small butternut squash (about 1¼ lbs.), peeled, seeded, and cut into ½-inch cubes

About 2½ cups fat-free reduced-sodium chicken broth

¼ teaspoon ground allspice

¼ teaspoon ground cinnamon

¼ teaspoon ground nutmeg

Salt and white pepper

2 teaspoons whipping cream (optional)

1. Melt butter in a 2- to 3-quart pan over medium-high heat. Add onion and apple; cook, stirring occasionally, until onion begins to brown (7 to 10 minutes). Add squash, ½ cup of the broth, allspice, cinnamon, and nutmeg. Cover and cook, stirring often, until squash is tender when pierced (10 to 12 minutes); if pan becomes dry, add a little more broth.

2. In a blender or food processor, whirl squash mixture, a portion at a time, until smoothly puréed. Return purée to pan and add remaining 2 cups broth. Bring just to a simmer over high heat, stirring; season to taste with salt and white pepper.

3. Ladle soup into 2 warm soup bowls. If desired, drizzle 1 teaspoon of cream decoratively over each serving of soup.

PER SERVING: 238 calories, 6 g total fat, 4 g saturated fat, 16 mg cholesterol, 846 mg sodium, 44 g carbohydrates, 6 g fiber, 7 g protein, 138 mg calcium, 2 mg iron

BROTH BASICS

WHEN HECTIC SCHEDULES DELAY THE DINNER HOUR, CANNED CHICKEN OR BEEF BROTH CAN BE A REAL LIFESAVER: IT'S THE FOUNDATION FOR HOMEMADE SOUPS THAT CAN BE TABLE-READY IN MINUTES. THE OTHER INGREDIENTS ARE BASIC, TOO; YOU CAN USUALLY CALL ON PANTRY STAPLES OR USE LEFTOVER MEATS AND VEGETABLES YOU HAVE ON HAND IN THE REFRIGERATOR. IN A FEW CASES, YOU MAY HAVE TO MAKE A QUICK STOP AT THE MARKET. COMPLETE A SATISFYING MENU WITH A GREEN SALAD, WARM BREAD, AND A SIMPLE DESSERT.

PASTA, PROSCIUTTO & PEA SOUP

20 TO 25 MINUTES

- 2 cans (about 14½ oz. *each*) fat-free reduced-sodium chicken broth
- ⅓ cup dry white wine
- ½ cup dried orzo or other tiny pasta shapes
- 2 teaspoons butter or margarine
- 1½ ounces thinly sliced prosciutto, cut into thin slivers
- ½ cup frozen tiny peas
- ½ cup lightly packed fresh basil leaves, cut into thin slivers
- Freshly grated Parmesan cheese

1. In a 1½- to 2-quart pan, combine broth, wine, and pasta. Cover and bring to a boil over high heat; then reduce heat and simmer, covered, until pasta is tender to bite (15 to 18 minutes total).

2. While pasta is cooking, melt butter in a small frying pan over medium-high heat. Add prosciutto and stir until brown and crisp (4 to 5 minutes). Remove from pan with a slotted spoon and drain on paper towels.

3. Stir peas and basil into soup and simmer until peas are heated through (1 to 2 minutes). Ladle into 2 warm soup bowls; sprinkle with prosciutto and cheese.

PER SERVING: 314 calories, 6 g total fat, 2 g saturated fat, 22 mg cholesterol, 1,544 mg sodium, 40 g carbohydrates, 5 g fiber, 19 g protein, 53 mg calcium, 3 mg iron

MEXICAN CHICKEN SOUP

15 MINUTES

- 2 cans (about 14½ oz. *each*) fat-free reduced-sodium chicken broth
- ⅔ cup tomato salsa
- 2 tablespoons lime juice
- 1 cup shredded cooked chicken
- ½ cup frozen corn kernels
- ½ cup quick-cooking white rice
- 2 tablespoons minced cilantro
- Lime wedges
- Avocado wedges
- Sour cream

1. In a 1½- to 2-quart pan, combine broth, salsa, and lime juice. Cover and bring to a boil over high heat. Stir in chicken, corn, rice, and cilantro. Return to a boil; then reduce heat and simmer, covered, until rice is tender to bite (3 to 5 minutes).

2. Ladle into 2 warm soup bowls. Offer lime wedges, avocado, and sour cream to season soup to taste.

PER SERVING: 315 calories, 6 g total fat, 1 g saturated fat, 62 mg cholesterol, 1,691 mg sodium, 37 g carbohydrates, 1 g fiber, 28 g protein, 19 mg calcium, 2 mg iron

ASIAN DUMPLING SOUP

15 MINUTES

- 1½ cups lightly packed packaged triple-washed spinach
- 2 cans (about 14½ oz. *each*) fat-free reduced-sodium chicken broth
- 1½ tablespoons minced fresh ginger
- 1 clove garlic, minced or pressed
- 1 tablespoon seasoned rice vinegar
- 1½ teaspoons soy sauce
- 8 ounces frozen potstickers or won tons
- ¼ cup diagonally sliced green onions

  Asian sesame oil

1. Remove and discard any coarse stems from spinach; set spinach aside.

2. In a 1½- to 2-quart pan, combine broth, ginger, garlic, vinegar, and soy sauce. Cover and bring to a boil over high heat. Add potstickers and simmer, uncovered, until hot in center; cut to test (6 to 8 minutes). Stir in spinach and onions. Remove from heat, cover, and let stand until spinach is wilted (about 2 minutes).

3. Ladle soup into 2 warm soup bowls; offer sesame oil to add to taste.

PER SERVING: 269 calories, 6 g total fat, 1 g saturated fat, 20 mg cholesterol, 1,969 mg sodium, 38 g carbohydrates, 2 g fiber, 17 g protein, 87 mg calcium, 2 mg iron

BLACK BEAN SOUP

20 MINUTES

- 2 cups fat-free reduced-sodium chicken broth
- 2 cans (about 15 oz. *each*) black beans, rinsed and drained
- ½ cup chopped onion
- 1 clove garlic, minced or pressed
- ¼ teaspoon ground cumin
- ¼ teaspoon ground coriander
- 1 tablespoon tomato paste
- 1 cup coarsely chopped cooked lean beef, such as leftover roast beef or steak

  Chopped cilantro

  Crushed tortilla chips

  Shredded pepper jack cheese

1. In a 2½- to 3-quart pan, combine broth, beans, onion, garlic, cumin, coriander, and tomato paste. Cover and bring to a boil over high heat.

2. For a thicker soup, scoop about half the beans into a blender or food processor. Add some of the broth and whirl until puréed; then return to pan.

3. Add beef to soup and bring to a simmer over medium-high heat. Ladle into 2 warm soup bowls; offer cilantro, tortilla chips, and cheese to add to taste.

PER SERVING: 372 calories, 12 g total fat, 4 g saturated fat, 57 mg cholesterol, 1,275 mg sodium, 33 g carbohydrates, 12 g fiber, 33 g protein, 84 mg calcium, 7 mg iron

MIXED GRAIN & LAMB SOUP WITH SHERRY

30 MINUTES

- 8 ounces lean ground lamb
- ½ cup chopped onion
- ½ cup chopped carrot
- ⅔ cup grain mix (use equal parts quick-cooking barley, quick-cooking brown rice, bulgur, and rinsed quinoa; or use all one kind of grain)
- 2¾ cups fat-free beef broth
- ½ cup dry sherry
- 2 tablespoons finely chopped parsley

  Freshly ground pepper

1. Crumble lamb into a 1½- to 2-quart pan; add onion and carrot. Cook over medium-high heat, stirring occasionally, until lamb is well browned (about 10 minutes). Spoon off and discard any fat.

2. To pan, add grain mix, broth, and sherry. Bring to a boil over medium-high heat; then reduce heat, cover, and simmer until all grains are tender to bite (about 12 minutes). Stir in parsley and season to taste with pepper.

PER SERVING: 614 calories, 28 g total fat, 12 g saturated fat, 83 mg cholesterol, 963 mg sodium, 46 g carbohydrates, 7 g fiber, 29 g protein, 56 mg calcium, 4 mg iron

CARAMELIZED FRENCH ONION SOUP WITH GRUYÈRE CROUTONS IMAGINE PREPARING AND SERVING A MELLOW, RICH-TASTING FRENCH ONION SOUP IN JUST 30 MINUTES! THIS RECIPE ALLOWS YOU TO DO JUST THAT. THE SECRET IS PREPARED BEEF DEMI-GLACE, SOLD IN THE SOUPS AISLE OR FREEZER CASE OF WELL-STOCKED SUPERMARKETS AND GOURMET FOOD SHOPS.

30 MINUTES

1 tablespoon butter (do not use margarine)

2 large onions (about 1 lb. *total*), thinly sliced

About 1 teaspoon sugar

2 cups fat-free beef broth

1 tablespoon prepared beef demi-glace (beef stock reduction)

⅓ cup dry white wine

1 tablespoon cognac (optional)

Salt and freshly ground pepper

4 diagonal slices French bread baguette (*each* about ¾ inch thick)

1 teaspoon olive oil

¾ cup shredded Gruyère cheese

1. Melt butter in a 2- to 3-quart pan over medium-high heat. Add onions and cook, stirring often, until golden brown and very soft (about 20 minutes). About halfway through cooking, stir 1 teaspoon of the sugar into onions.

2. To pan, add broth, demi-glace, wine, and cognac (if used). Bring to a boil; then boil, stirring often, until flavors are blended (about 5 minutes). If you prefer a sweeter flavor, add a little more sugar. Season onions to taste with salt and pepper.

3. While onions are cooking, brush both sides of each baguette slice with oil. Place on a baking sheet and broil 4 to 6 inches below heat, turning once, until lightly browned on both sides (1 to 2 minutes).

4. Ladle soup into 2 ovenproof soup bowls. Top each serving with 2 slices of toast; sprinkle toast with cheese. Place bowls on baking sheet and broil about 6 inches below heat until cheese is bubbly and lightly browned, 2 to 3 minutes. (If desired, top each bowl of soup with just one slice of cheese-topped toast; broil remaining 2 slices on baking sheet and serve alongside the soup.)

PER SERVING: 504 calories, 23 g total fat, 12 g saturated fat, 62 mg cholesterol, 1,136 mg sodium, 46 g carbohydrates, 5 g fiber, 22 g protein, 512 mg calcium, 2 mg iron

WINTER SQUASH SOUP WITH FONTINA & SAGE

VELVETY IN TEXTURE, DEEP GOLDEN ORANGE IN COLOR, AND RICH IN FLAVOR, THIS SOUP IS APPEALING IN EVERY WAY. FOR A DELICIOUS FINISHING TOUCH, IT'S LADLED INTO BOWLS OVER DICED FONTINA CHEESE, THEN GARNISHED WITH CRISP-FRIED FRESH SAGE LEAVES. IF YOU LIKE, USE BUTTERNUT, KABOCHA, RED KURI, OR BUTTERCUP SQUASH IN PLACE OF THE BANANA SQUASH.

30 MINUTES

1 tablespoon olive oil

6 fresh sage leaves (*each* about 1½ inches long)

1 small onion (about 4 oz.), chopped

2 cloves garlic, minced or pressed

1 pound banana squash, peeled, seeded, and cut into ¾-inch cubes

1 tablespoon minced parsley

1 teaspoon minced fresh sage

¼ teaspoon minced fresh thyme or dried thyme

2 cups fat-free reduced-sodium chicken broth or regular-strength vegetable broth

Salt

¼ cup diced fontina cheese

Freshly ground pepper

1. Heat oil in a 2- to 3-quart pan over medium-high heat until it ripples. Add sage leaves and stir often until they turn darker green and begin to curl at edges (about 1 minute). Lift leaves from pan with a slotted spoon and drain on paper towels.

2. Add onion and garlic to pan; cook, stirring occasionally, until onion begins to brown (7 to 10 minutes). Add squash, parsley, minced sage, thyme, and ⅔ cup of the broth. Cover and cook, stirring often, until squash is tender when pierced (6 to 8 minutes). Uncover; continue to simmer until liquid has evaporated and vegetables begin to stick to pan (about 5 more minutes).

3. Remove pan from heat and mash squash mixture with a potato masher until smooth. Stir in remaining 1⅓ cups broth. Place over high heat and bring soup to a boil, stirring often. Season to taste with salt.

4. Divide cheese between 2 warm soup bowls. Ladle soup into bowls; top with fried sage leaves and sprinkle with pepper.

PER SERVING: 217 calories, 12 g total fat, 4 g saturated fat, 16 mg cholesterol, 743 mg sodium, 22 g carbohydrates, 4 g fiber, 10 g protein, 154 mg calcium, 1 mg iron

TOMATO-BASIL SOUP WITH RICE

NOTHING IS A BETTER ACCENT FOR SWEET VINE-RIPENED TOMATOES THAN AROMATIC FRESH BASIL. WHEN BOTH ARE IN SEASON DURING THE SUMMER MONTHS, TRY THIS SMOOTH PURÉE. (WHEN FRESH TOMATOES ARE NO LONGER AT THEIR BEST, USE CANNED DICED TOMATOES AND 2 TEASPOONS OF DRIED BASIL.)

30 MINUTES

1½ teaspoons butter or margarine

1 medium-size onion (about 6 oz.), chopped

1 small carrot (about 4 oz.), chopped

2 large ripe tomatoes (about 1 lb. *total*), coarsely chopped; or 1 can (about 14½ oz.) diced tomatoes

⅓ cup lightly packed fresh basil leaves, chopped; or 2 teaspoons dried basil

½ teaspoon salt

½ teaspoon sugar

1¼ cups fat-free reduced-sodium chicken broth

3 tablespoons quick-cooking white rice

Freshly ground pepper

Finely slivered fresh basil

1. Melt butter in a 2- to 3-quart pan over medium-high heat. Add onion and carrot; cook, stirring occasionally, until vegetables begin to brown (7 to 10 minutes). Add tomatoes, chopped basil, salt, and sugar. Bring mixture to a boil, stirring often; then reduce heat, cover, and simmer until tomatoes are soft (about 5 minutes).

2. In a blender or food processor, whirl tomato mixture, a portion at a time, until smoothly puréed.

3. Return purée to pan, add broth, and return to a boil; then stir in rice. Reduce heat, cover, and simmer until rice is tender to bite (about 5 minutes). Season to taste with pepper. Ladle soup into 2 warm soup bowls; garnish with slivered basil.

PER SERVING: 178 calories, 4 g total fat, 2 g saturated fat, 8 mg cholesterol, 1,038 mg sodium, 33 g carbohydrates, 7 g fiber, 6 g protein, 78 mg calcium, 2 mg iron

Tomato-Basil Soup with Rice

Northern Italian Minestrone with Polenta

NORTHERN ITALIAN MINESTRONE WITH POLENTA

EACH REGION IN ITALY HAS ITS OWN VARIATION OF THIS CLASSIC SOUP. OUR VERSION IS LOADED WITH VEGETABLES AND CANNELLINI BEANS; A LITTLE POLENTA GIVES THE BROTH EXTRA TEXTURE AND BODY. ACCOMPANIED WITH HERB-SEASONED FOCACCIA, IT'S HEARTY ENOUGH FOR A ONE-BOWL LUNCH OR SUPPER.

30 MINUTES

1 tablespoon olive oil

1 large clove garlic, minced or pressed

2 ounces thinly sliced prosciutto, finely chopped

½ cup thinly sliced carrot

½ cup thinly sliced celery

½ cup chopped onion

1 medium-size ripe tomato (about 6 oz.), chopped

3 cups fat-free beef broth

¼ teaspoon dried thyme

¼ cup polenta or yellow cornmeal

4 ounces Swiss chard

1 can (about 15 oz.) cannellini (white kidney beans), rinsed and drained

Freshly grated Parmesan cheese

1. Heat oil in a 2- to 3-quart pan over medium-high heat. Add garlic and stir until fragrant (about 30 seconds). Add prosciutto, carrot, celery, and onion; cook, stirring occasionally, until the vegetables begin to brown and stick to pan bottom (7 to 10 minutes).

2. Add tomato, broth, thyme, and polenta to pan. Bring to a boil, stirring; then reduce heat and simmer, uncovered, until polenta is soft (16 to 18 minutes).

3. Meanwhile, trim and discard discolored ends of chard stems. Rinse and drain chard; stack leaves and cut in half lengthwise, then cut crosswise into ¼-inch-wide strips.

4. About 5 minutes before soup is done, stir in chard and beans. When soup is done, ladle into 2 warm soup bowls; offer cheese to add to taste.

PER SERVING: 490 calories, 13 g total fat, 2 g saturated fat, 23 mg cholesterol, 1,889 mg sodium, 67 g carbohydrates, 16 g fiber, 29 g protein, 119 mg calcium, 5 mg iron

LEEK, POTATO & SWEET GARLIC CHOWDER

THIS SMOOTH, LIGHT LEEK-POTATO CHOWDER IS FILLING, TOO. IT MAY SEEM A BIT HEAVY ON THE GARLIC, BUT THE FLAVOR IS SURPRISINGLY SWEET: 20 MINUTES OF SIMMERING SOFTENS THE GARLIC'S PUNGENCY. SERVE WITH PORK CHOPS AND HOT SAUERKRAUT MIXED WITH GRATED TART APPLE; CONCLUDE THE MEAL WITH ICE CREAM WITH COGNAC & CARAMELIZED WALNUTS (PAGE 224).

30 MINUTES

3 slices thick-cut bacon (about 4 oz. *total*), cut crosswise into ¼-inch-wide strips

4 large cloves garlic, minced or pressed

1 small onion (about 4 oz.), chopped

2 medium-size leeks (white part only), halved lengthwise, then thinly sliced crosswise

1 large russet potato (about 8 oz.), peeled and finely diced

2½ cups fat-free reduced-sodium chicken broth

Salt and white pepper

2 teaspoons minced parsley

1. Cook bacon in a 2- to 3-quart pan over medium-high heat, stirring often, until brown and crisp (4 to 5 minutes). Lift out with a slotted spoon and drain on paper towels; set aside.

2. To pan, add garlic and onion. Cook, stirring occasionally, until onion begins to brown (about 5 minutes). Add leeks and potato; cook, stirring occasionally, for 2 minutes. Stir in broth and bring to a boil over high heat. Then reduce heat and simmer, uncovered, until potato is very tender when pierced (about 10 minutes).

3. In a blender or food processor, whirl soup, a portion at a time, until smoothly puréed. Return to pan. Season to taste with salt and white pepper. Increase heat to high and stir until soup is steaming. Ladle into 2 warm soup bowls; sprinkle with bacon and parsley.

PER SERVING: 520 calories, 33 g total fat, 12 g saturated fat, 38 mg cholesterol, 1,198 mg sodium, 43 g carbohydrates, 4 g fiber, 13 g protein, 98 mg calcium, 4 mg iron

ASPARAGUS-TARRAGON CREAM SOUP

SAVOR THIS DELICATE BOWLFUL IN SPRING, WHEN ASPARAGUS IS AT ITS PEAK; IT'S A PERFECT FIRST COURSE FOR A DINNER OF GRILLED LAMB. FOR DESSERT, YOU MIGHT OFFER STRAWBERRY SHORTCAKE.

15 MINUTES

12 ounces asparagus, tough ends
   snapped off
 2 teaspoons olive oil
 2 tablespoons chopped shallots
1½ tablespoons chopped fresh tarragon
 1 can (about 14½ oz.) vegetable
   broth
   Salt and white pepper
 2 tablespoons whipping cream

1. Coarsely chop asparagus and set aside.

2. Heat oil in a 1½- to 2-quart pan over medium-high heat. Add shallots and cook, stirring often, until soft (2 to 3 minutes). Add asparagus, 1 tablespoon of the tarragon, and broth. Increase heat to high and bring to a boil; boil until asparagus is tender-crisp when pierced (about 3 minutes).

3. In a blender or food processor, whirl soup, a portion at a time, until smooth. Season to taste with salt and white pepper.

4. Return purée to pan and stir in cream. Stir over high heat until steaming (about 2 minutes). Ladle into 2 warm soup bowls and sprinkle with remaining 1½ teaspoons tarragon.

PER SERVING: 140 calories, 10 g total fat, 4 g saturated fat, 17 mg cholesterol, 866 mg sodium, 10 g carbohydrates, 1 g fiber, 5 g protein, 54 mg calcium, 1 mg iron

CHIPOTLE CORN & CHICKEN SOUP

THE RICH, SMOKY HEAT OF CHIPOTLE CHILES COMES THROUGH—IN TEMPERED FORM!—IN THIS MELLOW CHICKEN-CORN SOUP. TO TAME THE CHILES' FIRE, REMOVE THE VEINS (WHERE THE HEAT IS CONCENTRATED) AND SEEDS. CHIPOTLES ARE SOLD CANNED IN ADOBADO, A SPICY TOMATO SAUCE. LOOK FOR THEM IN THE INTERNATIONAL FOODS SECTION OF YOUR SUPERMARKET OR IN A LATINO GROCERY STORE.

25 MINUTES

 1 or 2 canned chipotle chiles in
   adobado sauce
 3 cups fat-free reduced-sodium
   chicken broth
½ cup chopped onion
 1 clove garlic, minced or pressed
¼ teaspoon cumin seeds
 1 cup fresh or frozen corn kernels
 1 small pear-shaped (Roma-type)
   tomato (about 2 oz.), diced
 1 cup shredded cooked chicken
 1 tablespoon lime juice
 2 tablespoons cilantro leaves
1½ ounces cream cheese, cut into
   ½-inch cubes

1. Wearing rubber gloves, rinse chiles; gently pull off and discard stems, veins, and seeds. Tear chiles lengthwise into strips.

2. Place chiles in a 2- to 3-quart pan and add broth, onion, garlic, cumin seeds, and corn. Bring to a boil over high heat; then reduce heat, cover, and simmer until flavors are blended (about 15 minutes).

3. Stir in tomato and chicken. Increase heat to high and bring to a boil; then stir in lime juice and cilantro. Ladle into 2 warm soup bowls and top with cheese.

PER SERVING: 307 calories, 13 g total fat, 6 g saturated fat, 74 mg cholesterol, 1,154 mg sodium, 25 g carbohydrates, 4 g fiber, 26 g protein, 50 mg calcium, 2 mg iron

TORTELLINI IN BRODO WITH SPINACH & PESTO

A PROSCIUTTO- AND PESTO-SEASONED BROTH THICK WITH PLUMP MUSHROOM-FILLED TORTELLINI AND FRESH SPINACH MAKES A FAST AND FILLING MEAL. SERVE IT WITH SLICED CIABATTA, A CRUSTY ITALIAN BREAD WITH A CHEWY INTERIOR. FOR DESSERT, YOU MIGHT OFFER CAKE WITH MELTED FRUIT UNDER MARSALA CREAM (PAGE 230).

20 MINUTES

2 teaspoons olive oil

1½ ounces thinly sliced prosciutto, chopped

1 clove garlic, minced or pressed

1 small onion (about 4 oz.), chopped

1 can (about 14½ oz.) fat-free beef broth

1 cup water

2 teaspoons minced parsley

Half of 1 (about 9-oz.) package fresh mushroom- or cheese-filled tortellini

2 cups lightly packed packaged triple-washed baby spinach

1 tablespoon prepared pesto

Freshly grated Parmesan cheese

1. Heat oil in a 3- to 4-quart pan over medium-high heat. Add prosciutto, garlic, and onion; cook, stirring occasionally, until onion begins to brown (7 to 10 minutes).

2. Add broth and water. Increase heat to high and bring to a boil. Stir in parsley and tortellini; reduce heat and boil gently, uncovered, until pasta is just tender to bite (5 to 6 minutes).

3. Add spinach to soup; cover and simmer until spinach is wilted (about 2 minutes). Stir in pesto. Ladle into 2 warm soup bowls; offer cheese to add to taste.

PER SERVING: 369 calories, 16 g total fat, 4 g saturated fat, 46 mg cholesterol, 1,201 mg sodium, 39 g carbohydrates, 4 g fiber, 19 g protein, 114 mg calcium, 4 mg iron

COUNTRY BREAD & CABBAGE SOUP WITH FONTINA CROSTINI

THIS HEARTY ITALIAN SOUP HAS VERY HUMBLE BEGINNINGS. TO MAKE A MEAL OUT OF NOTHING, INVENTIVE COOKS BOILED A FEW VEGETABLES—TOMATO, CARROT, AND CELERY—IN WATER, THEN POURED THE MIXTURE OVER STALE BREAD. OVER TIME, THE DISH HAS BECOME MORE SOPHISTICATED, BUT IT RETAINS ITS ORIGINAL SIMPLICITY. ENJOY IT BESIDE A CRACKLING FIRE, WITH A GLASS OF CHIANTI AND A GREEN SALAD DRESSED IN OLIVE OIL AND BALSAMIC VINEGAR. FOR HEARTIER APPETITES, OFFER GRILLED ITALIAN SAUSAGE ALONGSIDE.

25 MINUTES

Country Bread & Cabbage Soup with Fontina Crostini

2 tablespoons olive oil

4 slices crusty Italian bread, such as
ciabatta, francese, or pane pugliese
(*each* about ¾ inch thick)

½ cup shredded fontina cheese

1 ounce thinly sliced pancetta or
bacon, chopped

1 large clove garlic, minced or
pressed

1 small onion (about 5 oz.), chopped

⅓ cup chopped carrot

⅓ cup chopped celery

1½ cups coarsely shredded green
cabbage

2 cups fat-free beef broth

1 tablespoon tomato paste

1 teaspoon minced fresh sage or
¼ teaspoon dried rubbed sage

1 teaspoon sugar

Salt and freshly ground pepper

Sage sprigs

1. Using 2 teaspoons of the oil, brush both sides of each slice of bread with oil. Arrange bread in a single layer in a small baking pan. Bake in a 350° oven until golden (about 10 minutes); then turn over and continue to bake until golden on other side and crisp throughout (about 5 more minutes). Sprinkle evenly with cheese and continue to bake until cheese is melted (about 2 more minutes).

2. While bread is toasting, combine remaining 4 teaspoons oil and pancetta in a 2- to 3-quart pan. Stir over medium-high heat until pancetta is brown and crisp (about 3 minutes). Remove from pan with a slotted spoon and drain on paper towels; set aside.

3. To pan, add garlic, onion, carrot, and celery. Cook over medium-high heat, stirring occasionally, until vegetables begin to brown and stick to pan bottom (7 to 10 minutes). Stir in cabbage, broth, tomato paste, minced sage, and sugar. Bring to a boil; then reduce heat and simmer, uncovered, until cabbage is tender to bite (about 5 minutes). Season to taste with salt and pepper.

4. To serve, place 2 crostini in each warm wide, shallow soup bowl. Ladle soup evenly over crostini, sprinkle with pancetta, and garnish with sage sprigs.

PER SERVING: 557 calories, 33 g total fat, 11 g saturated fat, 42 mg cholesterol, 1,403 mg sodium, 47 g carbohydrates, 6 g fiber, 19 g protein, 263 mg calcium, 3 mg iron

Cream of Porcini Mushroom Soup

CREAM OF PORCINI MUSHROOM SOUP

THIS CREAMY-TEXTURED SOUP GETS ITS INTENSELY MUSHROOMY FLAVOR FROM A COMBINATION OF DRIED PORCINI AND FRESH COMMON MUSHROOMS. A LITTLE GOAT CHEESE WHIRLED INTO THE SOUP (AND SPREAD ON TOAST FOR ENJOYING ALONGSIDE) ROUNDS OUT FLAVORS AND MAKES THIS A COMPLETE MEAL; JUST ADD A SALAD SUCH AS OUR SPINACH, PANCETTA & PINE NUT SALAD (PAGE 24). FOR THE SMOOTHEST PURÉE, USE A BLENDER RATHER THAN A FOOD PROCESSOR.

30 MINUTES

⅓ cup (about ½ oz.) dried porcini mushrooms

8 ounces fresh regular mushrooms, sliced

½ cup chopped onion

¼ cup dry white wine

2¼ cups fat-free reduced-sodium chicken broth

1 tablespoon dry sherry

1 cup peeled, chopped russet potato

2 tablespoons chopped parsley

⅛ teaspoon ground nutmeg

1 cup milk

6 slices slender French bread baguette (*each* about 2 inches in diameter and ⅓ inch thick)

2 ounces chive-flavored or plain soft fresh chèvre

1. In a small bowl, soak porcini mushrooms in ½ cup boiling water until softened (about 5 minutes).

2. Meanwhile, in a 2- to 3-quart pan, combine fresh mushrooms, onion, and 2 tablespoons of the wine. Cook over high heat, stirring often, until mushrooms are dry and juices stick to pan bottom and turn deep brown (7 to 9 minutes).

3. Lift soaked porcini from water with a slotted spoon and add to mushroom mixture in pan; reserve soaking liquid. Stir in remaining 2 tablespoons wine and again cook until pan is dry (2 to 3 more minutes). Lift out 6 fresh mushroom slices and reserve for garnish.

4. To pan, add broth, sherry, potato, 1½ tablespoons of the parsley, and nutmeg. Carefully pour most of porcini soaking liquid into pan, discarding sediment at bottom of bowl. Bring to a boil over high heat; then reduce heat, cover, and simmer until porcini are very tender when pierced (10 to 15 minutes). Add milk and stir until steaming (4 to 5 minutes).

5. Meanwhile, arrange baguette slices in a small baking pan and broil 4 to 6 inches below heat until golden (about 1 minute). Turn bread over, spread with half the chèvre, and broil until cheese is melted (about 30 seconds). Sprinkle with remaining 1½ teaspoons parsley.

6. In a blender, whirl soup and remaining chèvre until smoothly puréed. Pour into 2 warm soup bowls; garnish each serving with 3 of the reserved mushroom slices. Serve with chèvre-topped toast.

PER SERVING: 364 calories, 11 g total fat, 7 g saturated fat, 30 mg cholesterol, 950 mg sodium, 40 g carbohydrates, 6 g fiber, 20 g protein, 216 mg calcium, 4 mg iron

CREAM OF BROCCOLI SOUP

IF BROCCOLI IS NOT AT THE TOP OF YOUR "MOST-FAVORED VEGETABLE" LIST, THIS NOURISHING SOUP MIGHT CHANGE YOUR OPINION. IT'S GOOD ALONGSIDE HOT ROAST BEEF SANDWICHES AND BUTTERED EGG NOODLES. FOR A TANGY GARNISH, TOP EACH BOWLFUL WITH A SPOONFUL OF SOUR CREAM.

25 MINUTES

12 ounces broccoli
1 tablespoon butter or olive oil
1 small onion (about 5 oz.), chopped
1 small carrot (about 4 oz.), chopped
1 can (about 14½ oz.) fat-free reduced-sodium chicken broth or regular-strength vegetable broth
¾ cup milk
  Salt and freshly ground pepper
  Sour cream

1. Trim and discard tough ends of broccoli stalks; peel stalks, if desired. Coarsely chop stalks and flowerets; then arrange on a rack over about 1 inch of water in a 3- to 4-quart pan. Cover and bring water to a boil over high heat; then steam, covered, until broccoli is tender when pierced (3 to 5 minutes). Remove broccoli from pan and set aside. Pour off and discard water.

2. Melt butter in pan over medium-high heat. Add onion and carrot and cook, stirring occasionally, until vegetables begin to brown (7 to 10 minutes).

3. Scrape onion mixture into a blender or food processor. Add half the broth and whirl until smoothly puréed; return to pan. Transfer cooked broccoli to blender and add remaining broth; whirl until puréed, then add to onion mixture in pan.

4. Add milk to soup and stir often over medium-high heat until steaming (4 to 5 minutes); do not boil. Season to taste with salt and pepper. Ladle into 2 warm soup bowls; garnish each serving with a spoonful of sour cream.

PER SERVING: 200 calories, 9 g total fat, 6 g saturated fat, 28 mg cholesterol, 685 mg sodium, 22 g carbohydrates, 6 g fiber, 10 g protein, 90 mg calcium, 1 mg iron

PURÉE OF ZUCCHINI SOUP WITH PERNOD

THIS SMOOTH, PALE GREEN ZUCCHINI PURÉE IS ENHANCED WITH PERNOD, AN ANISE-FLAVORED LIQUEUR—JUST A SPLASH, ENOUGH TO ACCENT THE DELICATE FLAVOR OF THE SQUASH WITHOUT OVERPOWERING IT. FOLLOW THE SOUP WITH A HEARTY ENTRÉE SUCH AS VEAL CHOPS OSSO BUCO STYLE (PAGE 87) AND A LIGHT, FRUITY RED WINE.

20 MINUTES

1 tablespoon butter or margarine

2 cloves garlic, minced or pressed

¼ cup chopped shallots

3 medium-size zucchini (about 1 lb. *total*), coarsely chopped

2 cups fat-free reduced-sodium chicken broth

¼ teaspoon dried thyme

⅛ teaspoon ground nutmeg

1 tablespoon Pernod, Sambuca, or other anise-flavored liqueur (not sweet)

1½ tablespoons whipping cream

Salt and freshly ground pepper

1. Melt butter in a 2- to 3-quart pan over medium-high heat. Add garlic, shallots, and zucchini; cook, stirring occasionally, until zucchini begins to brown lightly (7 to 10 minutes).

2. Add broth, thyme, and nutmeg. Increase heat to high and bring soup to a boil; then reduce heat and simmer, uncovered, until flavors are blended (about 5 minutes).

3. In a blender or food processor, whirl zucchini mixture, a portion at a time, until smoothly puréed. Return to pan. Add Pernod and 1 tablespoon of the cream. Stir often over medium-high heat until steaming (2 to 3 minutes); do not boil. Season to taste with salt and pepper. Ladle into 2 warm soup bowls and drizzle with remaining 1½ teaspoons cream.

PER SERVING: 171 calories, 10 g total fat, 6 g saturated fat, 28 mg cholesterol, 693 mg sodium, 15 g carbohydrates, 1 g fiber, 7 g protein, 60 mg calcium, 1 mg iron

GINGER–FIVE SPICE CARROT SOUP AN AROMATIC BLEND OF CHINESE FIVE-SPICE AND FRESH GINGER TURNS PLAIN CARROT PURÉE INTO AN EXOTIC FIRST-COURSE SOUP THAT'S A NICE INTRODUCTION TO BROILED LAMB CHOPS. TO BRING OUT THE CARROTS' NATURAL SWEETNESS, YOU BROWN THEM LIGHTLY BEFORE SIMMERING TO SOFTNESS.

30 MINUTES

1 tablespoon butter or margarine

1 small onion (about 4 oz.), chopped

1 tablespoon minced fresh ginger

2½ cups thinly sliced carrots

3 cups fat-free reduced-sodium chicken broth or regular-strength vegetable broth

About ¼ teaspoon Chinese five-spice

1 tablespoon lemon juice

Plain yogurt

1. Melt butter in a 2- to 3-quart pan over medium-high heat. Add onion, ginger, and carrots; cook, stirring occasionally, until vegetables begin to brown (10 to 12 minutes). Add 1½ cups of the broth and ¼ teaspoon of the five-spice. Increase heat to high and bring to a boil; then reduce heat, cover, and simmer until carrots are very tender when pierced (about 10 minutes).

2. In a blender or food processor, whirl carrot mixture, a portion at a time, until puréed. Return purée to pan and stir in lemon juice and remaining 1½ cups broth. Stir over high heat until steaming.

3. Ladle soup into 2 warm soup bowls. Top each serving with a spoonful of yogurt and, if desired, a light sprinkling of five-spice.

PER SERVING: 176 calories, 6 g total fat, 4 g saturated fat, 16 mg cholesterol, 1,055 mg sodium, 26 g carbohydrates, 7 g fiber, 7 g protein, 62 mg calcium, 1 mg iron

MEATS

Basil Beef with Vietnamese Dipping Sauce (page 76)

SORT OF A BURRITO

A CROSS BETWEEN A MIDEASTERN-STYLE SANDWICH AND A TRADITIONAL BURRITO, THIS EAT-OUT-OF-HAND SUPPER CAN BE MADE WITH FLOUR TORTILLAS OR BIG FLATBREADS (BE SURE THEY'RE SOFT AND FRESH). YOU CAN USE GROUND LAMB OR PORK INSTEAD OF BEEF, IF YOU LIKE; FOR A HEFTIER BURRITO, ADD DICED AVOCADO OR A SPOONFUL OF SOUR CREAM. CHILLED PINEAPPLE STRIPS SPRINKLED WITH BROWN SUGAR ARE A REFRESHING DESSERT.

20 MINUTES

8 ounces lean ground beef

1 small onion (about 4 oz.), chopped

1 tablespoon chili powder

1½ teaspoons ground cumin

Salt

½ cup lightly packed cilantro leaves, minced

1 tablespoon lemon juice

1 medium-size tomato (about 6 oz.)

2 large flour tortillas (*each* about 10 inches in diameter); or use soft flatbreads of about the same size

2 inner romaine lettuce leaves

1. Heat a wide frying pan over medium-high heat. Crumble beef into pan; when fat begins to melt out of beef, add onion, chili powder, and cumin. Cook, stirring often, until onion is soft and beef is no longer pink (about 5 minutes). Season to taste with salt and remove from heat.

2. While beef is cooking, in a small bowl, toss together cilantro, lemon juice, and ⅛ to ¼ teaspoon salt; set aside. Also cut tomato in half; then cut each half lengthwise into ½-inch-thick strips.

3. To assemble each burrito, lay a tortilla on a work surface. Place half the tomato strips in a line from top of tortilla to center; top with half the beef mixture, then with a lettuce leaf. Roll up tortilla to make a cone-shaped sandwich; fold ends under to hold in juices. Add cilantro mixture to taste.

PER SERVING: 537 calories, 29 g total fat, 10 g saturated fat, 85 mg cholesterol, 610 mg sodium, 43 g carbohydrates, 5 g fiber, 27 g protein, 128 mg calcium, 6 mg iron

FLANK STEAK WITH CHÈVRE

SMOKY GRILLED BEEF IS TOPPED WITH A SIMPLE TOMATO SALAD IN THIS SUPPER FROM THE BARBECUE (THE MEAT CAN ALSO BE PAN-GRILLED, THOUGH IT WON'T HAVE THE SAME SMOKY FLAVOR). SERVE WITH RICE AND MUSHROOMS BAKED IN BUTTER AND CHARDONNAY; OFFER SPARKLING SORBET (PAGE 234) FOR DESSERT.

30 MINUTES

8 to 12 ounces flank steak

2 tablespoons soft fresh chèvre, such as Montrachet or Couturier

½ cup halved cherry tomatoes

⅓ cup coarsely chopped cilantro

2 teaspoons balsamic vinegar

Salt and freshly ground pepper

1. Place steak on a grill 3 to 4 inches above a solid bed of very hot coals (you can hold your hand at grill level for only 1 to 2 seconds) or over high heat on a gas grill. Close lid on gas grill. Cook until steak is browned on bottom (about 5 minutes). Turn steak over and crumble chèvre over top; cover barbecue or close lid on gas grill again. Continue to cook until steak is browned on other side and done to your liking; cut to test (about 5 more minutes for medium-rare). Transfer to a board and let stand for 5 minutes before slicing.

2. Meanwhile, in a small bowl, gently mix tomatoes, cilantro, and vinegar.

3. Slice steak across the grain and arrange on 2 warm dinner plates. Sprinkle with salt and pepper; top with tomato salad.

PER SERVING: 273 calories, 16 g total fat, 7 g saturated fat, 78 mg cholesterol, 132 mg sodium, 2 g carbohydrates, 0 g fiber, 30 g protein, 34 mg calcium, 3 mg iron

Flank Steak with Chèvre

STEAK HOUSE STEAK WITH
FRIED ONION RINGS & SAGE

OFFER THIS HEARTY FEAST WITH A SALAD OF SLICED TOMATOES TOPPED WITH CAPERS AND CHOPPED ANCHOVIES—AND DON'T FORGET CATSUP AND STEAK SAUCE FOR THE MEAT. FOR DESSERT, CONSIDER FRESH BLACKBERRIES SPRINKLED WITH SUGAR.

30 MINUTES

---

2 cups vegetable oil

1 large red onion (about 8 oz.), thinly sliced

⅓ cup fresh sage leaves

3 tablespoons all-purpose flour
Salt

1 beef rib-eye, New York, sirloin, T-bone, or porterhouse steak (about 1 lb. if boneless, about 1¼ lbs. if bone-in), about 1½ inches thick

1 teaspoon olive oil
Freshly ground pepper

1. Pour vegetable oil into a deep-fryer or deep, heavy 2-quart pan and heat, uncovered, to 360°F on a deep-frying thermometer. Meanwhile, mix onion, sage leaves, and flour in a large bowl, separating onion slices into rings.

2. Add onion mixture, 1 cup at a time, to hot oil and cook until onion just begins to brown (3 to 5 minutes). With tongs, lift onion and sage from oil to a plate lined with paper towels to drain; sprinkle lightly with salt. Loosely pile fried onion and sage on one side of 2 warm dinner plates, dividing equally. Keep warm.

3. While onion and sage are frying, place steak in a lightly oiled broiler pan, brush with olive oil, and sprinkle with salt and pepper. Broil 2 to 3 inches below heat until steak is a rich, crusty brown (about 10 minutes); then turn over and continue to broil until browned on other side (about 5 more minutes). Turn oven setting from broil to bake; set oven temperature at 400°. Leave steak in closed oven until a meat thermometer inserted in thickest part (not touching bone) registers 125°F for medium-rare (about 5 more minutes); or cut to test. Then remove steak from oven and let stand for a few minutes before slicing.

4. To serve, cut steak across the grain into ¼-inch-thick slices. Arrange sliced steak on plates alongside fried onions and sage.

PER SERVING: 749 calories, 54 g total fat, 17 g saturated fat, 139 mg cholesterol, 120 mg sodium, 20 g carbohydrates, 2 g fiber, 45 g protein, 77 mg calcium, 5 mg iron

CURRY STEAK SANDWICHES

CILANTRO AND MINT REPLACE THE FAMILIAR LETTUCE IN A SANDWICH WITH INDIAN FLAVORS. IF YOU HAVE TIME, CRISP THE HERBS BEFORE USING THEM: RINSE, ROLL IN PAPER OR CLOTH TOWELS, ENCLOSE IN A PLASTIC BAG, AND CHILL UNTIL SPRIGHTLY (ABOUT 30 MINUTES). JUICY ORANGES MAKE A GOOD DESSERT. FOR A PRETTY PRESENTATION, PEEL THEM BLOSSOM-FASHION—SLICE OFF THE TOP OF THE FRUIT AND SCORE THE RIND VERTICALLY; THEN PEEL PARTWAY DOWN, CURVING EACH STRIP IN TOWARD FRUIT AND TUCKING ITS TIP BETWEEN FRUIT AND PEEL.

25 MINUTES

12 ounces flank or skirt steak

1½ teaspoons curry powder

½ teaspoon sugar

Salt

2 teaspoons olive oil

¼ cup sliced onion

6 to 8 cherry tomatoes, cut into halves or quarters

3 tablespoons seasoned rice vinegar

4 slices crusty Italian bread (*each* about ¾ inch thick)

⅓ cup lightly packed cilantro sprigs

⅓ cup lightly packed mint sprigs

1. Rub steak on both sides with curry powder, sugar, and salt. Heat oil in a wide frying pan over medium-high heat. Add steak and cook, turning once, until browned on both sides and done to your liking; cut to test (about 10 minutes for medium-rare). Transfer to a board and let stand for 5 minutes before slicing.

2. Meanwhile, in a small bowl, gently mix onion, tomatoes, and vinegar.

3. Thinly slice steak across the grain. Pour any accumulated liquid on board back into frying pan and stir to loosen drippings. Place 2 slices of the bread in pan and let them absorb all pan juices.

4. To assemble sandwiches, place a slice of pan juice–soaked bread on each warm dinner plate. Arrange half the steak atop each slice of bread; top evenly with cilantro and mint sprigs. Drain tomato-onion mixture, reserving vinegar. Spoon drained vegetables over sandwiches; drizzle remaining 2 slices bread with reserved vinegar and set atop sandwiches, vinegar side down. Cut sandwiches in half to serve.

PER SERVING: 578 calories, 27 g fat, 9 g saturated fat, 89 mg cholesterol, 927 mg sodium, 41 g carbohydrates, 5 g fiber, 40 g protein, 117 mg calcium, 8 mg iron

Curry Steak Sandwiches

POUNDED STEAK WITH YAM KABOBS TOUGH CUTS OF BEEF

COOK UP QUICK AND TENDER ON THE GRILL IF YOU START BY POUNDING

THEM OUT THIN. ACCOMPANY WITH SKEWERED YAM CHUNKS AND TOMATO

WEDGES OR GRILLED CORN; FOR DESSERT, SERVE LEMON ICE WITH

SLICED MANGOES OR PAPAYAS. (IF YOU DON'T WANT TO BARBECUE, YOU

30 MINUTES CAN BROIL THE KABOBS AND PAN-FRY THE STEAK OVER HIGH HEAT.)

1⅓ pounds yams (*each* about 1¼ inches in diameter; or cut to this diameter), scrubbed

1 small onion (about 4 oz.)

1 clove garlic

1 tablespoon chopped parsley

2 tablespoons olive oil

Salt and freshly ground pepper

About 1 pound beef top or bottom round steak (about ¼ inch thick), cut into 2 equal pieces

Lemon and orange wedges

1. Use two 12-inch bamboo or metal skewers for kabobs. If using bamboo skewers, soak them in water for 15 to 20 minutes before using.

2. Place yams in a 2-quart pan and add water to cover (cut yams in half, if needed, to fit them into pan). Cover and bring to a boil over high heat; then reduce heat and simmer, covered, until yams are tender when pierced (about 15 minutes). Drain and immediately immerse in cold water to cool slightly. Then drain, peel, and cut into about 1¼-inch cubes. Thread yams equally on skewers and set aside.

3. While yams are cooking, mince together onion, garlic, and parsley. Place in a small bowl, stir in oil, and season to taste with salt and pepper. Set aside.

4. Place each piece of steak between 2 large sheets of plastic wrap (wrap should be 3 times larger on all sides than meat). With a heavy, flat-sided mallet, pound firmly to a thickness of about ⅛ inch. Remove top piece of plastic wrap and sprinkle steaks with half the onion mixture; set wrap in place again and pound onion mixture into steaks.

5. Press remaining onion mixture over and between skewered yams. Place steaks (onion side down) and yam kabobs on a lightly oiled grill 3 to 4 inches above a solid bed of very hot coals (you can hold your hand at grill level for only 1 to 2 seconds) or over high heat on a gas grill. Close lid on gas grill. Cook, turning steaks once and kabobs as needed, until edges are nicely browned (about 4 minutes for meat, 6 minutes for kabobs). Offer lemon and orange wedges to squeeze over foods.

PER SERVING: 802 calories, 30 g total fat, 8 g saturated fat, 139 mg cholesterol, 124 mg sodium, 78 g carbohydrates, 12 g fiber, 54 g protein, 72 mg calcium, 6 mg iron

BASIL BEEF WITH VIETNAMESE DIPPING SAUCE

Pictured on page 67

MARINATED BEEF STRIPS ARE WRAPPED IN FRAGRANT FRESH BASIL LEAVES, SKEWERED, AND QUICKLY BROILED TO MAKE AN APPEALING LIGHT MEAL. A BUTCHER CAN MAKE FAST WORK OF SLICING THE MEAT FOR YOU; A FRENCH MANDOLIN OR JAPANESE BOX GRATER WILL YIELD LONG THREADS OF CARROT (OR YOU CAN MAKE SHORTER SHREDS WITH A CONVENTIONAL GRATER). YOU MIGHT SERVE HOT RICE ALONGSIDE THE MEAT; FOR DESSERT, TRY COCONUT MACAROONS OR CHINESE ALMOND COOKIES.

30 MINUTES

---

12 ounces boneless beef sirloin, cut into strips about ¼ inch thick, 2 inches long, and 1 inch wide

1 teaspoon Asian fish sauce (*nuoc mam* or *nam pla*)

1 teaspoon soy sauce

1 teaspoon sugar

4 teaspoons vegetable oil

1 medium-size carrot (about 5 oz.)

Vietnamese Dipping Sauce (below)

About 15 large fresh basil leaves

VIETNAMESE DIPPING SAUCE

3 tablespoons Asian fish sauce (*nuoc mam* or *nam pla*)

2 tablespoons cider vinegar

2 tablespoons sugar

⅛ to ¼ teaspoon crushed red pepper flakes

1 clove garlic, minced or pressed

1. Soak six 12-inch bamboo skewers in water for 15 to 20 minutes. Meanwhile, in a bowl, mix beef, the 1 teaspoon fish sauce, soy sauce, the 1 teaspoon sugar, and 1 teaspoon of the oil; set aside. Also place a roasting pan 3 to 4 inches below heat and turn on broiler to highest heat. Pan should become very hot.

2. Peel carrot. Using a mandolin or Japanese box grater, shred carrot into long, thin threads (or use a conventional grater for short shreds).

3. Prepare Vietnamese Dipping Sauce and pour into 2 small bowls; add a small amount of shredded carrot to each. Set aside.

4. You should have about 30 small pieces of marinated beef. Fold each piece in half (you can fold scraps into the middle) and thread about 5 slices on each skewer; wrap every other slice with a basil leaf before skewering.

5. Brush remaining 1 tablepoon oil over bottom of hot roasting pan. Place skewered beef in pan and broil until done medium-rare; cut to test (4 to 6 minutes). To serve, arrange beef and carrot on 2 dinner plates (or serve carrot separately); set one bowl of dipping sauce on each plate.

VIETNAMESE DIPPING SAUCE

In a small bowl, stir together the 3 tablespoons fish sauce, vinegar, the 2 tablespoons sugar, red pepper flakes, and garlic.

PER SERVING: 538 calories, 31 g total fat, 9 g saturated fat, 104 mg cholesterol, 1,255 mg sodium, 26 g carbohydrates, 2 g fiber, 37 g protein, 39 mg calcium, 4 mg iron

FILLET STEAKS WITH MERLOT GLAZE

JUICY BEEF FILLET STEAKS WITH A RASPBERRY–RED WINE GLAZE MAKE AN ENTRÉE FIT FOR A CELEBRATION. SERVE WITH FLUFFY COUSCOUS AND MUSHROOMS SAUTÉED IN OLIVE OIL AND BALSAMIC VINEGAR. CHOCOLATE TRUFFLES ARE A SUITABLY ELEGANT DESSERT.

20 MINUTES

½ cup fat-free beef broth

¼ cup Merlot or other dry red wine

1 tablespoon seedless raspberry jam

¼ teaspoon freshly ground pepper

2 thin slices pancetta (about 2 oz. *total*)

2 beef fillet steaks (6 to 8 oz. *each*), *each* about 1½ inches thick

1. In a 1- to 2-quart pan, mix broth, wine, jam, and pepper. Bring to a boil over high heat; then boil until reduced to ⅓ cup (about 7 minutes). Reduce heat and keep warm, if needed.

2. While sauce is boiling down, wrap a slice of pancetta around rim of each steak. Arrange steaks on a rack in a broiler pan. Broil 4 to 6 inches below heat until browned (6 to 7 minutes). Then turn over and continue to broil until browned on other side and done to your liking; cut to test (6 to 7 more minutes for rare).

3. Place one steak on each warm dinner plate; spoon sauce over steaks.

PER SERVING: 467 calories, 31 g total fat, 12 g saturated fat, 122 mg cholesterol, 368 mg sodium, 7 g carbohydrates, 0 g fiber, 37 g protein, 17 mg calcium, 5 mg iron

RIB STEAKS WITH CRISPY DUTCH POTATOES

THIS STOVE-TOP SUPPER CALLS FOR TWO FRYING PANS—ONE FOR THE STEAKS, THE SECOND FOR THE CRUSTY, HERB-SEASONED POTATOES. BESIDES RIB-EYE STEAKS, YOU CAN USE OTHER TENDER CUTS SUCH AS SIRLOIN, NEW YORK, T-BONE, OR PORTERHOUSE. COMPLETE THE MEAL WITH A SALAD OF BABY SPINACH OR TENDER SPRING GREENS.

25 MINUTES

---

12 ounces thin-skinned potatoes, scrubbed

1 tablespoon olive oil

2 bone-in beef rib-eye steaks (about 8 oz. *each*), *each* about ½ inch thick

2 teaspoons Dijon mustard

2 tablespoons dry vermouth or dry white wine

1 teaspoon sugar

2 teaspoons vegetable oil

½ teaspoon dried thyme

3 tablespoons fine dry bread crumbs
Salt and freshly ground pepper

1. Cut potatoes into ¾-inch chunks. Place potatoes in a 2-quart pan and add enough water to cover. Cover and bring to a boil over high heat; then reduce heat and simmer, covered, until potatoes are almost tender when pierced (3 to 4 minutes). Drain potatoes well.

2. Heat olive oil in a wide frying pan over high heat. Add steaks and cook, turning once, until browned on both sides and done to your liking; cut to test (about 4 minutes for rare). Place one steak on each warm dinner plate. Add mustard and vermouth to pan and stir to loosen drippings; pour this sauce over steaks.

3. While steaks are cooking, sprinkle sugar into a second wide frying pan over high heat. When sugar is melted, add drained potatoes and stir to coat with melted sugar. Add vegetable oil, thyme, and bread crumbs; cook, stirring, until crumbs begin to brown and potatoes are tender when pierced (about 5 minutes). Season potatoes to taste with salt and pepper and spoon alongside steaks.

PER SERVING: 861 calories, 59 g total fat, 21 g saturated fat, 130 mg cholesterol, 320 mg sodium, 40 g carbohydrates, 3 g fiber, 36 g protein, 50 mg calcium, 6 mg iron

RED CHILI RACK OF LAMB

A FRESH-TASTING MIXED BEAN SALAD PERFECTLY COMPLEMENTS THE RICH, PUNGENT FLAVORS OF THIS SMALL RACK OF LAMB. SERVE WITH TOMATO WEDGES, WARM TORTILLAS, OR RICE. FOR DESSERT, SCOOP PASSION FRUIT FROM THE SKINS AND SPOON OVER LEMON SORBET. WHEN YOU BUY THE LAMB, HAVE THE BUTCHER REMOVE THE CHINE BONE.

30 MINUTES

---

1 small rack of lamb (1¾ to 2 lbs.), trimmed of fat, bones frenched

¼ cup canned or bottled roasted red peppers, drained

2 tablespoons ground dried California chiles

½ teaspoon dried oregano

1 clove garlic, minced or pressed

1 tablespoon olive oil

1 tablespoon red wine vinegar

Salt

Mixed Bean Salad (below)

MIXED BEAN SALAD

4 ounces thin green beans (ends removed), cut into 3-inch lengths

2 tablespoons olive oil

1½ tablespoons sherry vinegar

1 clove garlic, minced or pressed

¼ cup thin wedges of red onion

Salt and freshly ground pepper

1 can (about 1 lb.) baby lima beans, rinsed and drained

1. Cut lamb rack between bones into 2 small racks (2 or 3 bones each). In a blender or food processor, combine red peppers, chiles, oregano, 1 clove garlic, the 1 tablespoon oil, and wine vinegar; whirl until peppers are almost puréed. Season to taste with salt. Coat lamb with pepper mixture.

2. Place lamb racks, bone side down, in a foil-lined roasting pan. Roast in a 475° oven until a meat thermometer inserted in thickest part (not touching bone) registers 140°F for medium-rare (about 25 minutes); or cut to test.

3. Meanwhile, prepare Mixed Bean Salad.

4. Serve one small rack of lamb per person; or cut racks between bones into individual chops. Offer bean salad with lamb.

MIXED BEAN SALAD

1. In a covered 2-quart pan, bring about 1 inch of water to a boil over high heat. Drop green beans into boiling water; return to a boil and cook, uncovered, until tender-crisp when pierced (3 to 5 minutes). Drain, rinse with cold water until cool, and drain again.

2. In a medium-size bowl, stir together the 2 tablespoons oil, sherry vinegar, 1 clove garlic, and onion; season to taste with salt and pepper. Stir green beans and lima beans into dressing.

PER SERVING: 737 calories, 40 g total fat, 10 g saturated fat, 132 mg cholesterol, 288 mg sodium, 43 g carbohydrates, 14 g fiber, 52 g protein, 178 mg calcium, 7 mg iron

RACK OF LAMB WITH ISRAELI TOMATO SALAD

ROUND OUT THIS SATISFYING MEAL WITH WARMED PITA BREAD, CRISP INNER ROMAINE LETTUCE LEAVES, CALAMATA OLIVES, AND MIDEASTERN-STYLE SALADS AND RELISHES SUCH AS TABBOULI, HUMMUS, OR EGGPLANT SPREAD. MELON WEDGES WITH MINT MAKE A COOLING DESSERT. WHEN YOU BUY THE LAMB, HAVE THE BUTCHER REMOVE THE CHINE BONE.

30 MINUTES

---

1 small rack of lamb (1¾ to 2 lbs.), trimmed of fat, bones frenched

½ teaspoon caraway seeds

Salt and freshly ground pepper

Israeli Tomato Salad (below)

ISRAELI TOMATO SALAD

1 tablespoon olive oil

⅓ cup chopped onion

1 large clove garlic, minced or pressed

1 teaspoon caraway seeds, crushed

½ teaspoon ground coriander

¼ teaspoon ground red pepper (cayenne)

2 large ripe tomatoes (about 1 lb. *total*), chopped

2 teaspoons balsamic vinegar

Salt

1. Cut lamb rack between bones into 2 small racks (2 or 3 bones each); rub with the ½ teaspoon caraway seeds, salt, and pepper. Place lamb racks, bone side down, in a foil-lined roasting pan. Roast in a 475° oven until a meat thermometer inserted in thickest part (not touching bone) registers 140°F for medium-rare (about 25 minutes); or cut to test.

2. Meanwhile, prepare Israeli Tomato Salad.

3. Serve one small rack of lamb per person; or cut racks between bones into individual chops. Offer tomato salad with lamb.

ISRAELI TOMATO SALAD

Heat oil in a wide frying pan over medium-high heat. Add onion, garlic, the 1 teaspoon caraway seeds, coriander, and red pepper; cook, stirring often, until onion begins to soften (about 5 minutes). Add tomatoes and vinegar; cook, stirring, until liquid has evaporated and tomatoes begin to fall apart (about 15 minutes). Season to taste with salt. Place pan in a larger pan filled with ice and water. Let stand, stirring occasionally, until tomato mixture is cool.

PER SERVING: 461 calories, 26 g total fat, 8 g saturated fat, 122 mg cholesterol, 137 mg sodium, 17 g carbohydrates, 4 g fiber, 40 g protein, 69 mg calcium, 5 mg iron

Rack of Lamb with Israeli Tomato Salad

BREAKFAST MEATS

EAT FOR BREAKFAST IS AN AMERICAN TRADITION. WHEN MARK TWAIN SPOKE OF THE MORNING MEAL, HE DESCRIBED "A MIGHTY PORTERHOUSE STEAK" SPRINKLED WITH FRESHLY GROUND PEPPER AND SERVED SIZZLING-HOT FROM THE GRIDDLE, ITS SAVORY JUICES "... TRICKLING OUT AND JOINING THE GRAVY, ARCHIPELAGOED WITH MUSHROOMS..."—AND IT GOES ON! WHILE 1½-INCH-THICK STEAKS MAY NO LONGER BE OUR FIRST CHOICE FOR DINING BRIGHT AND EARLY, SMALL AMOUNTS OF MEAT REMAIN APPEALING AS A CHANGE OF PACE FROM—OR A COMPLEMENT TO—THE NOW TYPICAL CEREAL, YOGURT, FRUIT, OR EGGS.

POTATO PANCAKE WITH HAM
30 MINUTES

- 1 tablespoon all-purpose flour
- 2 teaspoons sliced green onion tops
- 3 tablespoons milk
- 1 large egg yolk or egg white
- 8 ounces thin-skinned potatoes, scrubbed
- ¼ cup diced ham or corned beef
  Salt and freshly ground pepper
- 1 tablespoon butter or margarine
  Sour cream
  Raspberry jam
  Fresh raspberries

1. In a bowl, beat together flour, onion, milk, and egg yolk to blend well. Coarsely shred unpeeled potatoes in a food processor. Mix potatoes and ham into batter; season to taste with salt and pepper.

2. Melt butter in a wide frying pan over medium-high heat. Pour batter into pan and spread to make a pancake 7 to 7½ inches in diameter (if pancake is wider and thinner, it's hard to turn). Reduce heat to medium-low and cook pancake, turning once, until golden and crisp on both sides (about 20 minutes).

3. To serve, cut pancake into 4 wedges. Place 2 wedges on each warm dinner plate; place a spoonful each of sour cream and jam alongside pancake wedges. Sprinkle with raspberries. Offer additional sour cream and jam to add to taste.

PER SERVING: 227 calories, 11 g total fat, 5 g saturated fat, 133 mg cholesterol, 269 mg sodium, 25 g carbohydrates, 2 g fiber, 7 g protein, 43 mg calcium, 1 mg iron

BREAKFAST BEEF & EGG PASTRIES
30 MINUTES

  Half of an 8-ounce sheet purchased frozen puff pastry
- 1 tablespoon vinegar
- 2 large eggs
- 2 ounces Swiss cheese, thinly sliced
- 2 ounces paper-thin slices corned beef

1. Lay pastry flat on a work surface (if pastry breaks, slightly overlap pieces and push or pinch back together). Cut pastry in half crosswise. Place pieces on an ungreased baking sheet and bake in a 400° oven until well puffed and golden brown (about 15 minutes).

2. Meanwhile, in a 2-quart pan, bring about 2 inches of water to a boil over high heat. Reduce heat to a simmer and add vinegar. Crack eggs, one at a time, into a small dish and gently slide them into water. Return to a simmer; then simmer until whites are set but yolks are still soft (about 3 minutes). Lift eggs from water with a slotted spoon, draining off as much water as possible. Keep warm in a warm bowl, if needed.

3. Gently pull each piece of pastry in half horizontally; set top pieces aside. Place cheese on bottom pieces. Return baking sheet to oven until cheese is softened (about 2 minutes). Lay beef atop cheese; top beef on each pastry with an egg. Then top with remaining pastry pieces, setting them slightly off center.

PER SERVING: 528 calories, 35 g total fat, 10 g saturated fat, 253 mg cholesterol, 635 mg sodium, 28 g carbohydrates, 1 g fiber, 25 g protein, 316 mg calcium, 3 mg iron

LAMB SAUSAGE WITH WILTED GREENS & DILL BREAD
30 MINUTES

- 8 ounces lean ground lamb
- 1 small clove garlic, minced or pressed
- ¾ teaspoon ground sage
- 1 tablespoon minced parsley
- ⅛ teaspoon crumbled dried rosemary
- ¼ teaspoon salt
  Freshly ground pepper
  Olive oil (if needed)
- 2 to 3 cups lightly packed 1-inch strips of beet greens, chard, or escarole; or use whole baby spinach leaves
- 2 slices dill rye or other rye bread (each about ¼ inch thick), toasted if desired

1. In a bowl, mix lamb, garlic, sage, parsley, rosemary, and salt to blend well. Season to taste with pepper. Shape lamb mixture into four 1-inch-thick patties.

2. Heat a wide frying pan over medium-high heat. Add patties to pan and reduce heat to medium. Cook, turning once, until patties are browned on both sides and no longer pink in center; cut to test (about 20 minutes; patties should still be juicy). Place 2 patties on each warm dinner plate; keep warm.

3. Measure drippings in pan; you need 2 teaspoons. If you have more than this, discard excess; if you have less, add enough oil to make 2 teaspoons total. Rinse and drain greens, then add to pan with water that clings to them. Increase heat to medium-high and stir until greens are wilted and a brighter green in color. Arrange greens alongside sausage patties; serve with bread.

PER SERVING: 420 calories, 28 g total fat, 12 g saturated fat, 86 mg cholesterol, 708 mg sodium, 19 g carbohydrates, 2 g fiber, 23 g protein, 136 mg calcium, 5 mg iron

BREAKFAST STEAK
25 TO 30 MINUTES

Stewed Vegetables (at right)

Salt and freshly ground pepper

2 frozen small beef skirt, boneless rib-eye, or fillet steaks (2 to 3 oz. *each*), *each* about ½ inch thick

2 large eggs

Minced parsley

STEWED VEGETABLES

1 tablespoon butter or olive oil

½ cup thin wedges of red onion

½ cup diced green bell pepper

1 clove garlic, minced or pressed

¼ teaspoon dried thyme

1 medium-size tomato (about 6 oz.), chopped

Salt and freshly ground pepper

1. Prepare Stewed Vegetables and keep warm.

2. Place a wide frying pan over high heat until very hot. Sprinkle pan with salt and pepper; add frozen steaks and sprinkle with salt and pepper. Cook, turning once, until steaks are well browned on both sides and done to your liking; cut to test (about 2 minutes for rare). Immediately remove from heat.

3. Spoon Stewed Vegetables into center of 2 warm dinner plates. Top each serving with a steak; keep warm in a low oven. Crack eggs into frying pan and sprinkle with salt and pepper; then cover and cook over low heat until whites are set but yolks are still soft (about 2 minutes). Place an egg atop each steak; sprinkle with parsley.

STEWED VEGETABLES

Melt butter in a 2- to 3-quart pan over medium-high heat. Add onion, bell pepper, garlic, and thyme. Cook, stirring occasionally, until vegetables begin to brown (about 7 minutes). Add tomato and cook, stirring occasionally, until tomato is soft and a little juicy (about 6 minutes). Season to taste with salt and pepper. Cover and remove from heat.

PER SERVING: 355 calories, 26 g total fat, 11 g saturated fat, 276 mg cholesterol, 174 mg sodium, 10 g carbohydrates, 2 g fiber, 21 g protein, 57 mg calcium, 3 mg iron

MORAGA RANCH SCRAMBLE
20 TO 25 MINUTES

1 medium-size thin-skinned potato (about 6 oz.), scrubbed

2 tablespoons butter or olive oil

¼ cup chopped green bell pepper

¼ cup thin wedges of red onion

4 ounces boneless beef sirloin, cut for stir-fry into pieces about ¾ inch square and ⅛ to ¼ inch thick

2 tablespoons prepared barbecue sauce

Salt and freshly ground pepper

4 large eggs

1 tablespoon water

2 slices sourdough bread (*each* about ½ inch thick), toasted

1. Cut potato into ¾-inch chunks. Melt 1 tablespoon of the butter in a wide frying pan over medium-high heat. Add potato and cook, stirring often, until browned on some edges (about 5 minutes). Reduce heat to medium; add bell pepper and onion. Continue to cook, stirring occasionally, until all vegetables are lightly browned and tender when pierced (5 to 7 more minutes).

2. Scrape vegetables into a bowl. Increase heat to high; add beef and 1 more teaspoon butter to pan and cook, stirring, until edges of beef pieces are nicely browned (about 3 minutes). Stir vegetables back into pan along with barbecue sauce. Season to taste with salt and pepper; remove from heat and keep warm.

3. In a small bowl, beat eggs with water to blend; season to taste with salt and pepper. Melt remaining 2 teaspoons butter in another wide frying pan over high heat. Add eggs and cook, lifting up cooked portions to allow uncooked eggs to flow underneath, until eggs are softly set.

4. Place one slice of toast on each warm dinner plate. Top evenly with eggs, then with beef mixture.

PER SERVING: 518 calories, 30 g total fat, 13 g saturated fat, 492 mg cholesterol, 561 mg sodium, 32 g carbohydrates, 2 g fiber, 29 g protein, 83 mg calcium, 4 mg iron

PICNIC LAMB MEATBALLS WITH GARLIC TOAST

ROUND OUT THIS MEAL WITH SALTED ALMONDS, SLICED CUCUMBERS AND TOMATOES, AND SOFT BUTTER LETTUCE CUPS TO PICK UP THE MEATBALLS OR TO USE AS WRAPPERS FOR TOAST, MEATBALLS, AND, IF YOU LIKE, A FEW PUNGENT CAPERS. FOR DESSERT, OFFER POMEGRANATES OR ORANGES WITH SOFT DRIED FIGS AND DATES.

25 MINUTES

8 ounces lean ground lamb

4 large cloves garlic, minced or pressed

¼ teaspoon dried tarragon

⅓ cup fine dry whole wheat bread crumbs

1 large egg yolk or egg white

1½ tablespoons catsup

1½ tablespoons fat-free beef broth or water

Salt and freshly ground pepper

2 tablespoons olive oil

¼ cup chopped parsley

Lemon wedges

4 ounces sweet French bread baguette (about half of a slender baguette), cut crosswise into ½-inch-thick slices

1. In a large bowl, mix lamb, ½ teaspoon of the garlic, tarragon, bread crumbs, egg yolk, catsup, and broth; season to taste with salt and pepper.

2. Heat oil in a wide frying pan over medium-high heat. Add remaining minced garlic and stir until warm. Drop 2-table-spoon-size balls of lamb mixture into pan, using all. Cook, turn-ing as needed, until meatballs are golden on all sides and done medium-rare in center; cut to test (about 7 minutes). Lift meat-balls from pan to a warm platter. Sprinkle with parsley and gar-nish with lemon wedges.

3. Add baguette slices to oil in pan. Toast over medium-high heat, turning once, until golden on both sides (about 4 minutes). Arrange toast around meatballs on platter.

PER SERVING: 674 calories, 45 g total fat, 15 g saturated fat, 189 mg cho-lesterol, 629 mg sodium, 40 g carbohydrates, 3 g fiber, 27 g protein, 112 mg calcium, 5 mg iron

CURRIED LAMB TURNOVERS
To make these savory turnovers, you bake the pastry before you fill it—an unconventional technique, but one that saves time and uses less pastry than the traditional method. Complete your meal with mixed greens and tomatoes in vinaigrette and a cool glass of fresh lemonade with plenty of minced mint.

25 MINUTES

Half of an 8-ounce sheet purchased frozen puff pastry
1 large egg yolk or egg white, beaten
½ cup water
⅓ cup long-grain white rice
2 teaspoons olive oil
1 small onion (about 4 oz.), chopped
2 teaspoons curry powder
1 medium-size tomato (about 6 oz.), chopped
⅛ teaspoon fennel seeds, crushed
8 ounces lean ground lamb
¼ cup fat-free beef broth
¼ cup frozen tiny peas
Salt

1. Lay pastry flat on a work surface (if pastry breaks, slightly overlap pieces and push or pinch back together). Cut pastry in half diagonally to make 2 triangles. Place on an ungreased baking sheet; brush with egg yolk. Bake in a 400° oven until well puffed and golden brown (about 15 minutes).

2. Meanwhile, in a 1- to 2-quart pan, bring water to a boil over high heat. Add rice and return to a boil; then reduce heat, cover, and simmer until water has been absorbed and rice is tender to bite (about 15 minutes).

3. While rice is cooking, heat oil in a wide frying pan over medium-high heat. Add onion and curry powder; cook, stirring occasionally, until onion begins to brown (about 5 minutes). Add tomato and fennel seeds to one side of pan; crumble lamb into other side. Cook, stirring occasionally and keeping lamb and tomato separate, until lamb is no longer pink, tomato has fallen apart, and tomato liquid has evaporated (about 6 minutes). Stir in broth and peas, mixing all foods together. Bring to a boil; then boil, stirring, until pan liquid is slightly thickened (about 3 minutes). Season to taste with salt. Remove from heat and keep warm.

4. Assemble turnovers: starting at center point, gently pull each pastry triangle apart just enough to open it completely but not so far that you tear it into 2 pieces. Place each pastry on a warm dinner plate; fill each with half the rice and half the lamb curry.

PER SERVING: 879 calories, 56 g total fat, 16 g saturated fat, 189 mg cholesterol, 334 mg sodium, 63 g carbohydrates, 5 g fiber, 30 g protein, 75 mg calcium, 6 mg iron

LAMB TACOS WITH JICAMA-CARROT SLAW

A SPICY LAMB FILLING CONTRASTS WITH TART, COOLING JICAMA-CARROT SLAW IN THESE FLAVORFUL SOFT TACOS. FOR DESSERT, YOU MIGHT OFFER A RIPE PLANTAIN ROASTED IN ITS SKIN UNTIL SOFT, THEN SLIT OPEN ON THE SERVING PLATE AND SPRINKLED GENEROUSLY WITH LIME JUICE.

25 MINUTES

---

8 corn tortillas (*each* about 6 inches in diameter)

1½ cups lightly packed coarsely shredded jicama

1 cup lightly packed coarsely shredded carrot

¼ cup unsweetened grapefruit juice

2 teaspoons olive oil

1 small onion (about 4 oz.), chopped

2 teaspoons chili powder

1 teaspoon ground cumin

1 large tomato (about 8 oz.), chopped

10 to 12 ounces lean ground lamb
Salt

4 medium-size romaine lettuce leaves, rinsed, crisped, and cut crosswise into thin shreds
Prepared fresh salsa

1. Stack tortillas and wrap them in 2 layers of paper towels; then wrap tightly in foil. Warm in a 350° oven until hot (about 15 minutes).

2. Meanwhile, in a medium-size bowl, mix jicama, carrot, and grapefruit juice; set aside.

3. Also while tortillas are heating, heat oil in a wide frying pan over medium-high heat. Add onion, chili powder, and cumin; cook, stirring often, until onion begins to brown (about 5 minutes). Add tomato to one side of pan; crumble lamb into other side. Cook, stirring occasionally and keeping lamb and tomato separate, until lamb is no longer pink, tomato has fallen apart, and tomato liquid has evaporated (about 6 minutes). Stir all foods together; season to taste with salt.

4. To assemble each taco, stack 2 tortillas on a plate; arrange a fourth of the lettuce in a strip down center of tortillas and top with a fourth of the lamb mixture. Fold tortillas in half. Arrange 2 tacos on each warm dinner plate; serve with jicama-carrot slaw and salsa to add to taste.

PER SERVING: 851 calories, 44 g total fat, 17 g saturated fat, 111 mg cholesterol, 326 mg sodium, 82 g carbohydrates, 18 g fiber, 35 g protein, 283 mg calcium, 7 mg iron

POUNDED LAMB CHOPS WITH TAPENADE & WHITE BEANS

PITTED OLIVES AND A FOOD PROCESSOR MAKE QUICK WORK OF TAPENADE; FOR EVEN FASTER PREPARATION, USE A PURCHASED PRODUCT. CRISP ROMAINE LEAVES OR WILTED GREENS OF ANY KIND (SUCH AS SPINACH, KALE, CHARD, OR BEET GREENS) ARE AN APPROPRIATE COMPLEMENT; SPRINKLE THEM WITH OLIVE OIL, LEMON JUICE, SALT, AND PEPPER.

25 MINUTES

Pounded Lamb Chops with Tapenade & White Beans

Tapenade (below)

4 lamb rib chops (6 to 8 oz. *each*), *each* about ¾ inch thick

2 tablespoons olive oil

1 can (about 15 oz.) large or small white beans, rinsed and drained

½ teaspoon sherry vinegar

1 small tomato (about 4 oz.), chopped

Salt and freshly ground pepper

TAPENADE

¼ cup drained, pitted calamata olives

2 tablespoons drained capers

1 teaspoon Dijon mustard

2 canned anchovy fillets, drained

¼ teaspoon dried thyme

1 small clove garlic, minced or pressed

1. Prepare Tapenade.

2. Slash any fat and connective tissue around edge of lamb chops at 1-inch intervals, cutting just to meat. Rub chops evenly on both sides with Tapenade, using all of it. Place each chop between 2 sheets of plastic wrap. Using a heavy, flat-surfaced mallet, pound chops firmly to a thickness of about ¼ inch.

3. Heat oil in a wide frying pan over medium-high heat. Add chops and cook, turning once, until browned on both sides and done to your liking; cut to test (4 to 5 minutes for medium). Transfer to a warm platter and keep warm.

4. Pour beans into frying pan and stir over medium-high heat to loosen pan drippings. Stir in vinegar and tomato; season to taste with and salt and pepper. Stir gently until beans are heated through. Spoon beans onto platter alongside lamb.

TAPENADE

In a blender or food processor, combine olives, capers, mustard, anchovies, thyme, and garlic. Whirl until olives are minced.

PER SERVING: 674 calories, 49 g total fat, 15 g saturated fat, 100 mg cholesterol, 1,314 mg sodium, 26 g carbohydrates, 6 g fiber, 31 g protein, 78 mg calcium, 5 mg iron

VEAL SCALLOPS WITH PEARS

HERE'S A COMPLETE MEAL IN ONE PAN: SAGE-SEASONED VEAL SCALLOPS, DARK RYE CROUTONS, AND FRESH PEAR HALVES, ALL BAKED TOGETHER BRIEFLY IN A HOT OVEN. FINISH THE MEAL WITH CHOCOLATE MARRONS (PAGE 232). WHEN YOU BUY THE VEAL, HAVE THE BUTCHER POUND IT $^1/_{16}$ INCH THICK (MEAT THAT'S POUNDED IS MORE TENDER THAN MEAT SLICED THINLY).

30 MINUTES

10 to 12 ounces boneless veal (such as top round), pounded ¹⁄₁₆ inch thick

½ teaspoon ground sage

About 1 tablespoon all-purpose flour

2 tablespoons plus 1 teaspoon olive oil

1 small clove garlic, minced or pressed

2 slices dark rye bread (*each* about ¼ inch thick), crusts trimmed off, each slice cut in half diagonally

1 small firm-ripe pear

1 teaspoon lemon juice

⅓ cup fat-free beef broth or fat-free reduced-sodium chicken broth

¼ cup dry white wine

¼ teaspoon Dijon mustard

Salt

Parsley sprigs

1. Rub veal on one side with sage. Coat lightly with flour and shake off excess.

2. Heat 1 tablespoon of the oil in a wide frying pan over medium-high heat. Add veal and cook, turning once, until browned on both sides (2 to 4 minutes), scraping pan as needed to prevent sticking. Transfer veal to a 10- by 15-inch baking pan.

3. Sprinkle garlic and 1 tablespoon of the oil over one side of bread slices, dividing equally. Place bread, oil side down, in baking pan. Peel, halve, and core pear; place in baking pan, cut side up. Mix remaining 1 teaspoon oil and lemon juice; drizzle over pear halves. Place pan in a 450° oven and bake until pear halves are warm, veal is hot, and bread is sizzling (about 10 minutes).

4. Meanwhile, to frying pan used to brown veal, add broth, wine, and mustard, stirring to loosen pan drippings. Bring to a boil; then boil, stirring occasionally, until reduced to ¼ cup. Season to taste with salt.

5. To serve, overlap veal slices on 2 warm dinner plates; spoon sauce evenly over veal. Arrange toast triangles and pear halves alongside veal. Garnish with parsley sprigs.

PER SERVING: 426 calories, 19 g total fat, 4 g saturated fat, 119 mg cholesterol, 385 mg sodium, 27 g carbohydrates, 3 g fiber, 35 g protein, 42 mg calcium, 2 mg iron

VEAL CHOPS OSSO BUCO STYLE

OSSO BUCO—VEAL SHANKS SLOW-COOKED TO MELTING TENDERNESS IN A CASSEROLE—IS A MILANESE CLASSIC. GREMOLATA, A MIXTURE OF GRATED LEMON PEEL, PARSLEY, AND GARLIC, IS ALWAYS SPRINKLED OVER THE MEAT FOR FRESHNESS AND COLOR; HERE, IT GIVES QUICKLY SAUTÉED VEAL CHOPS THE FLAVOR OF THE TRADITIONAL DISH. SERVE WITH A JULIENNE OF ENDIVE AND BIBB LETTUCE AND A SOFT BAGUETTE PULLED INTO BIG CHUNKS. FRESH FIGS AND CRISP AMARETTI WITH COFFEE MAKE A SATISFYING ENDING.

20 MINUTES

1 teaspoon grated lemon peel

2 teaspoons minced parsley

1 small clove garlic, minced or pressed

1 tablespoon olive oil

2 veal loin chops (about 8 oz. *each*), *each* about ¾ inch thick

½ cup fat-free reduced-sodium chicken broth

1 teaspoon lemon juice

Salt

1. To prepare gremolata, mix lemon peel, parsley, and garlic in a small bowl. Set aside.

2. Heat oil in a wide frying pan over high heat. Add chops and cook, turning once, until golden brown on both sides and still pink in thickest part; cut to test (about 10 minutes). Place one chop on each warm dinner plate; keep warm.

3. To frying pan, add broth and lemon juice. Bring to a boil, stirring to loosen pan drippings; then boil until reduced to about 2 tablespoons. Season to taste with salt. Pour reduced liquid through a fine wire strainer over veal chops; sprinkle with gremolata and serve.

PER SERVING: 304 calories, 20 g total fat, 7 g saturated fat, 115 mg cholesterol, 280 mg sodium, 1 g carbohydrates, 0 g fiber, 28 g protein, 28 mg calcium, 1 mg iron

Veal Chops Osso Buco Style

Sesame Pork Tenderloins

SESAME PORK TENDERLOINS
WHILE THE BARBECUE HEATS, YOU HAVE TIME TO PREPARE PORK TENDERLOINS FOR GRILLING, COOK A POT OF WHITE OR QUICK-COOKING BROWN RICE, AND CRISP SOME SALAD GREENS. YOU MIGHT GRILL FRESH FRUIT TO SERVE AS AN ADDITIONAL ACCOMPANIMENT; IT'S DELICIOUS WITH THE MEAT. HALVE OR QUARTER A PEACH AND TWO PLUMS AND PEEL A BANANA (CUT IT INTO THICK DIAGONAL SLICES, IF YOU LIKE); BRUSH THE FRUIT WITH A MIXTURE OF 2 TEASPOONS BROWN SUGAR AND 1 TEASPOON MELTED BUTTER BEFORE HEATING IT OVER THE COALS. (IF YOU DON'T WANT TO BARBECUE, YOU CAN PAN-GRILL THE PORK AND BROIL THE FRUIT.)

30 MINUTES

8 to 12 ounces pork tenderloin

2 tablespoons sesame seeds

1 tablespoon olive oil

1 tablespoon seasoned rice vinegar

1 tablespoon soy sauce

Curly-leaf greens such as frisée, oak leaf lettuce, or red leaf lettuce

1. Cut pork into 4 or 6 pieces, each about 1½ inches long. Pour sesame seeds into a small dish. Dip each piece of pork into seeds to coat bottom and top thoroughly. Drizzle seed-coated sides with oil.

2. In a small bowl, stir together vinegar and soy sauce; set aside.

3. Place pork slices on an oiled grill 3 to 4 inches above a solid bed of very hot coals (you can hold your hand at grill level for only 1 to 2 seconds) or over high heat on a gas grill. Close lid on gas grill. Cook, turning once, until seeds are golden and pork is no longer pink in thickest part; cut to test (10 to 12 minutes). Remove from grill and drizzle with soy mixture. Serve on a bed of lettuce.

PER SERVING: 314 calories, 19 g total fat, 4 g saturated fat, 90 mg cholesterol, 725 mg sodium, 4 g carbohydrates, 1 g fiber, 31 g protein, 94 mg calcium, 3 mg iron

PORK CHOPS WITH NEW POTATOES

MAKE A SIMPLE SAUCE FOR PORK CHOPS AND BOILED POTATOES BY REDUCING A LITTLE WHITE WINE IN THE PAN USED FOR SAUTÉING THE MEAT, MIXING IT WITH THE BROWNED PAN DRIPPINGS AS IT COOKS DOWN. CRISP LETTUCE TASTES REFRESHING ALONGSIDE; SERVE IT WITHOUT DRESSING OR SPRINKLED WITH OLIVE OIL, LEMON JUICE, SALT, AND PEPPER. OFFER SUGARED SLICED STRAWBERRIES FOR DESSERT.

25 MINUTES

10 to 12 ounces small red thin-skinned potatoes (*each* about 1½ inches in diameter), scrubbed

2 pork shoulder chops or steaks (about 8 oz. *each* for chops, ¾ to 1 lb. *each* for steaks), *each* about ½ inch thick

Salt and freshly ground pepper

2 teaspoons olive oil

⅓ cup dry white wine

About ¼ cup thinly sliced cornichons

Shredded romaine lettuce

Dijon mustard

1. Place potatoes in a 2-quart pan and add enough water to cover. Cover and bring to a boil over high heat; then reduce heat and simmer, covered, until potatoes are tender when pierced (10 to 15 minutes). Drain, cut into halves, and keep warm.

2. While potatoes are cooking, sprinkle chops lightly with salt and pepper. Heat oil in a wide frying pan over medium-high heat. Add chops and cook, turning once, until well browned on both sides and no longer pink in thickest part; cut to test (10 to 14 minutes). Place one chop on each warm dinner plate.

3. Drain and discard fat from pan. Pour in wine and bring to a boil over high heat; then boil, stirring to loosen drippings, until reduced to about 3 tablespoons.

4. Pour sauce evenly over chops; sprinkle chops with cornichons. Arrange potatoes and lettuce beside chops; offer mustard to add to taste.

PER SERVING: 654 calories, 41 g total fat, 14 g saturated fat, 135 mg cholesterol, 305 mg sodium, 28 g carbohydrates, 3 g fiber, 34 g protein, 13 mg calcium, 3 mg iron

SAUSAGE WITH POTATOES, BEETS & DILL

FRENCH GARLIC SALAMI IS A FULLY COOKED SAUSAGE THAT NEEDS ONLY REHEATING. IT'S OFTEN AVAILABLE IN SPECIALTY MEAT MARKETS; IF YOU CAN'T FIND IT, SUBSTITUTE POLISH SAUSAGE OR GARLIC KNOCKWURST. SERVE THIS MEDLEY OF SAUSAGE, POTATOES, AND BEETS ON A BED OF WATERCRESS, IF YOU LIKE; TRY PEARS BAKED IN CIDER FOR DESSERT.

30 MINUTES

8 ounces small red thin-skinned potatoes (*each* about 1¼ inches in diameter), scrubbed

8 ounces baby beets (*each* about 1¼ inches in diameter), unpeeled; or 8 ounces large beets, peeled and cut into ¾-inch chunks

¼ cup olive oil

2 tablespoons white wine vinegar

½ teaspoon Dijon mustard

2 green onions, minced

¼ teaspoon dried tarragon

2 tablespoons chopped fresh dill

Pinch of sugar

Salt and freshly ground pepper

8 to 11 ounces French garlic salami, Polish sausage (kielbasa), or garlic knockwurst

6 cornichons, thinly sliced lengthwise

1. Place potatoes in a 2-quart pan and add enough water to cover. Place beets in another 2-quart pan and add water to cover. Cover pans and bring to a boil over high heat; then reduce heat and simmer, covered, until vegetables are tender when pierced (10 to 15 minutes for potatoes, about 20 minutes for beets). Drain. Cut potatoes and baby beets into quarters.

2. While vegetables are cooking, combine oil, vinegar, mustard, onions, tarragon, dill, and sugar in a large bowl. Whisk together to blend; season to taste with salt and pepper and set aside.

3. Also while vegetables cook, bring 1 inch of water to a simmer in a 2- to 3-quart pan over high heat. Add salami; reduce heat, cover, and simmer until heated through, about 7 minutes (do not boil, or casings may burst). Drain salami and slice ¼ inch thick.

4. Add hot cooked potatoes and beets to dressing; add cornichons and stir to mix. Then mix in sliced salami and spoon into 2 warm wide, shallow bowls.

PER SERVING: 952 calories, 74 g total fat, 20 g saturated fat, 106 mg cholesterol, 2,712 mg sodium, 37 g carbohydrates, 3 g fiber, 35 g protein, 43 mg calcium, 4 mg iron

Sausage with Potatoes, Beets & Dill

POLENTA CAKES WITH SAUSAGE & ASPARAGUS

HERE'S A GOOD CHOICE FOR SAUSAGE LOVERS: JUICY BROWNED LINKS ARE SERVED WITH CREAMY POLENTA THAT'S STUDDED WITH SLICED ASPARAGUS AND SPICY SAUSAGE NUGGETS. YOU CAN USE ANY KIND OF SAUSAGE—LAMB, BEEF, OR PORK, SMOKED OR RAW (THE COOKING TIMES GIVEN ARE FOR RAW SAUSAGE). FOR A MILDER DISH, SERVE SAUTÉED BEEF STEAKS OR LAMB, PORK, OR VEAL CHOPS ALONGSIDE THE POLENTA. OFFER SLICED ORANGES DOUSED WITH GRAND MARNIER FOR DESSERT.

30 MINUTES

---

3 or 5 sausages (about 4 oz. *each*)

12 ounces prepared plain polenta roll

5 to 6 ounces asparagus

½ cup fat-free reduced-sodium chicken broth

1. Heat a wide frying pan over medium-low heat. With a fork, pierce casings of 2 or 4 sausages. Place pierced sausages in hot pan and cook, turning occasionally, until no longer pink in center; cut to test (about 25 minutes). As sausages cook, fat will begin to melt from them, and they'll brown in their own fat.

2. Meanwhile, slit casing of remaining sausage and pop out meat (or have the butcher do this for you when you buy the sausages). Cut polenta into 1- by 2-inch chunks. Snap off and discard tough ends of asparagus. Cut off and reserve top 4 inches of each spear; cut remainder of spears crosswise into ½-inch pieces.

3. Crumble sausage removed from casing into another wide frying pan. Cook over medium heat until fat melts from meat; then add polenta and sliced asparagus (do not add tips). Cook until polenta begins to soften (about 4 minutes); then mash polenta with back of a wooden spoon and stir to prevent sausage from scorching. Add broth to pan; mix polenta, sausage, and asparagus, stirring to loosen pan drippings. Cook, stirring, until mixture is very hot (1 to 2 minutes). Remove from heat and keep warm.

4. About 4 minutes before sausage links are done, add asparagus tips to pan with them. Cook, stirring, until asparagus turns bright green and is tender-crisp when pierced.

5. Press polenta mixture into 2 well-oiled, deep 1- to 1½-cup ramekins, then invert one ramekin onto each warm dinner plate. (Or simply scoop mixture from pan onto plates.) Arrange whole sausages and asparagus tips decoratively around polenta.

PER SERVING (BASED ON 3 SAUSAGES TOTAL): 578 calories, 40 g total fat, 14 g saturated fat, 84 mg cholesterol, 1,540 mg sodium, 28 g carbohydrates, 4 g fiber, 23 g protein, 44 mg calcium, 3 mg iron

TOFU & PORK IN HOT SAUCE
BAKED TOFU-PORK MEATBALLS ARE CLOAKED IN A LIGHT, SPICY SAUCE AND SERVED OVER FRESH SPINACH FOR A NOURISHING ONE-BOWL DINNER THAT NEEDS NO ACCOMPANIMENTS. FRESH FRUIT IS GOOD FOR DESSERT; IF YOU'RE IN THE MOOD FOR SOMETHING A BIT FANCY, OFFER ORANGE SEGMENTS DIPPED IN MELTED DARK CHOCOLATE (PAGE 226).

30 MINUTES

8 ounces firm tofu, rinsed and drained

4 ounces lean ground pork

1 large egg white or egg yolk

1 tablespoon cornstarch

⅛ teaspoon salt

2 tablespoons plus 1 teaspoon olive oil

½ cup fat-free reduced-sodium chicken broth

1½ teaspoons hot bean sauce; or ⅛ teaspoon ground red pepper (cayenne)

1½ teaspoons soy sauce

8 ounces packaged triple-washed baby spinach

1 clove garlic, minced or pressed

½ teaspoon minced fresh ginger
Thinly sliced green onions

1. Place tofu and pork in a medium-size bowl; mash together with a potato masher to blend well. Add egg white, 1 teaspoon of the cornstarch, and salt; mix well. Shape into 1½-inch balls.

2. Pour 2 tablespoons of the oil into another medium-size bowl; add meatballs and turn gently to coat. Arrange meatballs in a 10- by 15-inch baking pan. Bake in a 400° oven until no longer pink in center; cut to test (10 to 13 minutes).

3. While meatballs are baking, stir together broth, remaining 2 teaspoons cornstarch, bean sauce, and soy sauce in a small bowl; set aside.

4. When meatballs are almost done, rinse and drain spinach. Place spinach with water that clings to it in a wide frying pan. Cook over high heat, turning leaves with tongs, just until all spinach is wilted (1 to 2 minutes). With a slotted spoon, transfer spinach to 2 warm wide, shallow bowls. Keep warm.

5. Rinse and dry pan. Place over high heat and add remaining 1 teaspoon oil, garlic, and ginger. Cook, stirring, just until garlic is lightly browned. Stir broth mixture and pour into pan; stir until sauce boils and thickens. Add meatballs and stir to coat with sauce. Spoon over spinach, dividing equally. Garnish with onions.

PER SERVING: 497 calories, 36 g total fat, 8 g saturated fat, 41 mg cholesterol, 1,041 mg sodium, 15 g carbohydrates, 6 g fiber, 34 g protein, 900 mg calcium, 16 mg iron

HARVEST STIR-FRY
TO PUT THIS COLORFUL MEAT-AND-VEGETABLE MEDLEY TOGETHER AS QUICKLY AS POSSIBLE, HAVE THE BUTCHER SLICE THE PORK FOR YOU. SERVE WITH YELLOW RICE (COOK 1 CUP BASMATI RICE IN 1¼ CUPS WATER WITH ¼ TEASPOON GROUND TURMERIC); START THE WATER FOR THE RICE AS A FIRST STEP. THIS DISH STANDS ON ITS OWN, BUT YOU CAN ADD A GREEN SALAD IF YOU LIKE.

30 MINUTES

Harvest Stir-fry

1 tablespoon vegetable oil

6 ounces lean boneless pork (such as loin, shoulder or butt), cut across the grain into ¼-inch-thick slices

1 small onion (about 4 oz.), cut into wedges

1 medium-size carrot (about 5 oz.), cut into ¾-inch chunks or ¼- by 2-inch strips

1 medium-size parsnip (about 4 oz.), cut into ¾-inch chunks

5 brussels sprouts, outer leaves trimmed

2 tablespoons fat-free reduced-sodium chicken broth

Fennel Broth (below)

FENNEL BROTH

¼ cup fat-free reduced-sodium chicken broth

½ teaspoon fennel seeds, crushed

½ teaspoon unseasoned rice vinegar

½ teaspoon soy sauce

½ teaspoon chopped fresh thyme

½ teaspoon salt

½ teaspoon cornstarch

1. Heat oil in a wide frying pan over high heat. Add pork and cook, stirring, until browned (about 1 minute). Spoon pork into a bowl.

2. Reduce heat to medium-high and add onion, carrot, parsnip, and brussels sprouts to pan. Cook, stirring, until vegetables begin to brown on edges (about 2 minutes). Add the 2 tablespoons chicken broth; cover, reduce heat, and simmer until all vegetables are tender when pierced (about 10 minutes).

3. Meanwhile, prepare Fennel Broth.

4. Stir Fennel Broth and add to vegetable mixture; then stir in pork. Bring to a boil over high heat; boil, stirring, until sauce is thickened (about 1 minute). To serve, spoon into 2 warm wide, shallow bowls.

FENNEL BROTH

In a small bowl, stir together the ¼ cup chicken broth, fennel seeds, vinegar, soy sauce, thyme, salt, and cornstarch.

PER SERVING: 325 calories, 17 g total fat, 4 g saturated fat, 47 mg cholesterol, 855 mg sodium, 26 g carbohydrates, 8 g fiber, 19 g protein, 86 mg calcium, 2 mg iron

POULTRY

Braised Chicken & Artichokes (page 110)

CHICKEN WITH RED GRAPES RED GRAPES CONTRAST HANDSOMELY

WITH THE PALE, CREAMY WINE SAUCE, BUT YOU CAN USE GREEN GRAPES

IF YOU PREFER. ACCOMPANY WITH SHORT-GRAIN WHITE RICE OR QUICK-

COOKING BROWN RICE SIMMERED IN CHICKEN BROTH.

15 TO 20 MINUTES

2 small boneless, skinless chicken
breast halves (about 5 oz. *each*)

About 2 tablespoons all-purpose
flour

1 tablespoon butter or margarine

1 small shallot, thinly sliced

¼ cup dry white or rosé wine

¼ cup whipping cream

2 tablespoons fat-free reduced-
sodium chicken broth

2 teaspoons chopped fresh tarragon
or ½ teaspoon dried tarragon

1 cup seedless red or green grapes

Salt and white pepper

Tarragon sprigs

1. Rinse chicken and pat dry. Place each piece between 2 sheets of plastic wrap. With a heavy, flat-sided mallet, pound meat firmly but gently to a thickness of about ¼ inch. Coat chicken lightly with flour; shake off excess.

2. Melt butter in a wide nonstick frying pan over medium-high heat. When butter sizzles, add chicken and cook, turning once, until browned on both sides and no longer pink in center; cut to test (4 to 5 minutes). Transfer to warm plates and keep warm.

3. Add shallot to pan; cook, stirring, until soft (1 to 2 minutes). Add wine, cream, broth, and chopped tarragon. Increase heat to high, bring to a boil, and boil, stirring often, until reduced to about ⅓ cup (about 2 minutes).

4. Add grapes and cook, shaking pan often, just until grapes are hot (about 30 seconds). Season sauce to taste with salt and white pepper; pour over chicken. Garnish with tarragon sprigs.

PER SERVING: 385 calories, 17 g total fat, 10 g saturated fat, 131 mg cholesterol, 203 mg sodium, 22 g carbohydrates, 2 g fiber, 35 g protein, 56 mg calcium, 2 mg iron

HONEY MUSTARD CHICKEN BREASTS THIS BAKED CHICKEN

IS SEASONED WITH SPICY, HONEY-SWEETENED DIJON MUSTARD. YOU

MIGHT SERVE IT WITH KALE OR RED SWISS CHARD, SAUTÉED IN OLIVE OIL

JUST UNTIL WILTED, AND MICROWAVED SWEET POTATOES.

25 MINUTES

2 tablespoons honey Dijon mustard

2 teaspoons lemon juice

½ teaspoon ground ginger

1 small clove garlic, minced or
pressed

2 small boneless, skinless chicken
breast halves (about 5 oz. *each*)

Vegetable oil cooking spray

Watercress sprigs, rinsed and
crisped

1. In a medium-size, shallow bowl, stir together mustard, lemon juice, ginger, and garlic.

2. Rinse chicken and pat dry. Turn each piece in mustard mixture to coat completely.

3. Coat bottom of a 9-inch-square baking pan with cooking spray. Arrange chicken, skinned side up, in pan; spoon any mustard mixture remaining in bowl over chicken. Bake in a 450° oven until meat in thickest part is no longer pink; cut to test (18 to 20 minutes). Serve on warm dinner plates, garnished with watercress.

PER SERVING: 194 calories, 2 g total fat, 0 g saturated fat, 82 mg cholesterol, 109 mg sodium, 7 g carbohydrates, 0 g fiber, 33 g protein, 18 mg calcium, 1 mg iron

SLIVERED CHICKEN & WALNUTS   SERVE THIS STIR-FRIED MEDLEY

OF CHICKEN, BELL PEPPER, AND CRUNCHY WALNUTS OVER OR ALONGSIDE

15 MINUTES   HOT WHITE RICE. BRING ON A BASKET OF TANGERINES FOR DESSERT.

Sherry Cooking Sauce (below)

10 to 12 ounces boneless, skinless chicken breasts

1 tablespoon soy sauce

1 teaspoon cornstarch

2 tablespoons vegetable oil

½ cup walnut halves

1 medium-size green bell pepper (about 6 oz.), seeded and cut into 1-inch squares

½ teaspoon finely minced fresh ginger or ¼ teaspoon ground ginger

1 green onion, thinly sliced (optional)

SHERRY COOKING SAUCE

½ teaspoon cornstarch

¼ teaspoon crushed red pepper flakes

1 teaspoon seasoned rice vinegar

3 tablespoons dry sherry

1 tablespoon soy sauce

1. Prepare Sherry Cooking Sauce; set aside.

2. Rinse chicken, pat dry, and cut crosswise into ½-inch-wide strips. In a medium-size bowl, mix chicken, 1 tablespoon soy sauce, and the 1 teaspoon cornstarch; set aside.

3. Heat oil in a wide nonstick frying pan over medium-high heat. Add walnuts and cook, stirring, until browned (about 2 minutes); lift out with a slotted spoon and set aside. Add chicken to pan. Cook and stir until chicken is no longer pink in center; cut to test (4 to 6 minutes). Add bell pepper and ginger; cook, stirring, until pepper is just tender-crisp to bite (about 1 minute).

4. Stir Sherry Cooking Sauce and pour into pan. Cook, stirring, until sauce boils and thickens (about 30 seconds). To serve, sprinkle with walnuts and, if desired, onion.

SHERRY COOKING SAUCE

In a small bowl, stir together the ½ teaspoon cornstarch, red pepper flakes, vinegar, sherry, and 1 tablespoon soy sauce.

PER SERVING: 522 calories, 31 g total fat, 4 g saturated fat, 90 mg cholesterol, 1,187 mg sodium, 15 g carbohydrates, 3 g fiber, 41 g protein, 58 mg calcium, 3 mg iron

---

PINE NUT–CRUSTED BAKED CHICKEN   BRUSHED WITH PESTO

AND CRUSTED WITH A MIXTURE OF PINE NUTS, CHEESE, AND HERBS,

THIS CHICKEN IS SEASONED IN ITALIAN TRATTORIA STYLE. TO

COMPLETE THE MEAL, ADD MULTICOLORED CHERRY TOMATOES AND A

BOWL OF ORZO TOSSED WITH PAPER-THIN GARLIC SLICES SAUTÉED

25 TO 30 MINUTES   BRIEFLY IN OLIVE OIL.

¼ cup pine nuts

3 tablespoons grated Parmesan cheese

1 small clove garlic, sliced

2 tablespoons chopped Italian parsley

¼ teaspoon dried rosemary

2 small boneless, skinless chicken breast halves (about 5 oz. *each*)

Olive oil cooking spray

1 tablespoon prepared pesto

1. In a food processor, combine pine nuts, cheese, garlic, parsley, and rosemary; whirl until nuts are coarsely chopped.

2. Rinse chicken and pat dry. Coat a 9-inch-square baking pan with cooking spray. Spread skinned side of chicken pieces with pesto, dividing it equally. Arrange chicken, pesto side up, in pan. Spoon pine nut mixture over chicken, pressing it on lightly.

3. Bake in a 450° oven until coating is golden brown and meat in thickest part is no longer pink; cut to test (18 to 20 minutes).

PER SERVING: 328 calories, 17 g total fat, 4 g saturated fat, 89 mg cholesterol, 289 mg sodium, 4 g carbohydrates, 2 g fiber, 41 g protein, 151 mg calcium, 3 mg iron

QUICK KUNG PAO CHICKEN

STEAMED RICE IS THE PERFECT MILD FOIL FOR THE BOLD, RICH FLAVORS OF THIS CHINESE CLASSIC. SIP COLD CHINESE BEER TO COOL THE PIQUANCY OF THE SAUCE.

15 TO 20 MINUTES

10 to 12 ounces boneless, skinless chicken breasts, cut into strips ¼ inch wide and 2 inches long

2 cloves garlic, minced

⅛ to ¼ teaspoon crushed red pepper flakes

3 tablespoons fat-free reduced-sodium chicken broth

1 tablespoon soy sauce

1 tablespoon dry sherry

½ teaspoon cornstarch

½ teaspoon Asian sesame oil

3 green onions

2 teaspoons vegetable oil

¼ cup dry-roasted peanuts

Hot cooked rice

1. In a shallow bowl, mix chicken, garlic, and red pepper flakes; set aside.

2. In a small bowl, stir together broth, soy sauce, sherry, cornstarch, and sesame oil; set aside. Cut onions into 1½-inch lengths, then sliver each piece lengthwise; set aside.

3. Heat vegetable oil in a wide nonstick frying pan over medium-high heat. Add chicken and cook, stirring, until golden brown on outside and no longer pink in center; cut to test (4 to 5 minutes). Stir broth-soy mixture and pour into pan; then add peanuts. Cook, stirring, until sauce boils and thickens (about 30 seconds). Stir in onions. To serve, spoon over rice.

PER SERVING: 343 calories, 17 g total fat, 2 g saturated fat, 82 mg cholesterol, 671 mg sodium, 8 g carbohydrates, 2 g fiber, 38 g protein, 49 mg calcium, 2 mg iron

HERB CHEESE–STUFFED CHICKEN BREASTS

CLASSIC CHICKEN KIEV FEATURES CHICKEN BREASTS FOLDED AROUND SEASONED BUTTER, THEN DEEP-FRIED. IN THIS STREAMLINED OVEN-BAKED VERSION, NUGGETS OF CREAMY GARLIC- AND HERB-SEASONED CHEESE REPLACE THE BUTTER; USE BOURSIN OR ANOTHER SIMILAR CHEESE, SUCH AS ALOUETTE OR RONDELÉ. OFFER STEAMED ASPARAGUS AND QUARTERED SMALL RED POTATOES ALONGSIDE,

25 TO 30 MINUTES

SPOONING THE LUSCIOUS MELTED CHEESE OVER THEM.

2 boneless, skinless chicken breast halves (about 6 oz. *each*)

¼ cup (about 2 oz.) garlic-and-herb Boursin or other seasoned double cream cheese

1 large egg

¼ cup fine dry bread crumbs

2 teaspoons butter or margarine

1. Rinse chicken and pat dry. Place each piece between 2 sheets of plastic wrap. With a heavy, flat-sided mallet, pound meat firmly but gently to a thickness of about ¼ inch in center and ⅛ inch around edges. Mound half the cheese in center of each chicken piece. To form each bundle, lap a long side of chicken over cheese; then fold narrow ends of chicken toward center and slightly over cheese, making a bundle about 5½ inches long. Lap other long side of chicken over to completely enclose cheese.

2. In a shallow dish, beat egg with a fork to blend. Spread bread crumbs in another shallow dish. Coat each chicken bundle with egg, then roll in crumbs to coat evenly.

Herb Cheese–stuffed Chicken Breasts

3. In a wide frying pan with an ovenproof handle, melt butter over medium-high heat. When butter sizzles, add chicken bundles, folded side up; cook, turning once with a wide spatula, until well browned on both sides (2½ to 3 minutes).

4. Transfer pan to a 400° oven and bake until chicken is evenly browned all over and looks opaque on all edges, 8 to 10 minutes. (Do not cut chicken to test; this would allow melted cheese to spurt out.)

PER SERVING: 425 calories, 21 g total fat, 12 g saturated fat, 248 mg cholesterol, 467 mg sodium, 10 g carbohydrates, 1 g fiber, 46 g protein, 63 mg calcium, 2 mg iron

LEMON CHICKEN STIR-FRY
MADE WITH QUICK-COOKING RICE THAT STEEPS
WHILE YOU STIR-FRY THE CHICKEN, THIS COLORFUL ONE-DISH MEAL IS
GOOD SERVED WITH A SALAD OF LETTUCE AND SLICED CUCUMBERS.

25 MINUTES

---

1 cup quick-cooking white rice

1½ cups fat-free reduced-sodium chicken broth

2 teaspoons cornstarch

8 ounces boneless, skinless chicken breasts, cut into 1-inch chunks

½ cup ¼-inch-wide red bell pepper strips

3 ounces Chinese pea pods (also called snow or sugar peas), ends and strings removed

1 teaspoon minced fresh serrano or jalapeño chile

1½ teaspoons grated lemon peel

1 tablespoon lemon juice

2 green onions, thinly sliced

1. Place rice in a heatproof wide 1½- to 2-quart bowl. In a wide nonstick frying pan, bring 1 cup of the broth to a boil over high heat; pour over rice, cover, and let stand until liquid has been absorbed and rice is tender to bite (about 7 minutes). Meanwhile, in a small bowl, stir together cornstarch and remaining ½ cup broth; set aside.

2. Return pan to high heat, add chicken, and cook, stirring, until surface of chunks is no longer pink (1 to 2 minutes). Add bell pepper, pea pods, chile, and lemon peel. Continue to cook and stir just until chicken is no longer pink in center; cut to test (3 to 4 more minutes).

3. Stir broth mixture and add to pan. Stir until sauce boils and thickens (about 1 minute). Stir in lemon juice. Fluff rice with a fork, then pour chicken mixture over it; sprinkle with onions.

PER SERVING: 359 calories, 2 g total fat, 0 g saturated fat, 66 mg cholesterol, 549 mg sodium, 50 g carbohydrates, 3 g fiber, 34 g protein, 56 mg calcium, 4 mg iron

---

CHICKEN PICCATA
BONELESS CHICKEN BREASTS ARE A VERSATILE INGREDIENT;
HERE, THEY TAKE THE PLACE OF VEAL IN A POPULAR ITALIAN SAUTÉ. THE
LIGHT, LEMONY SAUCE IS SEASONED WITH FRESH SAGE.

12 TO 15 MINUTES

---

2 small boneless, skinless chicken breast halves (about 5 oz. *each*)

Freshly ground pepper

2 teaspoons butter or margarine

1 tablespoon olive oil

8 fresh sage leaves

¼ cup dry vermouth

1 tablespoon lemon juice

1 teaspoon grated lemon peel

Salt

1. Rinse chicken and pat dry. Place each piece between 2 sheets of plastic wrap. With a heavy, flat-sided mallet, pound meat firmly but gently to a thickness of ⅛ to ¼ inch. Lightly sprinkle each piece with pepper.

2. Melt butter in oil in a wide nonstick frying pan over medium-high heat. When butter sizzles, add chicken and cook, turning once, until browned on both sides and no longer pink in center; cut to test (4 to 5 minutes).

3. Meanwhile, stack sage leaves; then cut crosswise with a sharp knife to make thin slivers.

4. Lift chicken from pan, transfer to 2 warm dinner plates, and keep warm. To pan, add vermouth, lemon juice, lemon peel, and sage. Bring sauce to a boil, stirring to loosen pan drippings; then boil until reduced by about half (about 1 minute). Season sauce to taste with salt, then pour over chicken.

PER SERVING: 283 calories, 12 g total fat, 4 g saturated fat, 93 mg cholesterol, 134 mg sodium, 1 g carbohydrates, 0 g fiber, 33 g protein, 27 mg calcium, 1 mg iron

RED, WHITE & GREEN CHICKEN BREASTS

THE COLORS OF THE MEXICAN FLAG COME TOGETHER IN THESE SAUTÉED CUMIN-SEASONED CHICKEN BREASTS. FOR A SUMMER SUPPER, ADD ACCOMPANIMENTS OF CORN ON THE COB, WARM TORTILLAS, AND FROSTY GLASSES OF ICED TEA WITH LIME.

15 TO 20 MINUTES

2 small boneless, skinless chicken breast halves (about 5 oz. *each*)

Ground cumin

2 teaspoons butter or margarine

1 tablespoon olive oil

¼ cup sour cream

2 tablespoons chopped cilantro

1 small fresh jalapeño chile, seeded and minced

1 small pear-shaped (Roma-type) tomato (about 3 oz.), seeded and chopped

1 clove garlic, minced or pressed

2 tablespoons lime juice

Salt

Cilantro sprigs

1. Rinse chicken and pat dry. Place each piece between 2 sheets of plastic wrap. With a heavy, flat-sided mallet, pound meat firmly but gently to a thickness of about ¼ inch. Sprinkle each piece with cumin to taste.

2. Melt butter in oil in a wide nonstick frying pan over medium-high heat. When butter sizzles, add chicken and cook, turning once, until browned on both sides and no longer pink in center; cut to test (4 to 5 minutes). Meanwhile, in a small bowl, stir together sour cream and chopped cilantro.

3. Lift chicken from pan, transfer to 2 warm dinner plates, and keep warm. To pan, add chile, tomato, garlic, and lime juice. Cook, stirring to loosen pan drippings, just until tomato is heated through (about 1 minute). Season to taste with salt.

4. Spoon tomato mixture over chicken; top each serving with half the sour cream mixture. Garnish with cilantro sprigs.

PER SERVING: 329 calories, 19 g total fat, 8 g saturated fat, 105 mg cholesterol, 154 mg sodium, 6 g carbohydrates, 1 g fiber, 34 g protein, 59 mg calcium, 1 mg iron

Red, White & Green Chicken Breasts

From Freezer to Table in 30 Minutes

STARTING ICE-HARD FROM THE FREEZER, BONELESS, SKINLESS CHICKEN BREAST HALVES CAN BE TRANSFORMED INTO SENSATIONAL WEEKNIGHT ENTRÉES IN HALF AN HOUR OR LESS. YOU CAN ACCOMPLISH THIS FEAT BY EITHER BAKING OR POACHING; WE PRESENT IDEAS FOR FLAVORING CHICKEN COOKED BOTH WAYS. SERVE ANY OF THESE DISHES WITH STEAMED RICE, PASTA, OR A SIMPLE PILAF. YOU CAN SPLURGE A BIT ON COMPLEMENTS SUCH AS A FAVORITE WINE OR A FINE LOAF OF CRUSTY BREAD, TOO, SINCE INDIVIDUALLY FROZEN BREAST HALVES OFFER A REAL BARGAIN AT THE SUPERMARKET OR A DISCOUNT STORE. THE PIECES TYPICALLY RANGE IN WEIGHT FROM 6 TO 10 OUNCES; FOR BEST RESULTS, COOK TWO OF ABOUT THE SAME SIZE.

Baked Chicken with Capers & Fresh Tomatoes
30 MINUTES

- 2 frozen boneless, skinless chicken breast halves (about 8 oz. *each*)
- 1½ cups chopped ripe tomatoes
- 1½ tablespoons drained capers
  Salt and freshly ground pepper
- ¼ cup slivered fresh basil
- 2 tablespoons freshly shredded Parmesan cheese

1. Place chicken pieces in a single layer in an 8- or 9-inch-square baking pan. Bake, uncovered, in a 400° oven until meat in thickest part is no longer pink; cut to test (25 to 30 minutes).

2. When chicken is nearly done, combine tomatoes and capers in a 1- to 1½-quart pan; stir over medium heat until hot (2½ to 3 minutes). Season to taste with salt and pepper.

3. Transfer chicken to 2 warm dinner plates and top with tomato mixture. Sprinkle with basil and cheese.

PER SERVING: 312 calories, 5 g total fat, 2 g saturated fat, 136 mg cholesterol, 558 mg sodium, 8 g carbohydrates, 2 g fiber, 56 g protein, 132 mg calcium, 3 mg iron

Chicken Baked with Prosciutto & Cheese
30 MINUTES

- 2 frozen boneless, skinless chicken breast halves (about 6 oz. *each*)
- 2 teaspoons olive oil
- ⅛ teaspoon coarsely ground pepper
- 2 teaspoons minced fresh sage or ¾ teaspoon dried sage
- ⅓ cup shredded provolone cheese
- 2 thin slices prosciutto (about 1 oz. *total*)
  Sage sprigs (optional)

1. Place chicken pieces in a single layer in an 8- or 9-inch-square baking pan. Bake, uncovered, in a 400° oven for 15 minutes. Meanwhile, in a small bowl, stir together oil, pepper, and minced sage.

2. After chicken has baked for 15 minutes, brush with oil mixture. Continue to bake until meat in thickest part is no longer pink; cut to test (about 12 minutes).

3. Top each chicken piece with half the cheese and one prosciutto slice. Return to oven; continue to bake until cheese is melted and prosciutto begins to crisp (about 3 minutes).

4. Transfer chicken to 2 warm dinner plates. Garnish with sage sprigs, if desired.

PER SERVING: 327 calories, 14 g total fat, 5 g saturated fat, 123 mg cholesterol, 538 mg sodium, 1 g carbohydrates, 0 g fiber, 48 g protein, 166 mg calcium, 2 mg iron

BAKED HOISIN CHICKEN
30 MINUTES

- 2 frozen boneless, skinless chicken breast halves (about 8 oz. *each*)
- 2 tablespoons hoisin sauce
- 2 tablespoons apricot jam
- 2 tablespoons minced cilantro
- 2 green onions, thinly sliced on the diagonal
- 1 teaspoon shredded lemon peel

1. Place chicken pieces in a single layer in an 8- or 9-inch-square baking pan. Bake, uncovered, in a 400° oven for 15 minutes. Meanwhile, in a small bowl, stir together hoisin sauce and jam.

2. After chicken has baked for 15 minutes, spoon hoisin mixture over it. Continue to bake until meat in thickest part is no longer pink; cut to test (12 to 15 more minutes).

3. Meanwhile, in a small bowl, mix cilantro, onions, and lemon peel. Transfer chicken to 2 warm dinner plates; stir pan juices to blend, then spoon evenly over chicken. Sprinkle with cilantro mixture.

PER SERVING: 349 calories, 3 g total fat, 1 g saturated fat, 132 mg cholesterol, 473 mg sodium, 23 g carbohydrates, 1 g fiber, 53 g protein, 42 mg calcium, 2 mg iron

POACHED MANGO CHICKEN
20 TO 25 MINUTES

- ⅔ cup mango nectar
- ½ cup fat-free reduced-sodium chicken broth
- 2 tablespoons lime juice
- 2 teaspoons minced fresh ginger
- ½ teaspoon ground cinnamon
- 2 frozen boneless, skinless chicken breast halves (6 to 8 oz. *each*)
- 1½ teaspoons cornstarch blended with 2 tablespoons water
- Salt
- Thin lime slices (optional)

1. In a wide frying pan, stir together mango nectar, broth, lime juice, ginger, and cinnamon. Add chicken to broth mixture, cover, and bring to a boil over high heat. Reduce heat and simmer, covered, until meat in thickest part is no longer pink; cut to test (15 to 20 minutes). Transfer chicken to a warm platter and keep warm.

2. Bring cooking liquid to a boil over high heat; then boil, uncovered, stirring occasionally, until reduced to about ½ cup (2 to 3 minutes). Stir cornstarch mixture, then pour into pan; return to a boil, stirring until sauce is thickened. Season to taste with salt.

3. Spoon sauce over chicken. Garnish with lime slices, if desired.

PER SERVING: 285 calories, 3 g total fat, 1 g saturated fat, 115 mg cholesterol, 289 mg sodium, 16 g carbohydrates, 0 g fiber, 47 g protein, 40 mg calcium, 2 mg iron

WINE-POACHED CHICKEN & MUSHROOMS
25 TO 30 MINUTES

- 8 small white mushrooms (about 4 oz. *total*), cut into quarters
- ⅓ cup fat-free reduced-sodium chicken broth
- ½ cup dry white wine
- ⅛ teaspoon white pepper
- ½ teaspoon dried tarragon
- 2 frozen boneless, skinless chicken breast halves (6 to 8 oz. *each*)
- ⅓ cup whipping cream
- Salt
- Chopped parsley (optional)

1. In a wide frying pan, combine mushrooms, broth, wine, white pepper, and tarragon. Add chicken to broth mixture, cover, and bring to a boil over high heat. Reduce heat and simmer, covered, until meat in thickest part is no longer pink; cut to test (15 to 20 minutes). Transfer chicken to a warm platter and keep warm.

2. Add cream to cooking liquid and mushrooms in pan. Bring to a boil over high heat. Then boil, stirring occasionally, until sauce is reduced to about ½ cup (6 to 8 minutes). Season to taste with salt.

3. Pour mushroom sauce over chicken. Sprinkle with parsley, if desired.

PER SERVING: 354 calories, 15 g total fat, 8 g saturated fat, 159 mg cholesterol, 250 mg sodium, 5 g carbohydrates, 1 g fiber, 48 g protein, 62 mg calcium, 2 mg iron

CHICKEN IN ORANGE & WINE SAUCE SAUTÉED CHICKEN

BREAST STRIPS IN AN ORANGE-ACCENTED SAUCE TASTE GOOD WITH HOT

FETTUCCINE; YOU MIGHT TOSS THE PASTA WITH RIBBONS OF PROSCIUTTO

FRIZZLED WITH MINCED GARLIC IN A LITTLE OLIVE OIL. ALONGSIDE, SERVE

15 MINUTES   STEAMED FRESH GREENS SUCH AS SPINACH OR SWISS CHARD.

---

10 to 12 ounces boneless, skinless
   chicken breasts
   Salt and freshly ground pepper
   About 2 tablespoons all-purpose
   flour
1 tablespoon olive oil
½ cup dry white wine
1 teaspoon lemon juice
2 tablespoons orange marmalade
   Chopped Italian parsley

1. Rinse chicken, pat dry, and cut crosswise into ½-inch-wide strips. Season to taste with salt and pepper, then coat lightly with flour on all sides; shake off excess.

2. Heat oil in a wide nonstick frying pan over medium-high heat. Add chicken and cook, stirring often, until golden brown on all sides (4 to 5 minutes).

3. Add wine and lemon juice to pan, stirring to loosen drippings. Cook, stirring often, until liquid is reduced by about half and chicken is no longer pink in center; cut to test (about 2 minutes). Stir in marmalade. Spoon chicken and sauce onto 2 warm dinner plates and sprinkle with parsley.

PER SERVING: 334 calories, 9 g total fat, 1 g saturated fat, 82 mg cholesterol, 107 mg sodium, 20 g carbohydrates, 0 g fiber, 34 g protein, 30 mg calcium, 2 mg iron

---

QUICK COQ AU VIN TURN OUT THIS FAMILIAR FRENCH BISTRO DISH IN A HURRY

BY USING CHUNKS OF CHICKEN THIGH SAUTÉED WITH PANCETTA AND

MUSHROOMS AND SAUCED WITH BROTH AND RED WINE. WIDE NOODLES

20 TO 25 MINUTES   AND BRUSSELS SPROUTS COMPLEMENT THE CLASSIC FLAVORS.

---

10 to 12 ounces boneless, skinless
   chicken thighs
   Salt and freshly ground pepper
   About 2 tablespoons all-purpose
   flour
1 teaspoon butter or margarine
2 teaspoons olive oil
4 medium-size mushrooms (about
   3 oz. *total*), cut into quarters
1 small shallot, slivered
1 thin slice pancetta (about 1½ oz.),
   cut into thin strips
½ teaspoon dried thyme
1 clove garlic, minced or pressed
⅓ cup fat-free reduced-sodium
   chicken broth
⅓ cup dry red wine

1. Rinse chicken, pat dry, and cut into 1-inch chunks. Season to taste with salt and pepper, then coat lightly with flour on all sides; shake off excess.

2. Melt butter in oil in a wide nonstick frying pan over medium-high heat. When butter sizzles, add chicken and cook, stirring often, until golden brown on all sides (about 5 minutes).

3. To chicken, add mushrooms, shallot, pancetta, thyme, and garlic. Continue to cook, stirring often, until mushrooms are tinged with brown (about 3 more minutes). Pour in broth and wine, stirring to loosen pan drippings. Cook, stirring often, until liquid is reduced by about half and chicken is no longer pink in center; cut to test (3 to 5 minutes). Spoon into a warm serving bowl.

PER SERVING: 368 calories, 20 g total fat, 6 g saturated fat, 147 mg cholesterol, 483 mg sodium, 10 g carbohydrates, 1 g fiber, 36 g protein, 35 mg calcium, 3 mg iron

DANISH CHICKEN MEATBALLS WITH BLUE CHEESE SAUCE

POACHING PRODUCES REMARKABLY MOIST AND TENDER MEATBALLS. THESE, FEATURING A DILL-SCENTED BLUE CHEESE SAUCE, ARE DELICIOUS SPOONED OVER HOT EGG NOODLES.

15 MINUTES

- 8 ounces lean ground chicken
- 2½ teaspoons cornstarch
- 1 large egg white
- ⅛ teaspoon salt
- ¼ teaspoon grated lemon peel
- 1 tablespoon chopped fresh dill or ½ teaspoon dried dill weed
- 1¼ cups fat-free reduced-sodium chicken broth
- ½ cup (about 2 oz.) crumbled blue-veined cheese
- 2 to 3 cups hot cooked egg noodles

1. In a medium-size bowl, combine chicken, ½ teaspoon of the cornstarch, egg white, salt, lemon peel, and half the dill. Using a fork, mix until well combined.

2. In a 10-inch frying pan, bring broth to a simmer over medium-high heat. As broth heats, drop chicken mixture into it by level tablespoons, keeping meatballs slightly apart. After all meatballs have been added, reduce heat, cover, and simmer until meatballs are white in center; cut to test (3 to 4 minutes).

3. In a small bowl, blend remaining 2 teaspoons cornstarch with 2 tablespoons water. With a slotted spoon, transfer meatballs to a bowl. Whisk cornstarch mixture into hot broth. Increase heat to high and add cheese; whisk until sauce is smooth.

4. Return meatballs and any accumulated liquid to sauce, mix gently, and heat for 30 seconds. Spoon meatballs and sauce over noodles in a warm serving bowl. Sprinkle with remaining dill.

PER SERVING: 571 calories, 21 g total fat, 8 g saturated fat, 181 mg cholesterol, 1,063 mg sodium, 54 g carbohydrates, 4 g fiber, 39 g protein, 206 mg calcium, 6 mg iron

BRAISED CHICKEN & ARTICHOKES

Pictured on page 95

25 TO 30 MINUTES

THIS COMFORTING DISH IS GOOD WITH SOFT POLENTA, COOKED SPEEDILY IN THE MICROWAVE AND SPRINKLED WITH PARMESAN CHEESE. ROUND OUT THE MEAL WITH GREEN BEANS, CRUSTY BREAD, AND A GLASS OF RED WINE.

10 to 12 ounces boneless, skinless chicken thighs

1 jar (about 6½ oz.) marinated artichoke hearts, drained (reserve marinade)

4 medium-size mushrooms (about 3 oz. *total*), cut into quarters

½ cup slivered onion

1 tablespoon tomato paste

½ cup fat-free reduced-sodium chicken broth

1 teaspoon balsamic vinegar

1. Rinse chicken; pat dry. Heat 1 tablespoon of the artichoke marinade in a wide nonstick frying pan over medium-high heat. Add chicken and cook, turning as needed, until golden brown on all sides (4 to 5 minutes). Remove from pan and set aside.

2. To pan, add mushrooms and onion; cook, stirring occasionally, until mushrooms are lightly browned (about 3 minutes). Then stir in tomato paste, broth, and 1 more tablespoon artichoke marinade. Return chicken and any accumulated liquid to pan. Arrange drained artichokes around chicken pieces.

3. Bring sauce to a boil; then reduce heat, cover, and simmer until chicken is tender when pierced and no longer pink in thickest part; cut to test (12 to 15 minutes).

4. Using a slotted spoon, transfer chicken and artichokes to a warm serving bowl and keep warm. Stir vinegar into sauce and bring to a boil; boil, stirring, until sauce is slightly thickened (1 to 2 minutes). Pour sauce over chicken.

PER SERVING: 310 calories, 13 g total fat, 3 g saturated fat, 129 mg cholesterol, 831 mg sodium, 14 g carbohydrates, 5 g fiber, 35 g protein, 49 mg calcium, 3 mg iron

MU SHU ROLLS

12 TO 15 MINUTES

TO MAKE SPEEDY ROLLED-UP SANDWICHES WITH THE FLAVORS OF A CHINESE RESTAURANT FAVORITE, FILL WARM TORTILLAS WITH SHREDDED CABBAGE, PLUM SAUCE, AND LEFTOVER SLICED ROAST CHICKEN OR TURKEY. NO LEFTOVERS? PICK UP A ROTISSERIE CHICKEN AT THE DELI COUNTER (IF IT'S STILL WARM, SO MUCH THE BETTER).

1½ to 2 cups thin bite-size strips roast chicken or turkey

4 to 6 flour tortillas (*each* 7 to 9 inches in diameter)

1½ to 2 cups finely shredded red or green cabbage (or a combination)

3 green onions, thinly sliced

Asian plum sauce

Red pickled ginger (optional)

1. Place chicken in a 1- to 1½-quart microwave-safe container. Cover and microwave on medium (50%) for 3 to 5 minutes or until heated through. Remove from microwave and keep warm.

2. Stack tortillas and wrap loosely in paper towels. Microwave on high (100%) for 30 to 45 seconds or until heated through.

3. To assemble each roll, set a hot tortilla on a plate. Spoon on chicken and cabbage; then top with onions, plum sauce, and, if desired, ginger. Roll up and eat out of hand.

PER SERVING: 541 calories, 15 g total fat, 3 g saturated fat, 109 mg cholesterol, 534 mg sodium, 54 g carbohydrates, 4 g fiber, 44 g protein, 175 mg calcium, 5 mg iron

POTATO "RISOTTO" WITH SAUSAGE & BROCCOLI

IT'S MADE WITH FROZEN SHREDDED POTATOES, NOT RICE—BUT THIS DISH ACHIEVES A SURPRISINGLY RISOTTO-LIKE TEXTURE NONETHELESS. SERVE IT IN WIDE, SHALLOW BOWLS. GARLIC-STUDDED FOCACCIA AND A SLICED TOMATO SALAD MAKE GOOD ACCOMPANIMENTS.

20 TO 25 MINUTES

2 or 3 fresh chicken-apple or chicken-basil sausages (8 to 10 oz. *total*)

1½ cups (about 6 oz.) fresh broccoli flowerets

3 cups frozen hash-brown-cut (shredded) potatoes

½ cup finely chopped onion

1 tablespoon chopped fresh sage or **1 teaspoon** dried sage

1½ cups reduced-fat (2%) milk

Salt

Freshly shredded Parmesan cheese (optional)

1. Remove casings from sausages and crumble meat into a wide nonstick frying pan. Cook over medium-high heat, stirring often with a wooden spoon to break up chunks, until meat is no longer pink (about 3 minutes). Add broccoli and continue to cook, stirring often, until sausage is well browned and broccoli is tender-crisp to bite (about 5 more minutes). Pour into a warm bowl and keep warm.

2. To pan, add potatoes and onion; cook, stirring often, until onion is soft (about 2 minutes). Reduce heat to medium. Add sage and milk; cook, stirring often, just until potatoes are tender to bite (6 to 8 minutes). Season to taste with salt.

3. Pour potato mixture into 2 warm wide, shallow bowls, dividing it equally; top with sausage-broccoli mixture. Sprinkle with cheese, if desired.

PER SERVING: 644 calories, 25 g total fat, 8 g saturated fat, 128 mg cholesterol, 1,078 mg sodium, 74 g carbohydrates, 8 g fiber, 35 g protein, 313 mg calcium, 5 mg iron

Potato "Risotto" with Sausage & Broccoli

BUFFALO CHICKEN DRUMMETTES

YOU MAY THINK OF TINY CHICKEN DRUMMETTES AS PARTY FARE. BUT WHO'S TO SAY DINNER FOR TWO CAN'T CONSIST OF FESTIVE FINGER FOOD? IT'S TRADITIONAL TO DIP THE HOT CHICKEN INTO CREAMY BLUE CHEESE DRESSING; IF THIS APPEALS TO YOU, USE YOUR FAVORITE RECIPE OR—EASIER STILL—ENJOY A PURCHASED DRESSING. COMPLETE THE MENU WITH CRUNCHY COLESLAW AND WARM CORNBREAD.

30 MINUTES

2 pounds chicken drummettes (15 to 20 pieces)

Vegetable oil cooking spray

¼ cup seasoned rice vinegar

2 tablespoons water

2 tablespoons tomato paste

1 tablespoon liquid hot pepper seasoning

1 teaspoon ground red pepper (cayenne)

¼ to ⅓ cup blue cheese dressing (optional)

1. Rinse chicken and pat dry. Coat a 9- by 13-inch baking pan with cooking spray. Arrange chicken in a single layer in pan. Bake in a 500° oven for 10 minutes.

2. Meanwhile, in a small bowl, stir together vinegar, water, tomato paste, hot pepper seasoning, and red pepper.

3. After chicken has baked for 10 minutes, remove pan from oven. Spoon off and discard fat; then pour vinegar mixture over chicken. Using tongs, turn chicken to coat well. Return pan to oven and continue to bake until chicken is well browned and meat near bone is no longer pink; cut to test (about 15 more minutes).

4. Brush chicken with sauce remaining in pan, then serve on a hot platter. Offer blue cheese dressing for dipping, if desired.

PER SERVING: 511 calories, 25 g total fat, 7 g saturated fat, 196 mg cholesterol, 1,114 mg sodium, 10 g carbohydrates, 1 g fiber, 59 g protein, 33 mg calcium, 3 mg iron

GRILLED TURKEY LOCO FILLETS WITH BLACK BEANS

TURKEY LOCO IS A CASUAL THANKSGIVING FAVORITE: A GRILLED WHOLE, BUTTERFLIED BIRD FLAVORED WITH LIME AND OREGANO. HERE, WE USE THE SAME SEASONINGS IN A DISH THAT'S MORE PRACTICAL FOR TWO—SUCCULENT BARBECUED TURKEY FILLETS. SERVE WITH SIMMERED BLACK BEANS, QUESADILLAS, AND A SALAD OF TORN ROMAINE AND DICED AVOCADO.

25 MINUTES

Grilled Turkey Loco Fillets with Black Beans

2 turkey breast tenderloins (5 to 6 oz. each), *each* about ½ inch thick

1 lime, cut in half

¾ teaspoon dried oregano

Salt and freshly ground pepper

2 teaspoons olive oil

½ cup thinly sliced onion

1 clove garlic, minced or pressed

1 teaspoon ground cumin

1 cup canned black beans (undrained)

1 small pear-shaped (Roma-type) tomato (about 3 oz.), seeded and chopped

Finely minced fresh jalapeño chile (optional)

1. Rinse turkey and pat dry. Squeeze and rub one lime half over turkey on all sides; reserve remaining lime half for garnish. Sprinkle turkey all over with ½ teaspoon of the oregano, then season lightly with salt and pepper. Set aside.

2. Heat oil in a small nonstick frying pan over medium heat. Add onion, garlic, cumin, and remaining ¼ teaspoon oregano; cook, stirring occasionally, until onion is soft but not brown (3 to 5 minutes). Stir in beans and their liquid, then tomato. Continue to cook, stirring occasionally, until almost all liquid has evaporated (about 10 minutes).

3. While beans are simmering, place turkey on a lightly greased grill 4 to 6 inches above a solid bed of medium-hot coals (you can hold your hand at grill level for 3 to 4 seconds) or over medium-high heat on a gas grill. Close lid on gas grill. Cook, turning once, until turkey is nicely browned on outside and no longer pink in thickest part; cut to test (10 to 12 minutes).

4. Transfer turkey to 2 warm dinner plates; spoon beans alongside and sprinkle with minced chile, if desired. Cut remaining lime half into wedges; garnish each serving with lime wedges.

PER SERVING: 335 calories, 7 g total fat, 1 g saturated fat, 88 mg cholesterol, 477 mg sodium, 26 g carbohydrates, 8 g fiber, 43 g protein, 91 mg calcium, 6 mg iron

Turkey Cutlets with Brandied Green Peppercorn–Tarragon Cream

Pop frozen slender French fries in the oven to crisp while you sauté tender turkey and stir together an elegant creamy sauce. Steamed broccoli spears and a crusty baguette make good accompaniments.

15 MINUTES

10 to 12 ounces turkey breast cutlets or slices (*each* about ¼ inch thick)

About 2 tablespoons all-purpose flour

1 tablespoon butter or margarine

2 teaspoons vegetable oil

¼ cup brandy

1 teaspoon drained bottled green peppercorns

1 tablespoon minced fresh tarragon or 1 teaspoon dried tarragon

⅓ cup whipping cream

Salt

Tarragon sprigs (optional)

1. Rinse turkey and pat dry. Lightly coat each piece with flour; shake off excess.

2. Melt butter in oil in a wide nonstick frying pan over medium-high heat. When butter sizzles, add turkey and cook, turning once, until golden brown on both sides and no longer pink in center; cut to test (5 to 6 minutes). Transfer to a warm platter and keep warm.

3. Add brandy to pan, stirring to loosen drippings. Cook until reduced by half (about 45 seconds); then stir in peppercorns, minced tarragon, and cream. Continue to cook until sauce is slightly reduced and forms large, shiny bubbles (about 2 more minutes). Season sauce to taste with salt, then pour over turkey. Garnish with tarragon sprigs, if desired.

PER SERVING: 448 calories, 24 g total fat, 12 g saturated fat, 156 mg cholesterol, 199 mg sodium, 8 g carbohydrates, 0 g fiber, 40 g protein, 55 mg calcium, 2 mg iron

Turkey Scaloppine with Garlic & Rosemary Potatoes

This Italian-inspired main dish calls for two frying pans. Pounded turkey breast slices are sautéed in the first, while quartered, steamed new potatoes cook to savory crustiness in the second. Serve with a loaf of ciabatta and a platter of juicy sliced tomatoes.

25 MINUTES

Turkey Scaloppine with Garlic & Rosemary Potatoes

8 ounces small red thin-skinned potatoes (*each* about 2 inches in diameter), scrubbed and cut into quarters

10 to 12 ounces turkey breast cutlets or slices (*each* about ¼ inch thick)

Salt, white pepper, and nutmeg

About 2 tablespoons all-purpose flour

1½ tablespoons olive oil

1 clove garlic, thinly sliced

¼ teaspoon crumbled dried rosemary

1 teaspoon butter or margarine

¼ teaspoon paprika

¼ cup dry vermouth

½ teaspoon grated lemon peel

2 tablespoons chopped parsley

1. Place potato quarters on a steamer rack above about 1 inch of water in a 2-quart pan. Cover and bring to a boil over high heat; then steam, covered, until potatoes are almost tender when pierced (about 10 minutes).

2. Meanwhile, rinse turkey and pat dry. Place each piece between 2 sheets of plastic wrap. With a heavy, flat-sided mallet, pound meat firmly but gently to a thickness of about ⅛ inch. Lightly sprinkle each slice with salt, white pepper, and nutmeg; then lightly coat with flour and shake off excess. Set aside.

3. Heat 1 tablespoon of the oil in a small nonstick frying pan over medium heat. Add steamed potatoes, garlic, and rosemary. Cook, stirring occasionally, until potatoes are golden brown and tender when pierced (8 to 10 minutes).

4. Meanwhile, in a wide nonstick frying pan, melt butter in remaining 1½ teaspoons oil over medium-high heat. When butter sizzles, stir in paprika. Then add turkey and cook, turning once, until browned on both sides and no longer pink in center; cut to test (4 to 5 minutes). Transfer turkey to 2 warm dinner plates and keep warm.

5. Add vermouth and lemon peel to pan, stirring to loosen drippings. Increase heat to high, bring to a boil, and boil until reduced by half (about 1 minute). Pour sauce evenly over turkey; sprinkle with parsley. Spoon potatoes alongside turkey.

PER SERVING: 435 calories, 13 g total fat, 3 g saturated fat, 102 mg cholesterol, 108 mg sodium, 28 g carbohydrates, 2 g fiber, 42 g protein, 30 mg calcium, 3 mg iron

SANTA FE SMOKED TURKEY SANDWICHES WITH PRONTO APRICOT CHUTNEY

ONCE YOU'VE MADE THE SPICY CHUTNEY, THE REST IS A SNAP: JUST STUFF SAVORY ONION-SPRINKLED KAISER ROLLS WITH SLICED SMOKED TURKEY AND A SPOONFUL OR TWO OF CHUTNEY, THEN ENJOY. FOR A RELAXED SUPPER ON A WARM EVENING, POUR TALL GLASSES OF BEER TO SIP; OFFER A COOLING DESSERT OF LIME SORBET AND COCONUT MACAROONS. (IF YOU MAKE THE CHUTNEY AHEAD, LET IT COOL SLIGHTLY, THEN TRANSFER TO A GLASS CONTAINER AND REFRIGERATE FOR UP TO A MONTH.)

30 MINUTES

Pronto Apricot Chutney (below)

2 onion Kaiser rolls (*each* about 4½ inches in diameter), split

Dijon mustard

Mayonnaise

6 ounces thinly sliced smoked turkey breast

2 to 4 lettuce leaves, rinsed and crisped

PRONTO APRICOT CHUTNEY

¾ cup coarsely chopped dried apricots

½ cup cider vinegar

½ cup sugar

¼ cup canned diced green chiles

¼ cup dried sweet cherries

¼ cup chopped red onion

1 cinnamon stick (about 2½ inches long)

½ teaspoon mustard seeds

¼ teaspoon salt

1. Prepare Pronto Apricot Chutney; set aside to cool.

2. Spread cut sides of rolls with mustard and mayonnaise to taste. Heap half the turkey on bottom half of each roll. Dollop on chutney to taste, then top each with half the lettuce. Add top halves of rolls and serve.

PER SERVING WITH 1 TABLESPOON CHUTNEY: 309 calories, 6 g total fat, 2 g saturated fat, 36 mg cholesterol, 1,149 mg sodium, 42 g carbohydrates, 2 g fiber, 23 g protein, 73 mg calcium, 3 mg iron

PRONTO APRICOT CHUTNEY

In a 1½- to 2-quart pan, combine apricots, vinegar, sugar, chiles, cherries, onion, cinnamon stick, mustard seeds, and salt. Bring to a boil over high heat; then reduce heat to low, cover, and simmer until apricots are very soft when pierced (15 to 20 minutes). Uncover and bring to a gentle boil; then cook, stirring occasionally, until almost all liquid has evaporated (about 5 more minutes). Remove from heat and let cool; remove and discard cinnamon stick. Makes about 1¼ cups.

PER TABLESPOON: 38 calories, 0 g total fat, 0 g saturated fat, 0 mg cholesterol, 40 mg sodium, 10 g carbohydrates, 0 g fiber, 0 g protein, 4 mg calcium, 0 mg iron

TURKEY-SAGE MEATBALL SANDWICHES

OVEN-FRIED TURKEY MEATBALLS ARE A QUICK START FOR HEARTY SANDWICHES MADE WITH CRUSTY FRENCH ROLLS. ALONGSIDE, OFFER YOUR FAVORITE DRY WHITE WINE OR SPARKLING CIDER AND A SELECTION OF RAW VEGETABLES SUCH AS BABY CARROTS, RADISHES, AND BROCCOLI FLOWERETS, ARRANGED ON A BED OF CRUSHED ICE TO KEEP THEM COLD AND CRISP.

25 MINUTES

1 large egg white

1 tablespoon fat-free reduced-sodium chicken broth or dry white wine

2 tablespoons fine dry bread crumbs

½ teaspoon dried sage

¼ teaspoon salt

8 ounces lean ground turkey

2 tablespoons chopped dried cranberries

1 green onion, thinly sliced

Vegetable oil cooking spray

2 sesame-seed French rolls (*each about 6 inches long*), split

1 cup lightly packed arugula, rinsed and crisped

About 2 ounces thinly sliced Gouda cheese

Dijon mustard

1. In a medium-size bowl, combine egg white, broth, bread crumbs, sage, and salt; mix until well combined. Add turkey, cranberries, and onion; mix lightly. Shape turkey mixture into 1½-inch balls.

2. Spray a shallow baking pan with cooking spray; arrange meatballs, slightly apart, in pan. Bake in a 450° oven until meatballs are no longer pink in center; cut to test (12 to 15 minutes). Wrap rolls in foil and place in oven to warm 6 to 8 minutes before meatballs are done.

3. Place half the arugula on bottom half of each warm roll. Set half the hot meatballs on arugula on each roll, then top with half the cheese. Add top halves of rolls; offer mustard to add to taste.

PER SERVING: 490 calories, 20 g total fat, 8 g saturated fat, 115 mg cholesterol, 1,079 mg sodium, 41 g carbohydrates, 3 g fiber, 35 g protein, 313 mg calcium, 4 mg iron

Turkey-Sage Meatball Sandwiches

GREEN PAPAYA–TURKEY TUMBLE
STIR-FRIED GROUND TURKEY IN A FRUITED CURRY SAUCE FILLS CRISP LETTUCE LEAVES FOR A REFRESHING WARM-WEATHER SUPPER. GREEN (IMMATURE) PAPAYAS ARE FIRM, WITH A WHITE INTERIOR; SOUTHEAST ASIANS USE THEM AS A VEGETABLE, RAW OR COOKED, FOR THEIR CRUNCHY, CUCUMBER-LIKE TEXTURE. LOOK FOR THEM IN ASIAN MARKETS.

20 TO 25 MINUTES

2 teaspoons vegetable oil

12 ounces lean ground turkey

⅓ cup finely chopped onion

2 teaspoons curry powder

1 cup peeled, seeded, diced green papaya

1 clove garlic, minced or pressed

½ cup fat-free reduced-sodium chicken broth

2 tablespoons Major Grey's chutney, chopped

¾ teaspoon cornstarch blended with 1 tablespoon water

Salt

8 to 10 butter or iceberg lettuce leaves, rinsed and crisped

1. Heat oil in a wide nonstick frying pan over medium-high heat. Crumble in turkey, then add onion; cook, stirring often, until turkey is lightly browned (about 7 minutes).

2. Mix in curry powder and stir until fragrant (about 30 seconds). Then stir in papaya, garlic, broth, and chutney. Reduce heat to medium. Cover and cook, stirring occasionally, until papaya is tender when pierced (5 to 7 minutes).

3. Stir cornstarch mixture into turkey mixture; stir until sauce boils and thickens (about 1 minute). Season to taste with salt. Spoon turkey mixture into a warm serving bowl.

4. To eat, spoon turkey mixture into lettuce leaves and roll to enclose; eat out of hand.

PER SERVING: 402 calories, 18 g total fat, 4 g saturated fat, 124 mg cholesterol, 492 mg sodium, 27 g carbohydrates, 2 g fiber, 32 g protein, 81 mg calcium, 3 mg iron

WHITE TURKEY CHILI
WARM CORNMEAL MUFFINS AND COLD BEER OR ICED TEA ARE GOOD WITH THIS OUT-OF-THE-ORDINARY CHILI, MADE WITH LEAN TURKEY AND SEASONED WITH CUMIN AND FRESH GREEN CHILE.

15 MINUTES

2 teaspoons vegetable oil

8 ounces lean ground turkey

About 1 tablespoon minced fresh serrano or jalapeño chile

¾ teaspoon ground cumin

½ cup chopped onion

1 can (about 15 oz.) small white beans, rinsed and drained

½ cup low-fat (1%) or fat-free milk

1 small can (about 8 oz.) cream-style corn

Ground dried California or New Mexico chiles

Salt

1 small tomato (3 to 4 oz.), seeded and chopped (optional)

Lime wedges

1. Heat oil in a 2-quart pan over medium-high heat. Crumble in turkey; then add serrano chile, cumin, and onion. Cook, stirring often, until turkey begins to brown and onion is soft (about 5 minutes).

2. Stir in beans, milk, and corn; cook, stirring, just until steaming (2 to 3 minutes). Season to taste with ground chiles and salt.

3. Ladle chili into 2 warm wide bowls. Sprinkle with tomato, if desired. Offer lime wedges to squeeze into chili to taste.

PER SERVING: 446 calories, 15 g total fat, 3 g saturated fat, 85 mg cholesterol, 806 mg sodium, 47 g carbohydrates, 8 g fiber, 32 g protein, 151 mg calcium, 5 mg iron

TURKEY JOE'S SPECIAL

GROUND TURKEY OR CHICKEN MAKES A LIGHTER VERSION OF THAT TRADITIONAL SAN FRANCISCO DISH, JOE'S SPECIAL. LONG A FAVORITE OF TIME-PRESSED COOKS, IT'S EASIER THAN EVER NOW THAT PREWASHED FRESH SPINACH IS READILY AVAILABLE. FOR A SATISFYING SUPPER, ADD THE SIMPLEST OF ACCOMPANIMENTS—A SOURDOUGH BAGUETTE AND A LIGHT RED WINE SUCH AS BEAUJOLAIS.

20 MINUTES

1 teaspoon olive oil

8 ounces lean ground turkey or chicken

1 medium-size onion (about 6 oz.), thinly sliced

1 clove garlic, minced or pressed

4 medium-size mushrooms (about 3 oz. *total*), sliced

3 ounces packaged triple-washed baby spinach

2 large eggs, lightly beaten
Salt and freshly ground pepper

2 tablespoons freshly shredded Parmesan cheese

1. Heat oil in a wide nonstick frying pan over medium-high heat. Crumble in turkey; then add onion, garlic, and mushrooms. Cook, stirring often, until mushrooms and onion are lightly browned (8 to 10 minutes).

2. Add spinach and cook, stirring often, just until wilted (1 to 2 minutes).

3. Reduce heat to low and pour in eggs; cook, stirring, until eggs are almost set (about 1 minute). Season to taste with salt and pepper; sprinkle with cheese.

PER SERVING: 347 calories, 18 g total fat, 5 g saturated fat, 299 mg cholesterol, 348 mg sodium, 16 g carbohydrates, 5 g fiber, 31 g protein, 161 mg calcium, 5 mg iron

BROILED MAPLE-GLAZED GAME HEN

ACCOMPANY THIS RICHLY BROWNED BIRD WITH THIN GREEN BEANS AND HOT BISCUITS. YOU'LL FIND CREAMY-TEXTURED MAPLE BUTTER IN THE HONEY AND SYRUP SECTION OF SPECIALTY GROCERY STORES; DESPITE THE NAME, IT'S PURE MAPLE SYRUP, CONTAINING NO BUTTER.

30 MINUTES

1 Rock Cornish game hen (1 to 1¼ lbs.)

1½ tablespoons maple butter

1 teaspoon Dijon mustard

1 teaspoon grated fresh ginger
Orange wedges

1. Reserve game hen neck and giblets for other uses. With poultry shears or a sharp knife, split hen in half, cutting along backbone and breastbone. Rinse hen halves and pat dry.

2. Place hen halves, skin side down, on a lightly oiled rack in a foil-lined broiler pan. Broil about 6 inches below heat until well browned (about 15 minutes). Meanwhile, in a small bowl, stir together maple butter, mustard, and ginger.

3. Brush browned sides of hen halves with some of the maple glaze. Then turn skin side up and brush lightly with maple glaze. Continue to broil until meat near thighbone is no longer pink; cut to test (about 10 more minutes). Brush with remaining glaze; broil until glaze is well browned (about 2 minutes).

4. Transfer each hen half to a warm dinner plate and garnish with orange wedges.

PER SERVING: 331 calories, 20 g total fat, 6 g saturated fat, 143 mg cholesterol, 130 mg sodium, 13 g carbohydrates, 0 g fiber, 24 g protein, 14 mg calcium, 1 mg iron

GRATIN OF TURKEY SAUSAGE & WHITE BEANS

JUICY SAUSAGES AND PLUMP WHITE BEANS COOKED IN OLIVE OIL WITH GARLIC AND A LITTLE FRESH TOMATO ARE A TIME-HONORED TUSCAN COMBINATION. IN THIS VERSION, THEY BAKE BRIEFLY BENEATH A CRISP CRUMB-AND-CHEESE TOPPING.

30 MINUTES

2 raw mild turkey Italian sausages (5 to 6 oz. *each*)

1 tablespoon olive oil

1 small onion (about 4 oz.), slivered

1 clove garlic, minced or pressed

½ teaspoon dried sage

1 can (about 15 oz.) cannellini (white kidney beans)

1 small pear-shaped (Roma-type) tomato (3 to 4 oz.), seeded and chopped

⅓ cup soft bread crumbs

2 tablespoons grated Parmesan cheese

Chopped parsley (optional)

1. Pierce sausages with a fork and place in a wide nonstick frying pan. Add ½ cup water. Bring to a boil over high heat; then reduce heat, cover, and simmer for 10 minutes.

2. Meanwhile, in another wide frying pan with an ovenproof handle, heat 2 teaspoons of the oil over medium-high heat. Add onion, garlic, and sage; cook, stirring often, until onion is soft and beginning to brown (3 to 5 minutes). Stir in beans and their liquid, then tomato; cook, stirring often, until liquid is reduced by about half (about 3 minutes). Remove pan from heat.

3. Drain and discard liquid from sausages. Increase heat to medium and cook, turning as needed, until sausages are lightly browned (4 to 5 minutes). Meanwhile, in a small bowl, mix bread crumbs, cheese, and remaining 1 teaspoon oil.

4. Arrange sausages atop bean mixture, pressing them down slightly into beans. Sprinkle with crumb mixture. Bake in a 450° oven until beans are bubbly and crumbs are golden brown (8 to 10 minutes). Sprinkle with parsley, if desired.

PER SERVING: 544 calories, 26 g total fat, 7 g saturated fat, 88 mg cholesterol, 1,567 mg sodium, 42 g carbohydrates, 9 g fiber, 37 g protein, 192 mg calcium, 7 mg iron

SEARED DUCK BREASTS WITH COUSCOUS & BLACK CHERRY SAUCE

START THE DUCK BREASTS IN A FRYING PAN ON THE RANGE TOP, THEN FINISH THEM IN A HOT OVEN WHILE YOU ASSEMBLE THE INGREDIENTS FOR THE STYLISH CHERRY SAUCE AND STEAM COUSCOUS TO SERVE ALONGSIDE. A GREEN VEGETABLE SUCH AS STIR-FRIED SWISS CHARD NICELY ROUNDS OUT THE PLATE. COMPLEMENT THE DUCK WITH A MERLOT OR BEAUJOLAIS.

20 TO 25 MINUTES

2 boneless Muscovy duck breast halves (10 to 12 oz. *each*)

Salt and freshly ground pepper

1 teaspoon butter or margarine

1 clove garlic, minced or pressed

¾ cup fat-free reduced-sodium chicken broth

½ cup couscous

½ cup dry red wine

¼ teaspoon ground coriander

1½ cups frozen pitted dark sweet cherries

Chopped parsley

1. Using a small knife, cut 3 or 4 diagonal slashes through skin and fat on each duck breast half; take care not to cut into meat. Sprinkle with salt and pepper. Heat a wide frying pan with an ovenproof handle over medium-high heat for about 30 seconds. Add duck, skin side down; cook, turning once, until well browned on both sides (4 to 5 minutes).

2. Carefully spoon or pour off fat, then transfer pan with duck to a 425° oven. Bake until meat in thickest part is just pink; cut to test (4 to 5 minutes).

3. Meanwhile, melt butter in a 1- to 1½-quart pan over medium heat. Add garlic and cook, stirring, until soft but not brown (about 1 minute). Add broth, increase heat to high, and bring mixture to a boil. Stir in couscous; then cover, remove from heat, and let stand for 5 minutes.

4. Remove pan with duck from oven. Lift duck to a warm platter and keep warm. Pour off and discard fat in pan. Place pan over high heat; add wine, stirring to loosen pan drippings. Stir in coriander and cherries; cook, stirring, until sauce is syrupy and slightly reduced (3 to 4 minutes).

5. Slice duck across the grain about ½ inch thick; fan out slices on warm plates. Fluff couscous with a fork, then mound alongside duck; spoon sauce over duck. Garnish with parsley.

PER SERVING: 917 calories, 44 g total fat, 17 g saturated fat, 392 mg cholesterol, 622 mg sodium, 58 g carbohydrates, 3 g fiber, 65 g protein, 36 mg calcium, 6 mg iron

TUSCAN-STYLE ROAST GAME HEN WITH BREAD DRESSING

A SPLIT ROCK CORNISH GAME HEN MAKES A FESTIVE DINNER FOR TWO. THE HEN HALVES ARE BRUSHED WITH HERB-SEASONED OIL AND ROASTED IN A HOT OVEN; A COLORFUL BREAD DRESSING, TOASTED IN THE SAME OVEN, IS AN IRRESISTIBLE ACCOMPANIMENT. SERVE A ROBUST CHIANTI TO MAKE IT AN OCCASION!

30 MINUTES

Tuscan-style Roast Game Hen with Bread Dressing

1 **Rock Cornish game hen (1 to 1¼ lbs.)**

1 **clove garlic, minced or pressed**

¼ **teaspoon dried marjoram**

2 **tablespoons olive oil**

3 **cups 1-inch chunks (about 6 oz.) sourdough bread**

½ **cup canned chopped Italian-style tomatoes in juice**

2 **teaspoons red wine vinegar**

1 **small shallot, slivered**

⅓ **cup coarsely chopped fresh basil or 1 tablespoon dried basil**

Salt and freshly ground pepper

Basil sprigs (optional)

1. Reserve game hen neck and giblets for other uses. With poultry shears or a sharp knife, split hen in half, cutting along backbone and breastbone. Rinse hen halves and pat dry.

2. Place hen halves, skin side up, in a shallow 7- by 11-inch baking pan. In a small bowl, mix garlic, marjoram, and 1 tablespoon of the oil. Brush mixture over all surfaces of hen halves. Bake in lower third of a 500° oven until meat near thighbone is no longer pink; cut to test (about 25 minutes).

3. Meanwhile, in a 9-inch-square baking pan, mix bread and remaining 1 tablespoon oil. Add to oven and bake, stirring once, until bread is golden and slightly crisp to the touch (about 8 minutes). Meanwhile, in a medium-size bowl, mix tomatoes, vinegar, shallot, and dried basil, if used (if using fresh basil, add later, as directed below).

4. To tomato mixture, add toasted bread and stir gently to coat evenly. Return mixture to pan, then return to oven. Continue to bake until dressing is deep golden brown (about 10 more minutes). Keep warm until hen is done.

5. To serve, place each hen half on a warm dinner plate. Pour pan juices into hot bread dressing, then add chopped fresh basil and mix lightly; season to taste with salt and pepper. Spoon dressing alongside hen halves. Garnish with basil sprigs, if desired.

PER SERVING: 657 calories, 36 g total fat, 8 g saturated fat, 143 mg cholesterol, 684 mg sodium, 48 g carbohydrates, 3 g fiber, 33 g protein, 125 mg calcium, 5 mg iron

SEAFOOD

Oven-roasted Chilean Sea Bass (page 137)

ASSYRIAN BARBECUED SALMON

SEASONINGS CHARACTERISTIC OF LEBANESE CUISINE FLAVOR THESE GRILLED SALMON STEAKS. YOU MIGHT SERVE THEM WITH NEW POTATOES AND A SALAD OF SLICED CUCUMBERS AND HALVED CHERRY TOMATOES.

15 TO 20 MINUTES

1 clove garlic, minced or pressed

1 tablespoon lemon juice

2 teaspoons olive oil

½ teaspoon ground cardamom

¼ teaspoon ground cloves

¼ teaspoon salt

2 tablespoons sesame seeds

1 tablespoon minced fresh dill

2 salmon steaks (about 8 oz. *each*), each ¾ to 1 inch thick

Dill sprigs and lemon wedges

1. In a shallow bowl, combine garlic, lemon juice, oil, cardamom, cloves, and salt. On a plate, mix sesame seeds and minced dill.

2. Rinse salmon steaks and pat dry. Place in lemon juice mixture, one at a time, and turn to coat. Then coat each steak on both sides with sesame seed mixture.

3. Place fish on a lightly greased grill 4 to 6 inches above a solid bed of medium coals (you can hold your hand at grill level for 4 to 5 seconds) or over medium heat on a gas grill. Close lid on gas grill. Cook, turning once with a wide spatula, until sesame seeds are browned and fish is just opaque but still moist in thickest part; cut to test (8 to 10 minutes).

4. Using spatula, lift fish to 2 warm dinner plates. Garnish with dill sprigs and lemon wedges.

PER SERVING: 463 calories, 31 g total fat, 6 g saturated fat, 118 mg cholesterol, 408 mg sodium, 4 g carbohydrates, 1 g fiber, 41 g protein, 120 mg calcium, 2 mg iron

Assyrian Barbecued Salmon

Oven-roasted Salmon & New Potatoes

Dried tarragon gives these roasted salmon steaks an intriguing flavor. Serve them with golden brown sliced potatoes (start the potatoes cooking while you get the fish ready for the oven). Steamed asparagus spears nicely round out the menu.

30 MINUTES

8 ounces small red thin-skinned potatoes, scrubbed and cut into about ½-inch-thick slices

2 teaspoons olive oil

1 clove garlic, minced or pressed

2 salmon steaks (about 8 oz. *each*), *each* about 1 inch thick

½ teaspoon dried tarragon

¼ teaspoon freshly ground pepper

Lemon wedges

1. In a 9-inch-square or larger baking pan, combine potatoes, 1 teaspoon of the oil, and garlic. Mix lightly to coat potatoes with oil; then spread potatoes out in a single layer. Bake in a 425° oven for 15 minutes.

2. Meanwhile, rinse fish and pat dry. In a small bowl, mix remaining 1 teaspoon oil, tarragon, and pepper. Spoon mixture evenly over fish, dividing it equally.

3. After potatoes have baked for 15 minutes, turn them browned side up and push to edges of pan. Place fish, seasoned side up, in center of pan. Return pan to oven and continue to bake until potatoes are tender when pierced and fish is just opaque but still moist in thickest part; cut to test (about 10 more minutes).

4. Using a wide spatula, lift fish and potatoes to 2 warm dinner plates. Garnish with lemon wedges.

PER SERVING: 501 calories, 26 g total fat, 5 g saturated fat, 118 mg cholesterol, 127 mg sodium, 21 g carbohydrates, 2 g fiber, 42 g protein, 32 mg calcium, 2 mg iron

Anise-broiled Salmon
& Creamed Spinach

THE SWEET, LICORICE-LIKE FLAVOR OF ANISE SUBTLY HIGHLIGHTS BOTH SUCCULENT BROILED SALMON AND THE IRRESISTIBLY RICH CREAMED SPINACH SERVED WITH IT. COMPLETE A SIMPLE, ELEGANT DINNER MENU WITH BABY YUKON GOLD POTATOES STEAMED IN THEIR JACKETS.

15 TO 20 MINUTES

Vegetable oil cooking spray

2 salmon fillets with skin (6 to 7 oz. each), *each* 1 to 1¼ inches thick

1 tablespoon butter or margarine

¼ teaspoon anise or fennel seeds, coarsely crushed

⅛ teaspoon white pepper

Creamed Spinach with Pernod (below)

Lemon wedges

CREAMED SPINACH WITH PERNOD

4 ounces packaged triple-washed baby spinach

½ cup whipping cream

¼ teaspoon freshly grated or ground nutmeg

1 tablespoon Pernod, Sambuca, or other anise-flavored liqueur (not sweet)

Salt and freshly ground pepper

1. Coat a shallow baking pan with cooking spray. Rinse fish and pat dry; then place in pan, skin side down. In a small bowl, combine butter, anise seeds, and white pepper; microwave on high (100%) for 30 seconds or until butter is melted. Brush butter mixture over fish.

2. Broil about 4 inches below heat until fish is well browned on outside and just opaque but still moist in thickest part; cut to test (10 to 12 minutes). Meanwhile, prepare Creamed Spinach with Pernod.

3. Spoon spinach onto 2 warm dinner plates; arrange fish alongside. Garnish with lemon wedges.

CREAMED SPINACH WITH PERNOD

Place spinach in a 2½- to 3-quart pan and stir over high heat until wilted (2½ to 3 minutes). Transfer about half the spinach to a food processor and whirl until puréed. To spinach remaining in pan, add cream, nutmeg, and half the Pernod. Bring to a boil over high heat; then boil, stirring often, until almost all liquid has evaporated (about 2 minutes). Add spinach purée and continue to cook, stirring, until mixture is hot and bubbly (about 1 minute). Stir in remaining Pernod; then season to taste with salt and pepper.

PER SERVING: 616 calories, 45 g total fat, 19 g saturated fat, 191 mg cholesterol, 294 mg sodium, 11 g carbohydrates, 3 g fiber, 39 g protein, 108 mg calcium, 3 mg iron

Salmon with Balsamic Onions

SALMON WITH BALSAMIC ONIONS
SAUTÉED RED ONION SIMMERED IN BALSAMIC VINEGAR AND FRESH ORANGE JUICE MAKES A SOPHISTICATED, TART-SWEET COUNTERPOINT TO PAN-BROWNED SALMON FILLETS. ENJOY A CREAMY RISOTTO DOTTED WITH FRESH GREEN PEAS OR SLICED ASPARAGUS ALONGSIDE.

20 MINUTES

2 teaspoons olive oil

1 medium-size red onion (about 6 oz.), thinly sliced

½ cup orange juice

¼ cup balsamic vinegar

2 skinless salmon fillets (about 6 oz. each), *each* 1¼ to 1½ inches thick

Salt and freshly ground pepper

Orange slices (optional)

1. Heat 1 teaspoon of the oil in a 1½- to 2-quart pan over medium-high heat. Add onion and cook, stirring often, until soft and lightly browned (about 4 minutes). Add orange juice and vinegar. Bring to a boil; then reduce heat to medium and boil gently, stirring occasionally, until onion is very tender and almost all liquid has evaporated (about 10 minutes).

2. Meanwhile, rinse fish and pat dry. Heat remaining 1 teaspoon oil in a wide nonstick frying pan over medium-high heat. Add fish and cook, turning once, until nicely browned on both sides and just opaque but still moist in thickest part; cut to test (8 to 10 minutes).

3. Using a wide spatula, lift fish to 2 warm dinner plates; season to taste with salt and pepper, then top evenly with onion mixture. Garnish with orange slices, if desired.

PER SERVING: 415 calories, 23 g total fat, 4 g saturated fat, 100 mg cholesterol, 105 mg sodium, 15 g carbohydrates, 1 g fiber, 35 g protein, 43 mg calcium, 1 mg iron

Fresh Fish Tacos—Fast Food for Fun

Though many Americans are only now learning to appreciate the simple pleasures of fish tacos, surfers and frequent travelers to Mexico have long considered them an integral part of the Baja California experience. In its most familiar form, the fish taco consists of lightly battered, deep-fried mild white fish wrapped in a corn tortilla (or often two) with shredded cabbage, a thin, creamy dressing, a bit of salsa, and an all-important squeeze of fresh lime juice.

If you don't want to fry the fish, you can grill it on the barbecue—either way, you'll have a fast and savory supper. Serve the tacos with your favorite purchased salsa; or, for variety (and if time allows), try one of the fresh salsas on the facing page.

CLASSIC BAJA FRIED-FISH TACOS
25 MINUTES

⅓ cup dark beer

⅓ cup all-purpose flour

⅛ teaspoon salt

10 to 12 ounces lingcod fillets (*each about ½ inch thick*)

Vegetable oil

8 warm corn tortillas (*each about 6 inches in diameter*)

About 1½ cups shredded cabbage

Mayonnaise thinned with a little water

Prepared salsa

Lime wedges

1. In a shallow bowl, combine beer, flour, and salt. Whisk to blend well.

2. Rinse fish, pat dry, and cut into 4 equal pieces.

3. In a deep, heavy pan, heat 1 inch of oil over medium-high heat to 360°F on a deep-frying thermometer. Using a fork to turn fish, coat 2 pieces of fish with beer batter; lift out and drain briefly. Slide batter-coated fish into oil; adjust heat to maintain oil temperature. Cook, turning once, until fish is golden (about 2 minutes). Lift from oil with a slotted spoon and drain briefly on paper towels. Keep warm while you batter and fry remaining 2 pieces of fish.

4. To assemble each taco, stack 2 tortillas; top with a piece of fish and a fourth of the cabbage. Spoon on mayonnaise and salsa to taste. Squeeze lime over filling; then fold tortillas to enclose filling and eat out of hand.

PER SERVING: 509 calories, 11 g total fat, 2 g saturated fat, 81 mg cholesterol, 411 mg sodium, 67 g carbohydrates, 7 g fiber, 36 g protein, 227 mg calcium, 3 mg iron

GRILLED SEA BASS TACOS
30 MINUTES

Pickled Cabbage Relish or Papaya-Mango Salsa (facing page)

10 to 12 ounces Chilean sea bass fillet (½ to ¾ inch thick)

Salt and freshly ground pepper

8 warm corn tortillas (*each about 6 inches in diameter*)

About ¼ cup sour cream

Lime wedges

1. Prepare relish and let stand as directed.

2. Rinse fish, pat dry, and place on a lightly greased grill 4 to 6 inches above a solid bed of hot coals (you can hold your hand at grill level for only 2 to 3 seconds) or over high heat on a gas grill. Close lid on gas grill. Cook, turning once with a wide spatula, until fish is lightly browned on both sides and just opaque but still moist in thickest part; cut to test (6 to 8 minutes). Transfer fish to a warm platter and cut into large chunks. Season to taste with salt and pepper.

3. To assemble each taco, stack 2 tortillas; top with chunks of fish, Pickled Cabbage Relish, and sour cream. Squeeze lime over filling; then fold tortillas to enclose filling and eat out of hand.

PER SERVING WITHOUT RELISH: 435 calories, 12 g total fat, 5 g saturated fat, 77 mg cholesterol, 282 mg sodium, 48 g carbohydrates, 5 g fiber, 35 g protein, 224 mg calcium, 2 mg iron

SALMON AVOCADO TACOS
25 MINUTES

Avocado Salsa (at right)

1 tablespoon lime juice

1 clove garlic, minced or pressed

⅛ teaspoon freshly ground pepper

1½ teaspoons olive oil

4 flour tortillas (*each* 7 to 9 inches in diameter)

10 to 12 ounces salmon fillet with skin (¾ to 1 inch thick)

Salt

About 1 cup finely shredded cabbage

¼ cup crumbled feta cheese

1. Prepare Avocado Salsa and set aside. In a shallow bowl, stir together lime juice, garlic, pepper, and oil.

2. Stack tortillas, wrap in foil, and set aside. Rinse fish and pat dry, then turn in lime juice mixture to coat well. Cut a piece of heavy-duty foil the same size as fish. Place fish skin side down on foil.

3. Place foil with fish on a grill 4 to 6 inches above a solid bed of medium coals (you can hold your hand at grill level for 4 to 5 seconds) or over medium heat on a gas grill. Set foil-wrapped tortillas at edge of grill. Close lid on gas grill; cover charcoal grill and open vents. Cook until fish is just opaque but still moist in thickest part; cut to test (10 to 12 minutes).

4. Pull off and discard skin from fish, then cut fish into 1-inch chunks and transfer to a warm serving bowl. Season to taste with salt.

5. To assemble each taco, place a warm tortilla on a plate; top with chunks of fish, salsa, cabbage, and cheese. Fold tortillas to enclose filling and eat out of hand.

PER SERVING WITHOUT SALSA: 600 calories, 26 g total fat, 7 g saturated fat, 107 mg cholesterol, 623 mg sodium, 43 g carbohydrates, 3 g fiber, 40 g protein, 210 mg calcium, 3 mg iron

PICKLED CABBAGE RELISH
30 MINUTES

½ cup thinly sliced red cabbage

¼ cup thinly sliced green cabbage

¼ cup thinly sliced onion

1 tablespoon minced fresh jalapeño chile

¼ cup distilled white vinegar

¼ teaspoon salt

¾ cup water

1. In a medium-size bowl, mix red cabbage, green cabbage, onion, chile, vinegar, salt, and water. Let stand for about 20 minutes.

2. To serve, lift cabbage mixture from bowl with a slotted spoon. Makes about 1 cup (drained).

PER TABLESPOON: 2 calories, 0 g total fat, 0 g saturated fat, 0 mg cholesterol, 36 mg sodium, 1 g carbohydrates, 0 g fiber, 0 g protein, 2 mg calcium, 0 mg iron

PAPAYA-MANGO SALSA
12 TO 15 MINUTES

½ cup diced papaya

¼ cup diced mango

¼ cup finely diced red bell pepper

2 teaspoons minced fresh jalapeño chile

1 tablespoon chopped cilantro

1 tablespoon lime juice

Salt

In a small bowl, combine papaya, mango, bell pepper, chile, cilantro, and lime juice. Mix lightly; season to taste with salt. Makes about 1 cup.

PER TABLESPOON: 4 calories, 0 g total fat, 0 g saturated fat, 0 mg cholesterol, 0 mg sodium, 1 g carbohydrates, 0 g fiber, 0 g protein, 2 mg calcium, 0 mg iron

AVOCADO SALSA
15 MINUTES

⅔ cup diced firm-ripe avocado

¼ cup chopped pear-shaped (Roma-type) tomato

¼ cup thinly sliced green onions

2 tablespoons chopped cilantro

1 tablespoon olive oil

2 teaspoons lemon juice

1 teaspoon minced fresh jalapeño chile

1 clove garlic, minced or pressed

Salt

In a small bowl, combine avocado, tomato, onions, cilantro, oil, lemon juice, chile, and garlic. Mix lightly; season to taste with salt. Makes about ¾ cup.

PER TABLESPOON: 26 calories, 2 g total fat, 0 g saturated fat, 0 mg cholesterol, 2 mg sodium, 1 g carbohydrates, 0 g fiber, 0 g protein, 3 mg calcium, 0 mg iron

RED PEPPER–SALMON PASTA

COOKING JUICES FROM LEMON-DRIZZLED BAKED SALMON FLAVOR A ROBUST SAUCE TO MIX WITH DELICATE ANGEL HAIR PASTA. SET OFF THE ENTRÉE WITH A GREEN VEGETABLE; SLENDER, TENDER-CRISP GREEN BEANS AND STIR-FRIED SLICED ZUCCHINI ARE BOTH GOOD CHOICES.

25 MINUTES

Vegetable oil cooking spray

2 skinless salmon fillets (about 6 oz. each), *each* 1¼ to 1½ inches thick

1 tablespoon lemon juice

¼ cup canned or bottled roasted red peppers, drained and patted dry

3 tablespoons grated Parmesan cheese

1½ teaspoons cornstarch

⅛ teaspoon crushed red pepper flakes

1 clove garlic, thinly sliced

2 tablespoons chopped cilantro

½ cup fat-free reduced-sodium chicken broth

4 ounces dried angel hair pasta (capellini)

Cilantro sprigs (optional)

1. Coat an 8- or 9-inch-square baking pan with cooking spray. Rinse fish, pat dry, and place in pan; drizzle with lemon juice. Cover pan tightly with foil and bake in a 450° oven until fish is just opaque but still moist in thickest part; cut to test (12 to 14 minutes).

2. Meanwhile, in a food processor or blender, combine roasted red peppers, cheese, cornstarch, red pepper flakes, garlic, chopped cilantro, and broth. Whirl until smoothly puréed. Pour purée into a 1- to 1½-quart pan and set aside.

3. Also while fish is baking, bring about 2 quarts water to a boil in a covered 3- to 4-quart pan over high heat. Stir in pasta and cook, uncovered, until just tender to bite (about 3 minutes). Or cook pasta according to package directions.

4. While pasta is cooking, bring red pepper purée to a boil over medium-high heat, stirring occasionally (2 to 3 minutes); reduce heat to very low and keep warm. When fish is done, stir juices from baking pan into purée; keep fish warm.

5. Drain pasta well, return to cooking pan, and lightly mix in about ⅔ cup of the red pepper sauce. Spoon pasta mixture onto 2 warm dinner plates or into 2 warm wide, shallow bowls. Top each serving with a piece of fish, then drizzle with remaining sauce. Garnish with cilantro sprigs, if desired.

PER SERVING: 581 calories, 22 g total fat, 5 g saturated fat, 106 mg cholesterol, 434 mg sodium, 48 g carbohydrates, 2 g fiber, 45 g protein, 139 mg calcium, 3 mg iron

BILL'S TROUT WITH STIR-FRIED PEPPERS

BASED ON A TRIED-AND-TRUE METHOD FOR PAN-FRYING FRESH-CAUGHT TROUT OVER THE CAMPFIRE, THIS RECIPE IS JUST AS GOOD COOKED ON THE RANGE AT HOME. TRY IT WITH A PLUMP LOAF OF SOURDOUGH BREAD AND A GLASS OF CHILLED CHARDONNAY.

20 TO 25 MINUTES

Bill's Trout with Stir-fried Peppers

2 slices bacon, cut crosswise into ½-inch-wide strips

2 tablespoons yellow cornmeal

2 tablespoons all-purpose flour
Salt and freshly ground pepper

2 cleaned whole trout (10 to 12 oz. *each*), heads removed, if desired

2 tablespoons vegetable oil

1 large red or yellow bell pepper (about 8 oz.), seeded and thinly sliced (or use ½ *each* red and yellow bell pepper)

1 clove garlic, minced or pressed

1 teaspoon grated lemon peel

1 teaspoon lemon juice

3 green onions, thinly sliced
Lemon wedges

1. Cook bacon in a wide nonstick frying pan over medium heat, stirring occasionally, until brown and crisp (5 to 6 minutes). Remove from pan with a slotted spoon and drain on paper towels; set aside. Spoon off and discard all but about 1 tablespoon of the drippings from pan.

2. While bacon is cooking, mix cornmeal and flour in a wide, shallow bowl; season to taste with salt and pepper. Rinse and drain fish, then turn each one in cornmeal mixture to coat well on all sides.

3. Add 1 tablespoon of the oil to bacon drippings in frying pan; heat over medium heat. Add fish and cook, carefully turning once with a wide spatula, until well browned on both sides and just opaque but still moist in thickest part; cut to test (12 to 15 minutes).

4. Meanwhile, heat remaining 1 tablespoon oil in a small frying pan over medium heat. Add bell pepper and garlic; cook, stirring often, until pepper is tender-crisp to bite (5 to 7 minutes). Stir in lemon peel, lemon juice, onions, and bacon; stir until bacon is hot (about 30 seconds).

5. Using spatula, lift fish to a platter or 2 warm dinner plates; spoon pepper mixture alongside. Garnish with lemon wedges.

PER SERVING: 613 calories, 36 g total fat, 7 g saturated fat, 133 mg cholesterol, 250 mg sodium, 21 g carbohydrates, 3 g fiber, 49 g protein, 122 mg calcium, 5 mg iron

TUNA WITH COCONUT CURRY SAUCE

THE EXOTIC FLAVORS OF TAMARIND AND THAI RED CURRY PASTE ACCENT GRILLED THICK TUNA STEAKS. LOOK FOR TAMARIND CONCENTRATE IN LATINO, MIDEASTERN, OR SOUTHEAST ASIAN FOOD MARKETS; THE SPICY CURRY PASTE IS SOLD IN ASIAN MARKETS AND MANY WELL-STOCKED SUPERMARKETS. SERVE THE FISH ON HOT WHITE RICE, WITH A COOLING SIDE SALAD OF SLICED CUCUMBERS.

25 MINUTES

1 tablespoon chopped cilantro

½ cup canned coconut milk

2 teaspoons tamarind concentrate or lime juice

¾ teaspoon Thai red curry paste or curry powder

2 ahi tuna steaks (about 6 oz. *each*), *each* 1 to 1¼ inches thick

¼ cup chopped roasted salted cashews

1½ cups hot cooked rice

2 tablespoons slivered fresh basil
Salt

1. In a shallow bowl, mix cilantro, coconut milk, tamarind concentrate, and curry paste.

2. Rinse fish, pat dry, and turn in coconut milk mixture to coat; lift out and set aside. Pour coconut milk mixture into a small pan and bring to a boil over high heat, stirring. Remove from heat and keep warm.

3. Place fish on a lightly greased grill 4 to 6 inches above a solid bed of very hot coals (you can hold your hand at grill level for only 1 to 2 seconds) or over high heat on a gas grill. Close lid on gas grill. Cook until bottom of fish is paler in color to a depth of about ¼ inch into fish; cut to test (about 2 minutes; fish will be red in center). Then turn fish with a wide spatula and continue to cook until side of fish on grill is the same color as top of fish and center is still pink to red; cut to test (about 1 more minute).

4. Stir cashews into rice, then spoon onto 2 warm dinner plates. Top each portion of rice with a tuna steak. Sprinkle with basil. Serve with warm coconut-curry sauce and season to taste with salt.

PER SERVING: 533 calories, 22 g total fat, 13 g saturated fat, 68 mg cholesterol, 329 mg sodium, 41 g carbohydrates, 2 g fiber, 43 g protein, 62 mg calcium, 5 mg iron

Tuna with Coconut Curry Sauce

PAN-GRILLED TUNA STEAKS WITH
SPINACH NOODLES PROVENÇAL

SAUTÉED FRESH TUNA WITH SPINACH PASTA IS AN UPSCALE TAKE ON THE FAMILIAR TUNA-NOODLE CASSEROLE—AND BETTER YET, IT'S FASTER TO PREPARE AND OFFERS MORE INTERESTING FLAVORS. START COOKING THE NOODLES FIRST; WHILE THEY BOIL, SAUTÉ THE TUNA AND WARM A BAGUETTE.

20 MINUTES

1½ tablespoons olive oil

3 canned anchovy fillets, drained and minced

2 cloves garlic, minced or pressed

1 medium-size onion (about 5 oz.), thinly sliced

1 can (about 14½ oz.) diced tomatoes

1 cup water

4 ounces dried spinach noodles

¼ cup sliced calamata olives

1½ teaspoons chopped fresh thyme or ½ teaspoon dried thyme

2 ahi tuna steaks (4 to 6 oz. *each*), *each* about 1 inch thick

Salt and freshly ground pepper

Chopped parsley (optional)

1. Heat half the oil in a wide nonstick frying pan over medium-high heat. Add anchovies, garlic, and onion; cook, stirring often, until onion is soft and lightly browned (3 to 4 minutes). Stir in tomatoes, water, noodles, olives, and thyme.

2. Bring to a boil; then reduce heat so mixture boils gently. Cook, stirring occasionally, until noodles are just tender to bite (about 10 minutes).

3. Meanwhile, rinse fish and pat dry. Heat remaining oil in another wide frying pan over medium-high heat. Add fish and cook, turning once, until browned on both sides but still red in thickest part; cut to test (5 to 8 minutes). Season to taste with salt and pepper.

4. Spoon noodles and sauce onto 2 warm dinner plates; top each serving with a tuna steak. Sprinkle with parsley, if desired.

PER SERVING: 618 calories, 23 g total fat, 4 g saturated fat, 51 mg cholesterol, 931 mg sodium, 61 g carbohydrates, 9 g fiber, 42 g protein, 122 mg calcium, 4 mg iron

GRILLED MAHIMAHI
WITH MACADAMIA PESTO

A POPULAR CHOICE FOR A QUICK DINNER FROM THE BARBECUE ON A WARM EVENING, MAHIMAHI IS A FIRM, DENSE FISH THAT CAN BE COOKED DIRECTLY ON THE GRILL. IT'S ALSO VERY LEAN, SO BE SURE TO OIL BOTH GRILL AND FISH BEFORE COOKING. FOR A MILDER FLAVOR, TRIM AWAY ANY DARK PORTIONS OF THE MAHIMAHI (OR HAVE YOUR FISHMONGER DO IT).

25 MINUTES

Macadamia Pesto (below)
1½ tablespoons olive oil
1 clove garlic, thinly sliced
⅛ teaspoon paprika
2 mahimahi fillets (5 to 6 oz. *each*), each ¾ to 1 inch thick
Lemon wedges (optional)

MACADAMIA PESTO

1½ cups lightly packed fresh basil leaves
1 tablespoon lemon juice
3 tablespoons olive oil
¼ cup roasted salted macadamia nuts
3 tablespoons grated Parmesan cheese
Salt

1. Prepare Macadamia Pesto; cover and set aside.

2. In a small pan, combine the 1½ tablespoons oil, garlic, and paprika. Heat over medium heat until oil is warm (about 1 minute). Remove from heat.

3. Rinse fish and pat dry; then brush both sides with garlic-seasoned oil. Place fish on a greased grill 4 to 6 inches above a solid bed of hot coals (you can hold your hand at grill level for only 2 to 3 seconds) or over high heat on a gas grill. Close lid on gas grill. Cook until lightly browned on bottom (4 to 5 minutes), then brush again with garlic-seasoned oil. Turn fish over with a wide spatula and continue to cook until lightly browned on other side and just opaque but still moist in thickest part; cut to test (4 to 5 more minutes).

4. Using spatula, lift fish to 2 warm dinner plates; spoon on pesto to taste. Garnish with lemon wedges, if desired.

PER SERVING WITH 1 TABLESPOON PESTO: 314 calories, 20 g total fat, 3 g saturated fat, 119 mg cholesterol, 192 mg sodium, 2 g carbohydrates, 1 g fiber, 31 g protein, 69 mg calcium, 3 mg iron

MACADAMIA PESTO

In a food processor or blender, combine basil, lemon juice, the 3 tablespoons oil, macadamias, and cheese; whirl until smooth. Season to taste with salt. Makes about ½ cup.

PER TABLESPOON: 90 calories, 9 g total fat, 1 g saturated fat, 6 mg cholesterol, 54 mg sodium, 2 g carbohydrates, 1 g fiber, 2 g protein, 66 mg calcium, 1 mg iron

OVEN-ROASTED CHILEAN SEA BASS

A HIT SINCE ITS INTRODUCTION TO THE WEST IN THE 1980S, CHILEAN SEA BASS IS NEARLY BONELESS, WITH A FAT CONTENT SIMILAR TO THAT OF KING SALMON—SO IT'S MOIST WHEN COOKED. FOR A HANDSOME DINNER DISH, BAKE THE SNOWY FILLETS WITH ASIAN SEASONINGS AND SERVE WITH WILTED GREENS AND JUICY GRAPEFRUIT SEGMENTS.

Pictured on page 125

25 MINUTES

1 teaspoon salted fermented black beans, rinsed and drained

1 teaspoon minced fresh ginger

1½ tablespoons unseasoned rice vinegar

1 medium-size ruby grapefruit (about 1 lb.)

2 tablespoons butter or margarine

10 to 12 ounces Chilean sea bass fillet (about 1 inch thick)

1 tablespoon slivered shallots

6 to 8 ounces mustard greens

1 tablespoon soy sauce

1. In a small bowl, mix beans, ginger, and vinegar with a fork, mashing slightly. Set aside. Cut peel and all white membrane from grapefruit. Then, holding fruit over a bowl to catch juice, cut between segments and inner membrane to release segments; set segments aside. Squeeze juice from membrane into bowl; discard membrane. Measure 2 tablespoons juice from bowl and set aside; reserve any remaining juice for other uses.

2. Place 1 tablespoon of the butter in an 8-inch-square baking pan; set pan in oven while it preheats to 500°. When butter is beginning to brown (about 2 minutes), remove pan from oven and tilt to coat with butter.

3. While butter is melting, rinse fish, pat dry, and cut into 2 equal pieces.

4. Turn fish in melted butter to coat both sides; sprinkle shallots around fish. Spoon black bean mixture and the 2 tablespoons grapefruit juice over fish. Return pan to oven and bake until fish is just opaque but still moist in thickest part; cut to test (8 to 10 minutes).

5. Meanwhile, rinse and drain mustard greens. Trim and discard coarse stems, then chop greens coarsely. Melt remaining 1 tablespoon butter in a wide nonstick frying pan over high heat. Add greens and soy sauce; cook, stirring often, until greens are wilted (1 to 2 minutes).

6. Using a wide spatula, lift fish to 2 warm dinner plates; pour pan juices over fish and spoon wilted greens alongside. Garnish with grapefruit segments.

PER SERVING: 325 calories, 15 g total fat, 8 g saturated fat, 95 mg cholesterol, 836 mg sodium, 16 g carbohydrates, 1 g fiber, 33 g protein, 140 mg calcium, 2 mg iron

GARLIC-LEMON RED SNAPPER
Crisp toasted almonds top fish fillets baked in a garlicky lemon butter. Serve with sliced fresh tomatoes or crumb-topped tomato halves that bake alongside the fish in their own shallow casserole. Complete a fresh, colorful menu with steamed broccoli spears and sliced ciabatta.

20 TO 25 MINUTES

2 tablespoons slivered almonds

12 to 14 ounces red snapper or ling-cod fillets (*each* about ½ inch thick)

2 tablespoons butter or margarine

3 cloves garlic, minced or pressed

2 tablespoons lemon juice

2 tablespoons chopped parsley

¼ teaspoon paprika

¼ teaspoon grated lemon peel

Lemon wedges

1. Spread almonds in an 8- or 9-inch-square baking pan. Bake in a 375° oven until golden (6 to 8 minutes), stirring once or twice. Meanwhile, rinse fish and pat dry.

2. Pour almonds out of pan and set aside. Add butter to same pan; return pan to oven until butter is melted (about 2 minutes). Remove pan from oven and add garlic, lemon juice, parsley, paprika, and lemon peel; stir to mix seasonings with melted butter. Add fish and turn in butter mixture to coat well.

3. Return pan to oven and bake until fish is just opaque but still moist in thickest part; cut to test (10 to 12 minutes).

4. Using a wide spatula, lift fish to 2 warm dinner plates. Spoon butter mixture from pan over fish to taste. Garnish with almonds and lemon wedges.

PER SERVING: 348 calories, 18 g total fat, 8 g saturated fat, 99 mg cholesterol, 241 mg sodium, 5 g carbohydrates, 1 g fiber, 40 g protein, 100 mg calcium, 1 mg iron

SEA BASS WITH GREEN LENTILS TARRAGON
Smaller and rounder than the familiar brown lentils, French green lentils make a savory accompaniment to rich-tasting Chilean sea bass when seasoned with sautéed shallot, chives, and a touch of tarragon vinegar. Serve with a butter lettuce salad, crunchy seeded rolls, and a dry white wine such as Sauvignon Blanc.

30 MINUTES

Sea Bass with Green Lentils Tarragon

½ cup French green lentils

10 to 12 ounces Chilean sea bass fillet (about 1 inch thick)

Salt and freshly ground pepper

Paprika

1 tablespoon olive oil

1 shallot, slivered

2 tablespoons tarragon vinegar

1 tablespoon whipping cream

1 small pear-shaped (Roma-type) tomato (about 3 oz.), seeded and chopped

2 tablespoons chopped chives

Whole chives

1. Rinse and sort lentils, discarding any debris. Then place lentils in a 1- to 1½-quart pan, add 1½ cups water, and bring to a boil over high heat. Reduce heat, cover, and simmer just until lentils are tender to bite (20 to 25 minutes).

2. Meanwhile, rinse fish, pat dry, and cut into 2 equal pieces. Season to taste with salt and pepper, then sprinkle lightly with paprika. Heat 2 teaspoons of the oil in a wide nonstick frying pan over medium-high heat. Add fish and cook, turning once, until browned on both sides and just opaque but still moist in thickest part; cut to test (about 10 minutes). Remove from heat and keep warm.

3. When lentils are almost done, heat remaining 1 teaspoon oil in a small nonstick frying pan over medium-high heat. Add shallot and cook, stirring, until lightly browned (about 2 minutes). Drain lentils and add to pan along with vinegar and cream. Bring to a boil, stirring; then boil until almost all liquid has evaporated (about 2 minutes). Stir in tomato and chopped chives; season to taste with salt and pepper.

4. Using a wide spatula, lift fish to 2 warm dinner plates. Spoon lentils around fish; garnish with whole chives.

PER SERVING: 405 calories, 13 g total fat, 3 g saturated fat, 72 mg cholesterol, 116 mg sodium, 30 g carbohydrates, 6 g fiber, 43 g protein, 54 mg calcium, 5 mg iron

HALIBUT WITH TOMATOES & CHILE

A VIVID SAUCE OF ROMA TOMATOES AND CILANTRO TOPS THESE EASY BAKED FISH FILLETS. IF HALIBUT ISN'T AVAILABLE, YOU CAN SUBSTITUTE CHILEAN SEA BASS OR A LEAN, WHITE-FLESHED FISH SUCH AS ROCKFISH OR SNAPPER.

25 MINUTES

Olive oil cooking spray

12 to 14 ounces halibut fillet (about ¾ inch thick)

About 1 tablespoon olive oil

1 small onion (about 4 oz.), slivered

1 clove garlic, minced or pressed

1½ to 2 tablespoons minced fresh jalapeño chile

8 ounces pear-shaped (Roma-type) tomatoes, diced

2 teaspoons lemon juice blended with ½ teaspoon cornstarch

Salt and freshly ground pepper

1 tablespoon chopped cilantro

1. Coat an 8- or 9-inch-square baking pan with cooking spray. Rinse fish, pat dry, and cut into 2 equal pieces; then brush lightly with a little of the oil and arrange in pan. Bake in a 425° oven until fish is just opaque but still moist in thickest part; cut to test (10 to 12 minutes).

2. Meanwhile, heat remaining oil (about 2 teaspoons) in a wide nonstick frying pan over medium-high heat. Add onion, garlic, and chile; cook, stirring often, until onion is soft and lightly browned (3 to 4 minutes). Mix in tomatoes; cover, reduce heat to medium, and cook until tomatoes are softened and juicy (about 5 minutes). Stir lemon juice–cornstarch mixture, then add to tomatoes; cook, stirring, until sauce boils and thickens (about 1 minute). Season to taste with salt and pepper.

3. Using a wide spatula, lift fish to 2 warm plates. Spoon tomato sauce over fish, then sprinkle with cilantro.

PER SERVING: 320 calories, 12 g total fat, 2 g saturated fat, 59 mg cholesterol, 113 mg sodium, 12 g carbohydrates, 3 g fiber, 40 g protein, 109 mg calcium, 2 mg iron

CUMIN-SAUTÉED SOLE
WITH GARLIC & LIME

THANKS TO THEIR MILD FLAVOR AND BRIEF COOKING TIME, SOLE FILLETS ARE PERENNIALLY POPULAR FOR DINNER IN A HURRY. FOR THIS RECIPE, LOOK FOR LARGE, FIRM FILLETS FROM A VARIETY SUCH AS PETRALE OR REX SOLE.

15 MINUTES

10 to 12 ounces sole fillets
   (*each* ½ to ¾ inch thick)
   Salt, ground cumin, and paprika
   About 2 tablespoons all-purpose flour
1½ tablespoons butter or margarine
1 tablespoon vegetable oil
3 cloves garlic, cut into paper-thin slices
1 tablespoon lime juice
   Cilantro sprigs and lime wedges

1. Rinse fish and pat dry. Season to taste with salt, cumin, and paprika; then coat lightly with flour and shake off excess.

2. Melt 1½ teaspoons of the butter in oil in a wide nonstick frying pan over medium-high heat. When butter sizzles, add fish and cook, turning once, until lightly browned on both sides and just opaque but still moist in thickest part; cut to test (6 to 8 minutes).

3. Using a wide spatula, lift fish to 2 warm dinner plates; keep warm. Pour off and discard any fat remaining in frying pan; then add remaining 1 tablespoon butter. Return to medium heat and swirl pan until butter is melted. Add garlic and cook, stirring, until it begins to brown (about 1 minute); add lime juice and stir until it bubbles. Pour butter-garlic sauce over fish; garnish with cilantro sprigs and lime wedges.

PER SERVING: 315 calories, 17 g total fat, 7 g saturated fat, 98 mg cholesterol, 216 mg sodium, 8 g carbohydrates, 0 g fiber, 31 g protein, 41 mg calcium, 1 mg iron

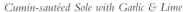

Cumin-sautéed Sole with Garlic & Lime

SKEWERED SWORDFISH WITH BAY & LEMON

SWORDFISH HAS A MILD YET DISTINCTIVELY RICH FLAVOR, AND ITS FIRM, MEATY TEXTURE MAKES IT A CLASSIC CHOICE TO SKEWER FOR KABOBS GRILLED ON THE BARBECUE. USE THE SAME GRILL TO COOK HALVED SMALL SUMMER SQUASH AND HEAT A SPLIT, GARLIC-BUTTERED BAGUETTE.

20 MINUTES

---

8 to 10 ounces boneless, skinless swordfish (about 1 inch thick)

1 lemon

5 fresh or dried bay leaves, cut crosswise into halves

1 tablespoon butter or margarine, melted

Coarse salt such as sea salt or kosher salt

1. Rinse fish, pat dry, and cut into 1-inch chunks. Cut lemon in half lengthwise. Set one half aside; cut remaining half crosswise into ¼-inch-thick slices. Discard seeds from slices.

2. Thread fish, lemon slices, and bay-leaf halves equally on two 10- to 12-inch metal skewers. To assemble each skewer, thread on a fish chunk, then a lemon slice, then another fish chunk, then a bay-leaf half; continue in this way until skewer is finished. Brush fish with butter; season to taste with salt.

3. Place skewers on a lightly greased grill 4 to 6 inches above a solid bed of hot coals (you can hold your hand at grill level for only 2 to 3 seconds) or over high heat on a gas grill. Close lid on gas grill. Cook, turning once, until fish is lightly browned on all sides and just opaque but still moist in thickest part; cut to test (about 8 minutes). Meanwhile, cut remaining lemon half into wedges.

4. Gently push fish and seasonings from skewers onto 2 warm dinner plates. Garnish with lemon wedges.

PER SERVING: 224 calories, 11 g total fat, 5 g saturated fat, 65 mg cholesterol, 176 mg sodium, 8 g carbohydrates, 0 g fiber, 26 g protein, 61 mg calcium, 2 mg iron

BUTTERFLIED GARLIC SHRIMP

SEASONED WITH PLENTY OF FRESH LIME AND GARLIC, THESE BIG BARBECUED SHRIMP ARE GOOD WITH ANY VEGETABLE THAT COOKS QUICKLY ON THE GRILL; YOU MIGHT TRY ZUCCHINI WEDGES OR SWEET WHITE CORN ON THE COB. SIP A SPICY TOMATO JUICE COCKTAIL, WITH OR WITHOUT VODKA OR TEQUILA, WHILE YOU WAIT FOR THE SIZZLING SHRIMP.

20 MINUTES

---

12 to 14 ounces large raw shrimp (12 to 15 per lb.), shelled

1½ tablespoons butter or margarine, melted

¼ cup fresh lime or lemon juice

3 or 4 cloves garlic, finely minced

2 teaspoons liquid hot pepper seasoning

Salt

Lime wedges

1. Cut down back of each shelled shrimp from head end to tail, cutting almost all the way through. Pull out and discard veins. Rinse shrimp and pat dry. Open each shrimp and place it cut side down in a shallow glass container, pressing shrimp to flatten; choose a container just large enough to hold all shrimp in a single layer.

2. In a small bowl, stir together butter, lime juice, garlic, and hot pepper seasoning. Spoon half the mixture evenly over shrimp; turn shrimp to coat well with marinade. Reserve remaining mixture to use for sauce.

3. Lift shrimp from marinade and place cut side down on a lightly greased grill 4 to 6 inches above a solid bed of hot coals (you can hold your hand at grill level for only 2 to 3 seconds) or over high heat on a gas grill. Close lid on gas grill. Cook, turning once and brushing with marinade after turning, until shrimp are pink on the outside and just opaque but still moist in center; cut to test (5 to 7 minutes). As shrimp are cooked, transfer them to a warm platter.

4. After you have turned shrimp, combine reserved lime juice mixture and any remaining shrimp marinade in a small pan; bring to a boil. Spoon sauce over grilled shrimp; season to taste with salt. Garnish with lime wedges.

PER SERVING: 225 calories, 11 g total fat, 6 g saturated fat, 215 mg cholesterol, 412 mg sodium, 5 g carbohydrates, 0 g fiber, 26 g protein, 81 mg calcium, 3 mg iron

Butterflied Garlic Shrimp

SHRIMP-FILLED PORTABELLA MUSHROOMS

IF YOU ENJOY STUFFED MUSHROOMS AS AN APPETIZER, YOU'LL APPRECIATE THIS MAIN-COURSE VERSION OF THE SAME DISH, MADE WITH BIG PORTABELLA MUSHROOMS FILLED WITH TINY SHRIMP AND JARLSBERG CHEESE. TRY THEM WITH A BUTTER LETTUCE SALAD, A WARM BAGUETTE, AND A CHILLED SAUVIGNON BLANC.

30 MINUTES

2 large portabella mushrooms (*each* about 4 inches in diameter; about 6 oz. *total*)

4 ounces small cooked shrimp

1 cup (about 4 oz.) shredded Jarlsberg or Swiss cheese

¼ cup thinly sliced green onions

1 teaspoon Worcestershire

Vegetable oil cooking spray

1. Rinse mushrooms and pat dry. Remove and chop stems; place in a medium-size bowl and mix in shrimp, cheese, onions, and Worcestershire.

2. Coat a 9-inch-square or 7- by 11-inch baking pan with cooking spray. Arrange mushrooms, cup side up, in pan. Spoon shrimp mixture on top of mushrooms, pressing it together lightly.

3. Bake in a 375° oven until cheese is melted and lightly browned (20 to 25 minutes). Serve hot.

PER SERVING: 288 calories, 17 g total fat, 10 g saturated fat, 151 mg cholesterol, 522 mg sodium, 6 g carbohydrates, 2 g fiber, 28 g protein, 438 mg calcium, 2 mg iron

KUNG PAO SHRIMP RISOTTO

COMBINING ASIAN AND ITALIAN FLAVORS AND COOKING TECHNIQUES, THIS COLORFUL DISH IS SURE TO SATISFY WHEN YOU'RE IN THE MOOD FOR A SPICY MEAL. SERVE IT WITH WARM FOCACCIA AND CHINESE BEER.

Pictured on page 8

25 MINUTES

8 to 10 ounces shelled, deveined raw shrimp (31 to 35 per lb.)

½ teaspoon vegetable oil

¼ cup diced red bell pepper

1½ teaspoons minced fresh ginger

2 small dried hot red chiles (*each* about 3 inches long)

½ cup arborio or other short-grain white rice

½ cup dry sherry

1 can (about 14½ oz.) fat-free reduced-sodium chicken broth

½ teaspoon Asian sesame oil

¼ cup slivered green or red bell pepper (or a combination)

1 tablespoon chopped roasted salted peanuts

Soy sauce

1. Rinse and drain shrimp. In a wide nonstick frying pan, stir shrimp over high heat until pink (about 2 minutes). Remove from pan and set aside.

2. To same pan, add vegetable oil, diced bell pepper, ginger, and chiles. Cook and stir until vegetables begin to soften (about 1½ minutes). Add rice and continue to cook, stirring, until grains are opaque (about 1 minute). Add sherry and broth. Bring to a boil; then reduce heat to medium-high and cook, stirring often, until rice is tender to bite (about 15 minutes). Remove and discard chiles (or reserve to use for garnish, if desired).

3. Return shrimp to pan and stir just until hot (1 to 2 minutes). Gently mix in sesame oil.

4. Spoon risotto into 2 warm wide bowls or onto warm dinner plates. Garnish with slivered bell pepper, peanuts, and (if desired) reserved chiles. Season to taste with soy sauce.

PER SERVING: 433 calories, 8 g total fat, 1 g saturated fat, 194 mg cholesterol, 746 mg sodium, 41 g carbohydrates, 4 g fiber, 33 g protein, 80 mg calcium, 6 mg iron

POACHED SHRIMP IN WINE SAUCE

LADLE A SIMPLE, SILKEN SAUCE OVER WARM SHRIMP ON A BED OF FRISÉE, AND YOU HAVE AN IDEAL CENTERPIECE FOR A CANDLELIT DINNER. TO COMPLETE THE MENU, ADD A CRISP-CRUSTED FRENCH BREAD BAGUETTE AND FLUTES OF CHAMPAGNE (LOOK FOR A BLANC DE NOIRS TO COMPLEMENT THE ROSY CRUSTACEANS).

15 MINUTES

1 cup fat-free reduced-sodium chicken broth

1 cup dry white wine

8 to 10 ounces shelled, deveined raw shrimp (31 to 35 per lb.)

6 tablespoons unsalted butter

2 teaspoons Dijon mustard

1 to 2 teaspoons lemon juice

1 to 1½ cups lightly packed frisée or small inner curly endive leaves, rinsed and crisped

1. In a wide frying pan, combine broth and wine. Bring to a boil over high heat. Meanwhile, rinse and drain shrimp.

2. Add shrimp to boiling broth-wine mixture. Cook, stirring occasionally, until just opaque but still moist in center; cut to test (1½ to 2 minutes). Using a slotted spoon, lift out shrimp and place in a bowl; keep warm.

3. Continue to boil wine mixture until it is reduced to about ⅔ cup (6 to 8 minutes). Then add butter (in a single chunk) and mustard. Continue to boil and stir until sauce is reduced to about ⅔ cup and is thick enough to coat a spoon in a velvety layer (about 3 minutes). Add lemon juice to taste.

4. Divide frisée between 2 dinner plates; top with shrimp. Pour hot sauce evenly over shrimp.

PER SERVING: 463 calories, 37 g total fat, 22 g saturated fat, 287 mg cholesterol, 638 mg sodium, 4 g carbohydrates, 1 g fiber, 28 g protein, 104 mg calcium, 4 mg iron

SHRIMP SAUTÉ WITH PROSCIUTTO & QUICK BAKED POLENTA

PREPARED POLENTA, SLICED AND BAKED WITH TWO CHEESES, MAKES A LUSCIOUS ACCOMPANIMENT FOR SHRIMP COOKED WITH TARRAGON AND WINE AND ACCENTED WITH SLIVERS OF PROSCIUTTO. ADD FRESH ASPARAGUS SPEARS AND A DRY WHITE WINE SUCH AS PINOT GRIGIO, AND YOU HAVE AN ELEGANT DINNER FOR TWO. BE SURE TO OFFER ITALIAN-STYLE BREAD TO SOAK UP THE FLAVORFUL SHRIMP JUICES.

20 TO 25 MINUTES

Shrimp Sauté with Prosciutto & Quick Baked Polenta

Quick Baked Polenta (below)

8 to 10 ounces shelled, deveined raw shrimp (31 to 35 per lb.)

2 teaspoons olive oil

1 large shallot, thinly slivered

1½ ounces thinly sliced prosciutto, cut into thin ribbons

¼ cup dry white wine

1 teaspoon chopped fresh tarragon or ¼ teaspoon dried tarragon

½ teaspoon shredded lemon peel

Freshly ground pepper

QUICK BAKED POLENTA

8 ounces prepared plain or herb-seasoned polenta roll

Olive oil cooking spray

⅓ cup shredded mozzarella cheese

2 tablespoons freshly shredded Parmesan cheese

1. Prepare Quick Baked Polenta.

2. While polenta is baking, rinse and drain shrimp; set aside. Heat oil in a wide nonstick frying pan over medium-high heat. Add shallot and prosciutto; cook, stirring, until shallot is soft but not brown (1½ to 2 minutes). Add shrimp, wine, tarragon, and lemon peel. Cook, stirring often, until shrimp are just opaque but still moist in center; cut to test (about 2 minutes). Season to taste with pepper, then spoon alongside polenta on warm plates.

QUICK BAKED POLENTA

1. Cut polenta into ½-inch-thick slices. Spray a shallow 3- to 4-cup baking dish with cooking spray. Arrange polenta slices in baking dish, slightly overlapping them if necessary. Bake in a 450° oven until polenta is hot and beginning to brown (6 to 8 minutes).

2. Sprinkle polenta evenly with mozzarella and Parmesan cheeses. Broil 4 to 6 inches below heat until cheeses are lightly browned (3 to 4 minutes). Using a wide spatula, lift servings of polenta to 2 warm dinner plates.

PER SERVING: 408 calories, 16 g total fat, 5 g saturated fat, 230 mg cholesterol, 947 mg sodium, 19 g carbohydrates, 2 g fiber, 40 g protein, 240 mg calcium, 4 mg iron

LONNY'S OYSTER STEW

PERFECT FOR A CHILLY AUTUMN EVENING, THIS CREAMY OYSTER STEW NEEDS ONLY WARM CORN MUFFINS AND GLASSES OF COLD BEER TO SET IT OFF. PANCETTA, LEEKS, AND FENNEL ACCENTUATE THE DISTINCTIVE FLAVOR OF THE OYSTERS.

20 MINUTES

1 small leek (about ¾ inch in diameter)

1 small head fennel (about 3 inches in diameter)

¼ cup diced pancetta or bacon

¼ teaspoon fennel seeds, coarsely crushed

2 cups half-and-half or whole milk

1 jar (about 10 oz.) small or medium-size oysters

1 to 2 teaspoons Pernod, Sambuca, or other anise-flavored liqueur (not sweet)

¼ cup chopped Italian parsley

Salt and freshly ground pepper

1 to 2 teaspoons butter or margarine

1. Trim and discard root end and green top from leek. Rinse leek well, then chop and place in a 2- to 2½-quart pan.

2. Rinse fennel and cut off coarse stalks; trim and discard base and any discolored or bruised parts from fennel bulb. Chop fennel bulb and add to leek in pan along with pancetta and fennel seeds. Cook over medium-high heat, stirring often, until fennel is softened but not browned (about 4 minutes).

3. Add half-and-half, then oysters and their liquid. Continue to cook, stirring often, just until stew is steaming (about 3 minutes); do not boil.

4. Stir in Pernod and 3 tablespoons of the parsley, then season to taste with salt and pepper. Ladle into 2 warm soup bowls and sprinkle with remaining 1 tablespoon parsley; top each serving with half the butter.

PER SERVING: 649 calories, 51 g total fat, 26 g saturated fat, 194 mg cholesterol, 594 mg sodium, 27 g carbohydrates, 2 g fiber, 22 g protein, 406 mg calcium, 12 mg iron

BAKED OYSTERS GRATIN

BAKED BETWEEN SPRINKLINGS OF BUTTERY CRACKER CRUMBS, THESE OYSTERS ARE A SUPPER TREAT FOR TWO. SERVE WITH A VERY DRY WHITE WINE SUCH AS A FRENCH MUSCADET AND A FAVORITE GREEN VEGETABLE, SUCH AS SLENDER WHOLE GREEN BEANS OR ASPARAGUS SPEARS. IF YOU MAKE YOUR OWN CRUMBS, YOU'LL NEED ABOUT TWELVE 2-INCH-SQUARE SALTINES.

20 MINUTES

⅔ cup fine saltine cracker crumbs

¼ cup butter or margarine, melted

⅛ teaspoon paprika

1 tablespoon chopped parsley

1 jar (about 10 oz.) small or medium-size oysters

Salt and white pepper

1. Sprinkle about half the crumbs over bottom of a lightly greased shallow, oval or round 1- to 1½-quart baking dish.

2. In a shallow bowl, stir together butter, paprika, and parsley. Drain oysters; then dip in butter mixture to coat well. Arrange oysters in a single layer over crumbs. Season to taste with salt and white pepper. Sprinkle evenly with remaining crumbs. Drizzle with any remaining butter mixture.

3. Bake in a 400° oven until crumbs are crisp and golden brown (12 to 15 minutes).

PER SERVING: 399 calories, 31 g total fat, 16 g saturated fat, 140 mg cholesterol, 628 mg sodium, 19 g carbohydrates, 1 g fiber, 12 g protein, 95 mg calcium, 11 mg iron

GOLD COUNTRY FRITTATA

TO MAKE THE LEGENDARY OMELET KNOWN AS HANGTOWN FRY EASIER TO PREPARE, WE'VE TRANSLATED IT INTO A NEW WORLD FRITTATA. IT'S AN AMPLE ENTRÉE, OFFERING SO MUCH VARIETY—EGGS, BACON, OYSTERS, CHEESE, AND FRESH SPINACH—THAT ONLY A BOWL OF CHERRY TOMATOES IS NEEDED TO COMPLETE THE MENU. OFFER THE TRADITIONAL ACCOMPANIMENTS OF SOURDOUGH BREAD OR ROLLS AND A CALIFORNIA CHARDONNAY AS WELL, IF YOU LIKE. NICE FOR SUNDAY SUPPER, THE DISH IS EQUALLY WELCOME AT A WEEKEND BRUNCH.

20 TO 25 MINUTES

3 slices bacon, coarsely chopped

1 tablespoon vegetable oil

½ cup chopped red onion

4 large eggs

2 tablespoons half-and-half or whole milk

¼ teaspoon salt

⅛ teaspoon freshly ground pepper

½ cup shredded Parmesan cheese

1 jar (about 10 oz.) small or medium-size oysters

1 cup lightly packed packaged triple-washed baby spinach, cut into ¼-inch-wide strips

1. In a 10-inch nonstick frying pan with an ovenproof handle, cook bacon over medium-high heat, stirring often, until lightly browned (about 4 minutes). Remove bacon from pan with a slotted spoon and drain on paper towels; set aside. Pour off and discard drippings from pan.

2. To pan, add oil and onion; cook over medium-high heat, stirring often, until onion is soft (2 to 3 minutes). Meanwhile, in a large bowl, combine eggs, half-and-half, salt, pepper, and about half the cheese; whisk until well blended, then set aside.

3. Drain oysters and pat dry. Arrange in a single layer in pan with onions. Cook until oysters are lightly browned on bottom (about 2 minutes); then turn over and sprinkle with spinach. Pour egg mixture into pan. Reduce heat to medium-low and cook, lifting cooked portion with a wide spatula to let uncooked eggs flow underneath, until eggs are just softly set (3 to 4 minutes).

4. Sprinkle bacon and remaining cheese over eggs. Then broil about 4 inches below heat until cheese is melted and lightly browned (2 to 3 minutes). Cut into wedges and serve at once.

PER SERVING: 502 calories, 33 g total fat, 11 g saturated fat, 532 mg cholesterol, 1,159 mg sodium, 15 g carbohydrates, 2 g fiber, 35 g protein, 437 mg calcium, 13 mg iron

CRISP CRAB CAKES WITH AVOCADO & BABY GREENS

HOT, CRISP SAUTÉED CRAB CAKES CONTRAST TEMPTINGLY WITH A COOL MEDLEY OF BABY GREENS AND SILKEN AVOCADO SLICES. OFFER FRENCH ROLLS AND FROSTY GLASSES OF ICED TEA OR MICROBREWERY BEER AS COMPLEMENTS.

15 TO 20 MINUTES

1 large egg

2 tablespoons whipping cream

½ cup soft bread crumbs

¼ cup grated Parmesan cheese

⅛ teaspoon white pepper

1 tablespoon minced parsley

1 clove garlic, minced or pressed

1 green onion, thinly sliced

8 ounces cooked crabmeat

1 tablespoon vegetable oil

1 small avocado (about 5½ oz.)

3 ounces mixed baby greens, rinsed and crisped

Lemon wedges

1. In a medium-size bowl, beat egg with cream to blend. Add bread crumbs, cheese, white pepper, parsley, garlic, and onion; mix well. Add crab and mix gently.

2. Heat oil in a wide nonstick frying pan over medium heat. To make each crab cake, mound a scant ¼ cup of the crab mixture in pan; then press down lightly to make a 3-inch-wide cake (you should have about 10 cakes). Cook, turning once, until golden brown on both sides (5 to 7 minutes).

3. While crab cakes are cooking, pit, peel, and slice avocado. Also divide greens between 2 dinner plates.

4. To serve, place hot crab cakes atop greens; arrange avocado slices alongside. Garnish with lemon wedges.

PER SERVING: 444 calories, 28 g total fat, 8 g saturated fat, 245 mg cholesterol, 612 mg sodium, 14 g carbohydrates, 2 g fiber, 33 g protein, 325 mg calcium, 3 mg iron

CRACKED CRAB POT

HOT GARLIC BREAD IS THE ACCOMPANIMENT OF CHOICE FOR AN EASY SHELLFISH STEW FEATURING THAT WEST COAST FAVORITE, CRACKED DUNGENESS CRAB. IF YOU HAVE THE CRAB CLEANED AND CRACKED AT THE FISH MARKET, DINNER CAN BE READY IN 15 MINUTES OR LESS.

12 TO 15 MINUTES

1 cup fat-free reduced-sodium chicken broth

⅓ cup dry vermouth

1 tablespoon butter or margarine

1 tablespoon chopped parsley

1½ teaspoons soy sauce

2 teaspoons lemon juice

2 cloves garlic, minced or pressed

1 cooked Dungeness crab (about 1½ lbs.), cleaned and cracked

1. In a 3½- to 4-quart pan, combine broth, vermouth, butter, parsley, soy sauce, lemon juice, and garlic. Bring to a boil over high heat.

2. Meanwhile, rinse crab under cold running water to remove any loose bits of shell. Pat dry with paper towels. Add crab to broth mixture. Cover, reduce heat to medium-low, and simmer just until crab is heated through (about 5 minutes).

3. Spoon crab pieces equally into 2 warm, wide bowls; ladle broth over crab.

PER SERVING: 200 calories, 7 g total fat, 4 g saturated fat, 97 mg cholesterol, 859 mg sodium, 4 g carbohydrates, 0 g fiber, 19 g protein, 99 mg calcium, 1 mg iron

PRONTO SCALLOP RISOTTO

A VEGETABLE-DOTTED RISOTTO BECOMES EVEN MORE TEMPTING IF YOU STIR IN SUCCULENT LITTLE BAY SCALLOPS, FROZEN PEAS, AND FRESH GINGER WHEN THE RICE IS ALMOST DONE. TO COMPLETE THE MENU, BRING ON A BASKET OF BREADSTICKS AND A ROMAINE AND ARUGULA SALAD.

25 TO 30 MINUTES

2 teaspoons olive oil

¼ cup chopped celery

¼ cup chopped red onion

⅔ cup arborio or other short-grain white rice

About 2 cups fat-free reduced-sodium chicken broth

6 to 8 ounces bay scallops

½ cup frozen tiny peas

1 teaspoon grated fresh ginger

2 teaspoons lemon juice

Salt and freshly ground pepper

1 tablespoon slivered fresh basil

Lemon wedges

1. Heat oil in a 1½- to 2-quart pan over medium heat. Add celery and onion and cook, stirring often, until soft (3 to 4 minutes). Add rice and stir until grains are opaque and well coated with oil mixture (about 1 minute).

2. Add 2 cups of the broth, increase heat to high, and bring to a boil, stirring often. Reduce heat to medium-low and continue to cook, stirring often, until rice is almost tender to bite (12 to 15 minutes). Meanwhile, rinse scallops and pat dry.

3. To rice, add scallops, peas, and ginger. Continue to cook and stir until scallops are just opaque but still moist in center; cut to test (3 to 4 minutes). Add lemon juice and, if a creamier texture is desired, a little more broth; mix well. Season to taste with salt and pepper.

4. Spoon risotto into 2 warm wide bowls. Sprinkle with basil and garnish with lemon wedges.

PER SERVING: 388 calories, 6 g total fat, 1 g saturated fat, 33 mg cholesterol, 859 mg sodium, 56 g carbohydrates, 7 g fiber, 27 g protein, 49 mg calcium, 5 mg iron

POACHED SCALLOPS WITH DRIED TOMATO ORZO

LIKE ALL THE BEST ONE-DISH MEALS, THIS ROSY SEAFOOD PASTA NEEDS ONLY A GREEN SALAD AND A LOAF OF YOUR FAVORITE BREAD AS ACCOMPANIMENTS. FOR DESSERT, SERVE BISCOTTI AND SEASONAL FRESH FRUIT—TANGERINES IN WINTER, SLICED WHITE PEACHES IN SUMMER.

20 MINUTES

Poached Scallops with Dried Tomato Orzo

1 cup fat-free reduced-sodium
  chicken broth

8 ounces sea scallops

2 tablespoons finely chopped dried
  tomatoes

½ cup dried orzo

2 teaspoons olive oil

1 teaspoon honey

1 teaspoon white wine vinegar

¾ teaspoon minced fresh thyme or
  ¼ teaspoon dried thyme

  Salt and freshly ground pepper

1. In a 2-quart pan, combine broth and 1 cup water. Bring to a boil over high heat. Meanwhile, rinse and drain scallops.

2. Add scallops to boiling broth-water mixture. When liquid returns to a boil, reduce heat to medium and cook until scallops are just opaque but still moist in center; cut to test (about 4 minutes). With a slotted spoon, transfer scallops to a bowl. Cover and keep warm.

3. Add tomatoes and pasta to pan; increase heat to high. Cook, stirring often, until almost all liquid has been absorbed and pasta is just tender to bite (10 to 12 minutes). Meanwhile, in a small bowl, stir together oil, honey, vinegar, and thyme.

4. Return scallops (and any liquid that has accumulated in bowl) to pan with pasta; stir gently just until heated through (about 1 minute).

5. Spoon pasta mixture into 2 warm wide, shallow bowls; drizzle with honey mixture. Season to taste with salt and pepper.

PER SERVING: 376 calories, 6 g total fat, 1 g saturated fat, 37 mg cholesterol, 499 mg sodium, 50 g carbohydrates, 2 g fiber, 28 g protein, 39 mg calcium, 3 mg iron

PASTA

30-minute Lasagne (page 176)

ASIAN NOODLE BOWLS

NOODLES IN A FLAVORFUL BROTH WITH TIDBITS OF MEAT, FISH, AND VEGETABLES ARE A POPULAR ASIAN CHOICE FOR FAST DINING. A BOWLFUL IS SATISFYING ENOUGH TO MAKE A WHOLE MEAL—AND BY VARYING THE TOPPINGS AND CONDIMENTS YOU USE, YOU CAN CREATE A VARIETY OF DIFFERENT DISHES FROM A SINGLE RECIPE. MANY SUPERMARKETS STOCK ASIAN SEASONINGS AND NOODLES; IF YOU CAN'T FIND A PARTICULAR INGREDIENT, LOOK FOR IT IN AN ASIAN OR GOURMET MARKET.

PICK & CHOOSE NOODLE BOWLS
20 MINUTES

> 6 ounces fresh or dried thin or thick Asian noodles, such as soba (buckwheat noodles), Chinese-style egg noodles, or udon
>
> 4 cups fat-free reduced-sodium chicken broth
>
> Toppings (suggestions follow)
>
> Condiments (suggestions follow)

1. Cook pasta according to package directions. Drain well and divide between 2 warm large soup bowls.

2. While pasta is cooking, bring broth to a boil in a 2-quart pan over high heat. Arrange toppings on a platter; arrange condiments in small bowls.

3. To serve, add desired toppings to pasta; then ladle hot broth into bowls and add condiments to taste.

Toppings. Choose 5 or 6 of the following: plain or marinated cubed **tofu;** finely shredded **carrot;** crisp **bean sprouts;** thinly sliced **shiitake, enoki, or button mushrooms; peas;** thinly sliced **green onion;** sliced **cucumber;** shredded **cooked chicken;** thinly sliced **cooked beef** or **pork;** small **cooked shrimp;** and shredded **nori.**

Condiments. Choose 2 or 3 of the following: **soy sauce; Asian fish sauce** (*nuoc mam* or *nam pla*); **prepared Asian peanut sauce; seasoned rice vinegar; chili oil; Asian sesame oil;** and **cilantro leaves.**

PER SERVING WITHOUT TOPPINGS OR CONDIMENTS: 316 calories, 1 g total fat, 0 g saturated fat, 0 mg cholesterol, 1,915 mg sodium, 65 g carbohydrates, 4 g fiber, 18 g protein, 30 mg calcium, 2 mg iron

SELF-STYLED NOODLE BOWLS
20 MINUTES

> 4 ounces dried vermicelli or angel hair pasta (capellini)
>
> Toppings (suggestions follow)
>
> 3 cups fat-free reduced-sodium chicken broth
>
> 3 tablespoons soy sauce
>
> 1½ tablespoons peanut butter
>
> 1½ tablespoons firmly packed brown sugar
>
> 1 tablespoon distilled white vinegar
>
> ½ teaspoon chili oil
>
> 1 tablespoon Asian sesame oil

1. In a 3- to 4-quart pan, bring about 2 quarts water to a boil over high heat; stir in pasta and cook, uncovered, until just tender to bite (7 to 8 minutes for vermicelli, about 3 minutes for angel hair). Or cook pasta according to package directions. Drain pasta and cover with cold water to cool quickly. Then divide pasta into 2 equal portions; twist each with your fingers to shape it into a mound and arrange on a small platter. Arrange toppings alongside pasta.

2. In pan used to cook pasta, combine broth, soy sauce, peanut butter, brown sugar, vinegar, and chili oil. Bring to a boil over high heat, stirring occasionally with a whisk. Add sesame oil, then pour broth into a warm serving bowl. Use at once, while still very hot.

3. To serve, place each portion of pasta in a warm large soup bowl. Add desired toppings, then ladle hot broth into bowls.

Toppings. Prepare the following: 2 **hard-cooked large eggs,** cut into halves; 2 ounces **baked ham,** cut into thin strips; 4 ounces **small cooked shrimp;** shredded **carrot;** thinly sliced **cucumber; sugar snap peas;** and slivered **green onion.**

PER SERVING: 613 calories, 23 g total fat, 5 g saturated fat, 340 mg cholesterol, 3,153 mg sodium, 59 g carbohydrates, 2 g fiber, 41 g protein, 77 mg calcium, 6 mg iron

UDON HOT POT FOR TWO
20 TO 25 MINUTES

> 3 cups fat-free reduced-sodium chicken broth
>
> 3 tablespoons dry white wine
>
> 3 tablespoons seasoned rice vinegar
>
> 1½ tablespoons soy sauce
>
> 3 cloves garlic, minced
>
> 3 quarter-size slices fresh ginger
>
> ⅓ cup slivered onion
>
> ⅓ cup thinly sliced carrot
>
> 5 ounces lean boneless beef (such as eye of round), cut into thin slices
>
> 5 ounces fresh or dried udon
>
> 3 tablespoons sliced green onions

1. In a 3- to 4-quart pan, combine broth, wine, vinegar, soy sauce, garlic, ginger, slivered onion, and carrot. Bring to a boil over high heat; then reduce heat, cover tightly, and simmer for 10 minutes. Meanwhile, cut beef into thin strips.

2. If desired, cut or break pasta strands in half. Add pasta to broth mixture and simmer, uncovered, until just tender to bite (2 to 5 minutes). Add beef and simmer just until cooked (30 seconds to 1 minute).

3. With a slotted spoon, remove ginger from soup; discard. Ladle soup into 2 warm large soup bowls and sprinkle with green onions.

PER SERVING: 493 calories, 12 g total fat, 4 g saturated fat, 43 mg cholesterol, 2,293 mg sodium, 61 g carbohydrates, 5 g fiber, 30 g protein, 58 mg calcium, 4 mg iron

PORK & CHICKEN NOODLES WITH TOASTED GARLIC OIL
20 MINUTES

> 1 tablespoon vegetable oil
>
> 1½ teaspoons minced garlic
>
> ½ small fresh jalapeño chile, seeded and thinly sliced
>
> 1½ teaspoons distilled white vinegar
>
> 1½ teaspoons soy sauce
>
> 3 ounces boneless, skinless chicken breast
>
> 3 ounces boneless pork loin, trimmed of fat
>
> 6 ounces fresh Chinese-style egg noodles or angel hair pasta (capellini)
>
> 4 cups fat-free reduced-sodium chicken broth
>
> Salt and freshly ground pepper
>
> About ½ teaspoon sugar
>
> ¼ cup sliced green onions
>
> Cilantro sprigs

1. In a small frying pan, combine oil and garlic. Stir occasionally over medium-low heat until garlic is light golden (about 5 minutes), watching carefully to prevent scorching. Remove from heat.

2. In a small bowl, combine chile, vinegar, and soy sauce; set aside. Rinse chicken and pat dry; then cut chicken and pork into thin slices about 1 inch wide and 3 inches long.

3. In a 3- to 4-quart pan, bring about 2 quarts water to a boil over high heat; stir in pasta and cook, uncovered, stirring occasionally, until just tender to bite (2 to 3 minutes). Or cook according to package directions. Drain pasta and divide between 2 warm large soup bowls.

4. While pasta is cooking, bring broth to a boil in a 2- to 3-quart pan over high heat. Stir in pork and chicken. Cook until meats are no longer pink in center; cut to test (2 to 3 minutes).

5. With a slotted spoon, lift meat from broth and arrange atop pasta in each bowl. Season broth to taste with salt, pepper, and sugar; then ladle into bowls. Sprinkle with onions and cilantro sprigs. Offer garlic oil and chile mixture to season soup to taste.

PER SERVING: 459 calories, 12 g total fat, 2 g saturated fat, 112 mg cholesterol, 1,573 mg sodium, 52 g carbohydrates, 2 g fiber, 35 g protein, 39 mg calcium, 4 mg iron

THAI HOT & SOUR SHRIMP NOODLES
25 MINUTES

> 4 cups fat-free reduced-sodium chicken broth
>
> 3 quarter-size slices fresh ginger
>
> 1 stalk fresh lemon grass (6 to 8 inches long), trimmed and cut into 3-inch lengths
>
> 2 fresh or dried kaffir lime leaves or ½ teaspoon finely shredded lime peel
>
> 1 small fresh jalapeño chile, seeded and thinly sliced
>
> 5 ounces dried rice noodles (mai fun, rice sticks, or rice vermicelli) or angel hair pasta (capellini)
>
> 6 ounces raw shrimp (31 to 35 per lb.), shelled and deveined
>
> 1½ tablespoons lime juice
>
> About 1 tablespoon Asian fish sauce (*nuoc mam* or *nam pla*)
>
> 3 tablespoons cilantro leaves
>
> 3 tablespoons sliced green onions
>
> Chili oil

1. In a 2- to 3-quart pan, combine broth, ginger, lemon grass, lime leaves, and chile. Bring to a boil over high heat. Reduce heat, cover, and simmer for 15 minutes.

2. Meanwhile, in a 3- to 4-quart pan, bring 2 quarts water to a boil over high heat; stir in pasta and cook, uncovered, stirring occasionally, until just tender to bite (about 3 minutes). Or cook pasta according to package directions. Drain well; divide between 2 warm large soup bowls. Keep warm.

3. With a slotted spoon, remove ginger, lemon grass, lime leaves, and chile from broth; discard. Stir shrimp into broth and cook until just opaque but still moist in thickest part; cut to test (2 to 3 minutes). With slotted spoon, lift shrimp from broth and place atop pasta in bowls.

4. Season broth to taste with lime juice and fish sauce. Ladle over shrimp and pasta in bowls. Sprinkle with cilantro and onions; offer chili oil to add to taste.

PER SERVING: 381 calories, 2 g total fat, 0 g saturated fat, 105 mg cholesterol, 1,770 mg sodium, 68 g carbohydrates, 0 g fiber, 22 g protein, 52 mg calcium, 2 mg iron

SPAGHETTI WITH ROASTED TOMATOES & TOASTED CRUMBS

To make this pasta sauce, you bake halved cherry tomatoes with olive oil, garlic, and parsley; the high heat firms the tomatoes' texture and concentrates their sweetness. For a wonderful weekday dinner, toss the hot tomatoes with spaghetti and chopped basil, then top with freshly toasted sourdough bread crumbs.

25 MINUTES

2 cups cherry tomatoes, halved
Salt and freshly ground pepper
2 tablespoons extra-virgin olive oil
1 large clove garlic, minced or pressed
2 tablespoons finely chopped parsley
6 ounces dried spaghetti
2 slices sourdough bread (about 2 oz. *total*), torn into pieces
2 tablespoons chopped fresh basil
Freshly grated Parmesan cheese

1. Place tomato halves, cut side up, in a 9- by 13-inch baking pan. Sprinkle lightly with salt and pepper. In a small bowl, stir together 2 teaspoons of the oil, garlic, and parsley; pat mixture evenly over cut sides of tomatoes, then drizzle with 2 more teaspoons oil. Bake in a 425° oven until tops of tomatoes are lightly browned (about 20 minutes).

2. Meanwhile, bring about 2 quarts water to a boil in a covered 3- to 4-quart pan over high heat; stir in pasta and cook, uncovered, until just tender to bite (8 to 10 minutes). Or cook pasta according to package directions.

3. Also while tomatoes bake, whirl bread in a food processor or blender until coarse crumbs form. Spread crumbs in an 8-inch baking pan and drizzle with remaining 2 teaspoons oil; stir well to coat completely with oil. Place in oven alongside tomatoes and bake until crumbs are crisp and golden brown (about 8 minutes). Remove from oven and let cool.

4. Drain pasta well and return to pan. Add tomatoes, half the bread crumbs, and basil; mix gently, using 2 forks. Season to taste with salt and pepper. Divide pasta mixture between 2 warm dinner plates and sprinkle with remaining bread crumbs. Offer cheese to add to taste.

PER SERVING: 500 calories, 12 g total fat, 2 g saturated fat, 0 mg cholesterol, 190 mg sodium, 84 g carbohydrates, 5 g fiber, 15 g protein, 58 mg calcium, 5 mg iron

MACARONI & AGED CHEDDAR AU GRATIN

What's the ideal comfort food? Everybody has a favorite, but old-fashioned macaroni and cheese surely ranks high on the list. In this version, extra-sharp Cheddar gives the creamy sauce a tangy bite, and a Parmesan-crumb topping adds a little crunch. Baked in individual ramekins, it's a perfect choice for a cozy night at home in front of the TV; just add a green salad alongside.

25 TO 30 MINUTES

Macaroni & Aged Cheddar au Gratin

6 ounces dried elbow macaroni

2 tablespoons butter or margarine

¼ cup soft bread crumbs

2 teaspoons grated Parmesan cheese

2 tablespoons all-purpose flour

1¼ cups milk

1 cup (about 4 oz.) shredded extra-sharp Cheddar cheese

Ground nutmeg, salt, and ground red pepper (cayenne)

1. In a covered 3- to 4-quart pan, bring about 2 quarts water to a boil over high heat; stir in pasta and cook, uncovered, until just tender to bite (8 to 10 minutes). Or cook pasta according to package directions.

2. Meanwhile, melt 1 teaspoon of the butter; stir in bread crumbs and Parmesan cheese. Set aside.

3. Melt remaining butter in a 1- to 1½-quart pan over medium-high heat. Add flour and stir until bubbly. Remove from heat and gradually add milk, whisking until smooth. Return to heat and bring to a boil, stirring often (4 to 5 minutes). Remove from heat, add Cheddar cheese, and stir until melted. Season sauce to taste with nutmeg, salt, and red pepper.

4. Drain pasta well; add to cheese sauce and mix well. Divide pasta mixture between 2 shallow 4- to 5-inch-diameter ramekins. Sprinkle with crumb mixture. Bake in a 500° oven until crumb topping is browned and sauce begins to bubble (6 to 8 minutes).

PER SERVING: 790 calories, 37 g total fat, 23 g saturated fat, 113 mg cholesterol, 608 mg sodium, 80 g carbohydrates, 2 g fiber, 32 g protein, 639 mg calcium, 4 mg iron

CHEESE-CRUSTED RIGATONI WITH TOMATO-PORCINI SAUCE

DIG BENEATH A GOLDEN-BROWN CRUST OF CHEESE TO REVEAL RIGATONI IN A RICH-FLAVORED TOMATO-WINE SAUCE DOTTED WITH MINCED VEGETABLES, PORCINI MUSHROOMS, AND NUGGETS OF BROWNED ITALIAN SAUSAGE. SUBSTITUTE TURKEY ITALIAN SAUSAGE FOR PORK SAUSAGE, IF YOU PREFER.

25 TO 30 MINUTES

¼ cup (about ⅜ oz.) dried porcini mushrooms

4 ounces mild Italian sausage, casings removed

1 large clove garlic, minced or pressed

⅓ cup finely chopped onion

⅓ cup finely chopped carrot

1 teaspoon dried basil

⅛ teaspoon crushed red pepper flakes

1 can (about 14½ oz.) crushed tomatoes

¼ cup dry red wine

6 ounces dried rigatoni

¾ cup shredded fontina cheese

1. In a small bowl, soak porcini mushrooms in ½ cup boiling water until softened (about 5 minutes). Lift from water with a slotted spoon, chop finely, and set aside. Reserve soaking liquid.

2. While mushrooms are soaking, crumble sausage into a wide frying pan. Cook over medium-high heat, stirring often with a wooden spoon to break up chunks, until sausage begins to brown and stick to pan bottom (5 to 6 minutes). Add garlic, onion, carrot, basil, and red pepper flakes. Cook, stirring often, until vegetables begin to brown (about 5 minutes).

3. To pan, add tomatoes, wine, and mushrooms. Carefully pour most of mushroom soaking liquid into pan, discarding sediment at bottom of bowl. Bring to a boil; then reduce heat and simmer, uncovered, until sauce is thickened (about 10 minutes).

4. Meanwhile, in a covered 3- to 4-quart pan, bring about 2 quarts of water to a boil over high heat; stir in pasta and cook, uncovered, until just tender to bite (10 to 12 minutes). Or cook pasta according to package directions.

5. Drain pasta well and return to cooking pan. Stir in sauce; mix well. Spoon half the pasta mixture into a deep 1-quart baking dish and sprinkle with half the cheese; then top with remaining pasta and sprinkle with remaining cheese. Broil about 6 inches below heat until cheese is bubbly and golden brown (about 2 minutes).

PER SERVING: 716 calories, 33 g total fat, 15 g saturated fat, 92 mg cholesterol, 1,105 mg sodium, 81 g carbohydrates, 6 g fiber, 33 g protein, 345 mg calcium, 7 mg iron

ASIAN-STYLE PASTA PRIMAVERA

INSPIRED BY THE WELL-KNOWN ITALIAN FAVORITE, THIS ASIAN INTERPRETATION OF PASTA PRIMAVERA REPLACES THE TRADITIONAL BOUQUET OF SPRING VEGETABLES WITH STIR-FRIED SHIITAKE MUSHROOMS, BABY BOK CHOY, AND CHINESE PEA PODS. SLIVERED HAM AND A SPRINKLING OF TOASTED SESAME SEEDS COMPLETE A COLORFUL DISH. FOR A LIGHT SUPPER, ADD ASIAN SLAW WITH COCONUT-PEANUT TOPPING (PAGE 34) OR COLD SLICED CUCUMBERS TOSSED WITH SEASONED RICE VINEGAR.

20 TO 25 MINUTES

3 large fresh shiitake mushrooms (*each* about 3 inches in diameter) or 2 ounces large regular mushrooms

¾ cup fat-free reduced-sodium chicken broth

1 tablespoon soy sauce

About 1 teaspoon seasoned rice vinegar

1 tablespoon sesame seeds

6 ounces dried angel hair pasta (capellini)

1 tablespoon vegetable oil

2 ounces thinly sliced baked ham, slivered

2 cloves garlic, minced or pressed

1 tablespoon minced fresh ginger

1 small head baby bok choy, trimmed and thinly sliced (about 1 cup)

4 ounces Chinese pea pods (also called snow or sugar peas), ends and strings removed

2 tablespoons dry sherry

1. Rinse mushrooms, then trim and discard bruised stem ends. Cut mushrooms lengthwise into ¼-inch-thick slices. Set aside. In a small bowl, mix broth, soy sauce, and vinegar; set aside.

2. Pour sesame seeds into a wide frying pan or wok. Toast over medium heat, shaking pan often, until seeds are golden (3 to 4 minutes). Pour out of pan and set aside.

3. In a covered 3- to 4-quart pan, bring about 2 quarts water to a boil over high heat; stir in pasta and cook, uncovered, until just tender to bite (about 3 minutes). Or cook pasta according to package directions.

4. Meanwhile, place pan used to toast sesame seeds over high heat; add oil and ham. Cook, stirring often, until ham is lightly browned (about 2 minutes). Remove ham from pan with a slotted spoon and set aside. Add garlic and ginger; cook, stirring often, until fragrant (about 30 seconds). Add mushrooms, bok choy, pea pods, and sherry. Cook, stirring often, until pea pods are bright green and tender-crisp to bite (about 2 minutes). Pour in broth mixture and bring to a boil. Remove from heat.

5. Drain pasta well. Add pasta to vegetable mixture; then add ham and mix gently, using 2 forks. Divide pasta between 2 warm dinner plates and sprinkle with sesame seeds.

PER SERVING: 525 calories, 13 g total fat, 2 g saturated fat, 17 mg cholesterol, 1,256 mg sodium, 75 g carbohydrates, 5 g fiber, 23 g protein, 131 mg calcium, 6 mg iron

ORECCHIETTE WITH BROCCOLI RABE

BROCCOLI RABE (ALSO CALLED RAPINI) IS INDEED RELATED TO ORDINARY BROCCOLI, BUT IT HAS LONGER, SKINNIER STEMS, SMALLER HEADS OF FLOWERETS, AND A BITTER FLAVOR SIMILAR TO THAT OF CHICORY OR MUSTARD GREENS. IN THE APULIA REGION OF SOUTHERN ITALY, IT'S OFTEN STIR-FRIED IN A LITTLE OLIVE OIL AND SERVED WITH ORECCHIETTE PASTA ("LITTLE EARS"). OUR VERSION ALSO INCLUDES CRISP PANCETTA SLIVERS AND PINE NUTS.

15 TO 20 MINUTES

Orecchiette with Broccoli Rabe

6 ounces dried orecchiette

8 ounces broccoli rabe

1½ ounces thinly sliced pancetta or bacon, cut into thin strips

2 tablespoons pine nuts

1 tablespoon olive oil

2 cloves garlic, minced or pressed

⅛ teaspoon crushed red pepper flakes

¾ cup fat-free reduced-sodium chicken broth

¼ cup freshly grated Pecorino Romano or Parmesan cheese

1. In a covered 3- to 4-quart pan, bring about 2 quarts water to a boil over high heat; stir in pasta and cook, uncovered, until just tender to bite (10 to 12 minutes). Or cook pasta according to package directions.

2. Meanwhile, trim and discard tough stem ends and yellowed leaves from broccoli rabe. Rinse and drain broccoli rabe and halve thick stems lengthwise; then cut all broccoli rabe into 1-inch lengths.

3. Also combine pancetta, pine nuts, and 1 teaspoon of the oil in a wide frying pan; stir often over medium-high heat until pancetta is crisp and nuts are golden (about 5 minutes). Remove pancetta and pine nuts from pan with a slotted spoon and set aside. To pan, add remaining 2 teaspoons oil and garlic; swirl pan until garlic is fragrant (about 30 seconds). Add broccoli rabe, red pepper flakes, and 2 tablespoons of the broth. Cook and stir until greens are just tender to bite (about 5 minutes).

4. Drain pasta well and add to pan along with remaining broth; stir until broth begins to boil. Remove from heat and stir in pancetta, pine nuts, and about half the cheese. Divide pasta mixture between 2 warm bowls or dinner plates; sprinkle with remaining cheese.

PER SERVING: 610 calories, 28 g total fat, 8 g saturated fat, 24 mg cholesterol, 525 mg sodium, 70 g carbohydrates, 3 g fiber, 23 g protein, 172 mg calcium, 5 mg iron

PASTA WITH MINT & PEAS

SIMPLE AND BEAUTIFUL, THIS DISH IS JUST RIGHT FOR A LAID-BACK SUPPER ON A WARM SUMMER EVENING. TOSS SLENDER ANGEL HAIR PASTA WITH SWEET, TENDER-CRISP SUGAR SNAP PEAS, SLIVERED MINT, AND LEMON; THEN EMBELLISH EACH PORTION WITH CRÈME FRAÎCHE, MORE MINT, AND A SQUEEZE OF LEMON JUICE.

15 MINUTES

6 ounces dried angel hair pasta (capellini)

7 ounces (about 1¾ cups) sugar snap peas, ends and strings removed

1 clove garlic, minced or pressed

1½ tablespoons butter or olive oil

2 teaspoons finely slivered lemon peel

3 tablespoons lemon juice

¼ cup slivered fresh mint

⅓ cup crème fraîche or sour cream

Salt and freshly ground pepper

1. In a covered 3- to 4-quart pan, bring about 2 quarts water to a boil over high heat; stir in pasta and cook, uncovered, for 1 minute. Add peas; cook until peas turn bright green and pasta is just tender to bite (about 2 more minutes). Drain peas and pasta well.

2. In pan used to cook pasta, combine garlic and butter; stir over high heat until butter is melted. Add drained peas and pasta; mix until pasta stops sizzling (about 1 minute). Add 1½ teaspoons of the lemon peel, 2 tablespoons of the lemon juice, and 1 tablespoon of the mint; mix well.

3. Divide pasta mixture between 2 warm wide soup bowls, swirling to make a well in the center of each portion. Spoon crème fraîche into center of each bowl, dividing equally; sprinkle with remaining ½ teaspoon lemon peel, 1 tablespoon lemon juice, and 3 tablespoons mint. Season to taste with salt and pepper.

PER SERVING: 591 calories, 25 g total fat, 15 g saturated fat, 56 mg cholesterol, 129 mg sodium, 75 g carbohydrates, 5 g fiber, 15 g protein, 174 mg calcium, 7 mg iron

ARTICHOKE, FENNEL & SAUSAGE FUSILLI

TENDER ARTICHOKES, FRESH FENNEL, AND SAVORY ITALIAN SAUSAGE SIMMERED IN A WINE-AND-CREAM BROTH MAKE A WINNING SAUCE FOR FANCIFUL CORKSCREW-SHAPED PASTA. (TO SAVE TIME, WE USE FROZEN ARTICHOKE HEARTS.) YOU MIGHT START THE MEAL WITH PURÉE OF ZUCCHINI SOUP WITH PERNOD (PAGE 64) AND FINISH WITH FRESH OR STEWED APRICOTS AND SHORTBREAD COOKIES.

30 MINUTES

1 small head fennel
  (about 3 inches in diameter)
4 ounces mild or hot Italian sausage,
  casings removed
⅓ cup chopped onion
1 clove garlic, minced or pressed
½ teaspoon fennel seeds
¼ cup slivered red bell pepper
  Half of 1 (about 9-oz.) package
  frozen artichoke hearts, thawed
  and drained
⅓ cup fat-free reduced-sodium
  chicken broth
2 tablespoons dry white wine
2 tablespoons whipping cream
6 ounces dried fusilli
  Freshly grated Parmesan cheese

1. Rinse fennel and cut off coarse stalks, reserving some of the feathery leaves. Trim and discard base and any discolored or bruised parts from fennel bulb; then thinly slice bulb crosswise and set aside.

2. Crumble sausage into a 2- to 3-quart pan. Cook over medium-high heat, stirring often with a wooden spoon to break up chunks, until sausage begins to brown and stick to pan bottom (5 to 6 minutes).

3. Add sliced fennel, onion, garlic, fennel seeds, and bell pepper to pan. Cook, stirring often, until vegetables just begin to brown (6 to 8 minutes). Add artichokes, broth, wine, and cream. Increase heat to high and bring to a boil; then reduce heat and simmer, uncovered, stirring occasionally, until artichokes are tender when pierced (about 5 minutes).

4. While you are preparing sauce, bring about 2 quarts water to a boil in a covered 3- to 4-quart pan over high heat; stir in pasta and cook, uncovered, until just tender to bite (10 to 12 minutes). Or cook pasta according to package directions.

5. Drain pasta well, then return to cooking pan. Top with sauce; mix gently, using 2 forks. Divide pasta between 2 warm dinner plates. Garnish with fennel leaves. Offer cheese to add to taste.

PER SERVING: 626 calories, 24 g total fat, 10 g saturated fat, 60 mg cholesterol, 663 mg sodium, 76 g carbohydrates, 8 g fiber, 23 g protein, 114 mg calcium, 6 mg iron

Artichoke, Fennel & Sausage Fusilli

THREE-CHEESE FARFALLE
WITH PROSCIUTTO & CHARD
SHAPED LIKE BOW TIES OR BUTTERFLIES, WHIMSICAL FARFALLE ARE COMBINED HERE WITH BOLD SWISS CHARD AND CLOAKED IN A MELLOW, VELVETY SAUCE MADE FROM THREE CHEESES—ASIAGO, FONTINA, AND BOCCONCINI. BOCCONCINI ARE BITE-SIZE BALLS OF FRESH MOZZARELLA; LOOK FOR THEM IN ITALIAN DELICATESSENS AND THE GOURMET CHEESE SECTION OF WELL-STOCKED SUPERMARKETS.

20 MINUTES

6 ounces dried farfalle
(bow-tie pasta)

1 tablespoon butter or olive oil

1½ ounces thinly sliced prosciutto,
chopped

¼ cup fat-free reduced-sodium
chicken broth

2 cups coarsely chopped Swiss chard

¼ cup freshly shredded Asiago cheese

¼ cup shredded fontina cheese

½ cup (about 3 oz.) bocconcini,
cut into quarters; or use 3 ounces
regular fresh mozzarella, cut into
bite-size pieces

Freshly ground pepper

1. In a covered 3- to 4-quart pan, bring about 2 quarts water to a boil over high heat; stir in pasta and cook, uncovered, until just tender to bite (8 to 10 minutes). Or cook pasta according to package directions.

2. Meanwhile, melt butter in a wide frying pan over medium-high heat. Add prosciutto and cook, stirring often, until brown and crisp (3 to 4 minutes). With a slotted spoon, remove half the prosciutto from pan; drain on paper towels and set aside.

3. Add broth and chard to pan; cover and simmer until chard is wilted (about 3 minutes). Remove from heat. Add Asiago and fontina cheeses and stir until melted.

4. Drain pasta well, then add to cheese sauce and stir until coated. Stir in bocconcini until evenly distributed (it should not melt). Divide pasta mixture between 2 warm dinner plates; sprinkle with reserved prosciutto and season to taste with pepper.

PER SERVING: 674 calories, 29 g total fat, 17 g saturated fat, 97 mg cholesterol, 1,058 mg sodium, 65 g carbohydrates, 3 g fiber, 35 g protein, 458 mg calcium, 5 mg iron

CHEESE TORTELLINI WITH
WILD MUSHROOM RAGOUT
TO MAKE AN EXQUISITE SAUCE FOR FRESH TORTELLINI, SAUTÉ AN ASSORTMENT OF WILD OR CULTIVATED FRESH MUSHROOMS, STIR IN A LITTLE WINE AND CREAM, AND SEASON WITH MIXED FRESH HERBS. ROUND OUT THE MEAL WITH MARINATED FENNEL & OIL-CURED OLIVES WITH ORANGES (PAGE 31).

30 MINUTES

Cheese Tortellini with Wild Mushroom Ragout

8 ounces assorted fresh mushrooms, such as chanterelle, crimini, morel, oyster, pompon, porcini, portabella, shiitake, and button (choose 3 or 4 kinds)

1 tablespoon olive oil

2 tablespoons finely chopped shallots

1 ounce prosciutto, finely diced
Salt and freshly ground pepper

1 package (about 9 oz.) fresh cheese-filled tortellini

¼ cup fat-free reduced-sodium chicken broth

¼ cup dry white wine

¼ cup whipping cream

2 teaspoons finely chopped mixed fresh herbs or 1 teaspoon mixed dried herbs, such as parsley, thyme, marjoram, and rosemary

¼ cup thinly shaved dry jack cheese

1. Place mushrooms in a plastic food bag. Fill bag with water; then seal bag and shake to wash mushrooms. Drain mushrooms well; if they are still gritty, repeat rinsing. Trim and discard bruised stem ends. Cut larger mushrooms lengthwise into ¼-inch-thick slices; leave small ones whole. Set aside.

2. Heat oil in a wide frying pan over medium-high heat. Add shallots and prosciutto; cook, stirring often, until shallots begin to brown (4 to 5 minutes). Add mushrooms and sprinkle with salt and pepper to taste. Increase heat to high and cook, stirring, until all liquid released from mushrooms has evaporated (10 to 12 minutes).

3. While shallots and mushrooms are cooking, bring about 2 quarts water to a boil in a covered 3- to 4-quart pan over high heat; stir in tortellini and cook, uncovered, until just tender to bite (5 to 6 minutes). Or cook according to package directions. Drain well; keep warm.

4. Add broth, wine, and cream to mushroom mixture; cook until liquid is reduced by half (about 3 minutes). Stir in herbs and drained tortellini; mix gently until hot (about 1 minute). Divide tortellini and sauce between 2 warm dinner plates; scatter cheese over each serving.

PER SERVING: 702 calories, 33 g total fat, 15 g saturated fat, 120 mg cholesterol, 920 mg sodium, 71 g carbohydrates, 3 g fiber, 30 g protein, 342 mg calcium, 4 mg iron

Sesame Noodles with Gingered Pork & Vegetables

SESAME NOODLES WITH GINGERED PORK & VEGETABLES

HEARTY WITH STRIPS OF LEAN, GINGERY PORK AND BRIMMING WITH COLOR FROM STIR-FRIED VEGETABLES—CARROTS, RED BELL PEPPERS, AND BRIGHT GREEN SUGAR SNAP PEAS—THIS LIVELY ASIAN-INSPIRED DISH MAKES A GREAT ONE-BOWL MEAL. SERVE WITH GLASSES OF CHILLED GINGER BEER; FOLLOW WITH LITCHIS & SYRUP WITH CRUSHED ICE (PAGE 227).

15 TO 20 MINUTES

5 ounces dried thin Asian noodles or linguine

1 teaspoon Asian sesame oil

1 tablespoon peanut or vegetable oil

6 ounces boneless pork loin, trimmed of fat and cut into matchstick pieces

1 small carrot (about 4 oz.), cut into matchstick pieces

½ cup slivered red bell pepper

2 ounces sugar snap peas or Chinese pea pods (also called snow or sugar peas), ends and strings removed

3 green onions, cut diagonally into 1-inch lengths

1 tablespoon minced fresh ginger

1 large clove garlic, minced or pressed

2 tablespoons prepared teriyaki sauce

1 tablespoon lime juice

1 tablespoon chopped cilantro

2 tablespoons coarsely chopped roasted salted peanuts

1. In a covered 3- to 4-quart pan, bring about 2 quarts water to a boil over high heat; stir in pasta and cook, uncovered, until just tender to bite (8 to 10 minutes). Or cook pasta according to package directions. Drain well, then return to cooking pan. Add sesame oil and toss to mix; keep warm.

2. While pasta is cooking, place a wide frying pan over high heat. When pan is hot, add peanut oil, then pork. Cook, stirring often, until pork is lightly browned (about 3 minutes). Remove from pan and keep warm.

3. To pan, add carrot, bell pepper, peas, and onions. Cook and stir until carrot is barely tender-crisp to bite (1½ to 2 minutes). Add ginger, garlic, teriyaki sauce, lime juice, pork, and pasta; mix gently, using 2 forks. Pour onto a platter or divide between 2 warm bowls. Sprinkle with cilantro and peanuts.

PER SERVING: 586 calories, 20 g total fat, 4 g saturated fat, 50 mg cholesterol, 756 mg sodium, 70 g carbohydrates, 6 g fiber, 33 g protein, 85 mg calcium, 5 mg iron

ASPARAGUS PASTA "RISOTTO"

SHAPED LIKE TINY TEARDROPS, DRIED ORZO MAKES A DELICIOUS STAND-IN FOR RICE IN THIS QUICK "RISOTTO." YOU SIMMER THE PASTA IN BROTH, THEN STIR IN SLICED ASPARAGUS AND PARMESAN CHEESE. FRESH WHOLE SAGE LEAVES, COOKED BRIEFLY IN VERY HOT OLIVE OIL UNTIL CRISP, ARE CRUMBLED OVER THE RISOTTO FOR A SENSATIONAL FINISH. IF YOU HAVE ENOUGH TIME, PREPARE A SALAD SUCH AS WILD MUSHROOMS & PANCETTA ON ARUGULA (PAGE 23) TO SERVE ALONGSIDE.

20 MINUTES

3 cups fat-free reduced-sodium
  chicken broth

1 cup dried orzo

2 cups 1- to 2-inch diagonal pieces
  thin asparagus

¼ cup grated Parmesan cheese

1 tablespoon extra-virgin olive oil

¼ cup fresh sage leaves
  Sage sprigs
  Freshly ground pepper

1. In a covered 2- to 3-quart pan, bring broth to a boil over high heat. Add pasta, reduce heat to medium-high, and cook, uncovered, for 8 minutes, stirring occasionally. Add asparagus and continue to cook, stirring occasionally, until pasta is barely tender to bite (2 to 4 more minutes). Stir in cheese and remove pan from heat.

2. While pasta is cooking, heat oil in a small frying pan over medium-high heat until it ripples. Add sage leaves and stir often until they turn darker green and begin to curl at edges (about 1 minute). Remove from heat. With a slotted spoon, remove leaves from pan; drain on paper towels. Reserve oil.

3. Crumble sage leaves and add to risotto along with oil; mix lightly. Spoon into 2 warm wide bowls and garnish with sage sprigs. Season to taste with pepper.

PER SERVING: 486 calories, 12 g total fat, 4 g saturated fat, 10 mg cholesterol, 1,167 mg sodium, 71 g carbohydrates, 3 g fiber, 25 g protein, 229 mg calcium, 5 mg iron

MEDITERRANEAN-STYLE SPINACH FETTUCCINE WITH CHICKEN

MEDITERRANEAN FLAVORS COME ALIVE IN A ROBUST, HERB-SEASONED COMBINATION OF BONELESS CHICKEN BREAST AND VEGETABLES TO SPOON OVER FRESH SPINACH FETTUCCINE.

25 MINUTES

¼ **cup pine nuts**

2 **tablespoons olive oil**

2 **cloves garlic, minced or pressed**

1 **small onion (about 5 oz.), minced**

¾ **teaspoon dried basil**

¾ **teaspoon dried oregano**

⅛ **to ¼ teaspoon crushed red pepper flakes**

1 **small boneless, skinless chicken breast half (about 4 oz.), cut into ½-inch chunks**

1 **small zucchini (about 4 oz.), cut diagonally into ¼-inch-thick slices**

4 **ounces mushrooms, sliced**

1 **large tomato (about 8 oz.), chopped**

8 **ounces fresh spinach fettuccine**

¼ **cup freshly grated Parmesan cheese**

1. Pour pine nuts into a small frying pan. Toast over medium heat, shaking pan often, until nuts are pale gold (2 to 3 minutes). Pour out of pan and set aside.

2. Heat oil in a wide frying pan over medium-high heat. Add garlic, onion, basil, oregano, and red pepper flakes. Cook, stirring often, until onion begins to brown (8 to 10 minutes). Add chicken, zucchini, mushrooms, and tomato. Cook, stirring occasionally, until mushrooms are soft and chicken is no longer pink in center; cut to test (about 5 minutes). Remove from heat and keep warm.

3. While vegetables and chicken are cooking, bring about 2 quarts water to a boil in a covered 3- to 4-quart pan over high heat; stir in pasta and cook, uncovered, until just tender to bite (3 to 4 minutes). Or cook pasta according to package directions.

4. Drain pasta well, then return to cooking pan and top with chicken mixture; mix gently, using 2 forks. Divide between 2 warm dinner plates and sprinkle with pine nuts and cheese.

PER SERVING: 720 calories, 29 g total fat, 6 g saturated fat, 124 mg cholesterol, 148 mg sodium, 83 g carbohydrates, 6 g fiber, 37 g protein, 223 mg calcium, 8 mg iron

Mediterranean-style Spinach Fettuccine with Chicken

RAVIOLI WITH QUICK BOLOGNESE SAUCE

THIS HEARTY MEAT SAUCE IS SO FLAVORFUL YOU'D SWEAR IT HAD BEEN SLOW-COOKED FOR HOURS. TO ACHIEVE THAT RICH TASTE FAST, BROWN THE VEGETABLES AND MEAT FIRST, THEN SIMMER THEM RAPIDLY WITH TOMATOES TO MELD THE FLAVORS. SERVE THE SAUCE OVER RAVIOLI OR ANY OTHER PASTA, WITH A GENEROUS SPRINKLING OF FRESHLY GRATED PARMESAN CHEESE.

30 MINUTES

1 tablespoon butter or olive oil

1 tablespoon olive oil

1 large clove garlic, minced or pressed

¼ cup finely chopped onion

¼ cup finely chopped carrot

¼ cup finely chopped celery

2 teaspoons minced parsley

4 ounces lean ground beef

4 ounces lean ground pork

1 can (about 14½ oz.) crushed tomatoes

⅛ teaspoon ground allspice

½ cup milk

Salt and freshly ground pepper

1 package (about 9 oz.) fresh cheese-filled ravioli

Freshly grated Parmesan cheese

1. In a 3- to 4-quart pan, melt butter in oil over medium-high heat. Add garlic, onion, carrot, celery, and parsley. Cook, stirring occasionally, until vegetables are soft (about 5 minutes). Add beef and pork; cook, stirring often with a wooden spoon to break up chunks, until meat begins to brown and stick to pan bottom (about 10 minutes).

2. To browned meat mixture, add tomatoes, allspice, and milk. Simmer rapidly, stirring often, until sauce is slightly thickened (about 10 minutes). Season to taste with salt and pepper.

3. Meanwhile, bring about 2 quarts water to a boil in a covered 3- to 4-quart pan over high heat; stir in ravioli and cook, uncovered, until ravioli rise to the surface and are just tender to bite (4 to 6 minutes). Or cook ravioli according to package directions.

4. Drain ravioli well and return to pan; top with sauce and toss lightly to mix. Divide between 2 warm wide bowls. Offer cheese to add to taste.

PER SERVING: 934 calories, 53 g total fat, 22 g saturated fat, 218 mg cholesterol, 1,037 mg sodium, 65 g carbohydrates, 6 g fiber, 45 g protein, 434 mg calcium, 5 mg iron

PAN-BROWNED GNOCCHI WITH SWISS CHARD & PROSCIUTTO

ALMOST AS VERSATILE AS PASTA ARE GNOCCHI—PLUMP, PASTALIKE DUMPLINGS THAT MAY BE BASED ON POTATOES, RICOTTA CHEESE, FARINA, OR OTHER INGREDIENTS. HERE, POTATO GNOCCHI ARE SAUTÉED IN SIZZLING SAGE BUTTER UNTIL GOLDEN, THEN TOSSED WITH THIN STRIPS OF PROSCIUTTO AND WILTED RED CHARD FOR A DELECTABLE MAIN COURSE. LOOK FOR GNOCCHI IN WELL-STOCKED SUPERMARKETS; THEY'RE SOLD VACUUM-PACKED (ALONGSIDE THE DRIED PASTAS), REFRIGERATED, AND FROZEN.

20 TO 25 MINUTES

Pan-browned Gnocchi with Swiss Chard & Prosciutto

4 ounces red Swiss chard

2 teaspoons olive oil

1 large clove garlic, minced
   or pressed

1½ ounces thinly sliced prosciutto,
   cut into ¼-inch-wide strips

12 ounces purchased potato gnocchi
   (almost three-fourths of a 17½-oz.
   package)

1 tablespoon butter or margarine

1 tablespoon finely chopped fresh
   sage or ½ teaspoon dried rubbed
   sage

   Sage leaves or sprigs

2 tablespoons freshly grated Asiago
   cheese

1. In a covered 4- to 5-quart pan, bring about 3 quarts water to a boil over high heat. Meanwhile, trim and discard discolored ends of chard stems. Rinse and drain chard; stack leaves and cut in half lengthwise, then cut crosswise into ½-inch-wide strips. Set aside.

2. Heat oil in a wide nonstick frying pan over medium-high heat. Add garlic and prosciutto and cook, stirring often, until prosciutto is brown and crisp (about 3 minutes). Stir in chard. Cover and cook, stirring occasionally, just until chard is wilted (2 to 3 minutes). Remove from pan and set aside.

3. Drop gnocchi into boiling water; once they have risen to the surface, continue to cook for 1 more minute (cooking time will be 3 to 4 minutes total). Or cook gnocchi according to package directions. Drain well.

4. Melt butter in frying pan over medium-high heat. Add chopped sage; swirl in butter for 1 minute. Add drained gnocchi and cook, turning occasionally, until light golden on all sides (3 to 5 minutes). Add chard mixture and stir gently just until heated through (about 3 minutes). Divide gnocchi between 2 warm dinner plates; garnish with whole sage leaves. Sprinkle with cheese.

PER SERVING: 536 calories, 17 g total fat, 7 g saturated fat, 63 mg cholesterol, 1,773 mg sodium, 75 g carbohydrates, 5 g fiber, 21 g protein, 147 mg calcium, 5 mg iron

PENNE WITH SAUSAGE, ROASTED PEPPERS & GREENS

START THE WATER FOR THE PENNE HEATING IN A COVERED PAN; THEN STIR UP A BOLD TOMATO-SAUSAGE SAUCE ENHANCED WITH FRESH GREENS AND ROASTED RED PEPPERS. FOR DESSERT, OFFER RIPE PEACHES POACHED IN RED WINE.

15 TO 20 MINUTES

6 ounces dried penne

4 ounces mild or hot turkey Italian sausage, casings removed

1 large clove garlic, minced or pressed

⅔ cup chopped onion

1 can (about 8 oz.) no-salt-added tomato sauce

¼ cup dry red wine

½ cup canned or bottled roasted red peppers, drained and cut into thin strips

1½ cups thinly sliced mustard greens

2 tablespoons freshly shredded Parmesan cheese

1. In a covered 3- to 4-quart pan, bring about 2 quarts water to a boil over high heat; stir in pasta and cook, uncovered, until just tender to bite (8 to 10 minutes). Or cook pasta according to package directions.

2. Meanwhile, crumble sausage into a 2- to 3-quart pan. Add garlic and onion. Cook over medium-high heat, stirring often with a wooden spoon to break up chunks, until sausage begins to brown and stick to pan bottom (5 to 6 minutes). Stir in tomato sauce, wine, and red peppers. Bring to a simmer; then simmer, stirring often, for about 5 minutes to blend flavors. Stir in mustard greens and about half the cheese.

3. Drain pasta well; add to tomato sauce. Mix well. Divide between 2 warm dinner plates. Sprinkle with remaining cheese.

PER SERVING: 540 calories, 10 g total fat, 3 g saturated fat, 35 mg cholesterol, 590 mg sodium, 84 g carbohydrates, 5 g fiber, 26 g protein, 151 mg calcium, 6 mg iron

PAPPARDELLE, SMOKED SALMON & ASPARAGUS IN LEMON-DILL CREAM

IMAGES OF SPRING WILL COME TO MIND WHEN YOU ENJOY THIS VERY PRETTY DISH OF BROAD PASTA RIBBONS, SMOKED SALMON, AND TENDER ASPARAGUS IN A DELICATE LEMON-DILL CREAM SAUCE. IF YOU CAN'T FIND PAPPARDELLE, SUBSTITUTE FETTUCCINE, USING THE THINNEST (IN TERMS OF THE PASTA'S THICKNESS, NOT ITS WIDTH) YOU CAN FIND.

20 TO 25 MINUTES

Pappardelle, Smoked Salmon & Asparagus in Lemon-Dill Cream

8 ounces asparagus, tough ends
snapped off, spears cut diagonally
into 1-inch lengths

6 ounces dried pappardelle

1 tablespoon butter or margarine

1 large shallot, finely chopped

⅓ cup whipping cream

1 teaspoon shredded lemon peel

2 tablespoons lemon juice

2 ounces sliced smoked salmon or
lox, cut into thin strips

1 tablespoon chopped fresh dill
Salt and freshly ground pepper

1 tablespoon salmon caviar (optional)
Dill sprigs

1. In a covered 3- to 4-quart pan, bring about 2 quarts water to a boil over high heat. Add asparagus and cook, uncovered, until just tender-crisp when pierced (2 to 3 minutes). Lift from water with a slotted spoon and immediately immerse in ice water until cool; then drain and set aside.

2. Add pasta to boiling water and cook, uncovered, until just tender to bite (7 to 8 minutes); or cook according to package directions. Drain well, reserving ½ cup of the cooking water.

3. While pasta is cooking, melt butter in a wide frying pan over medium-high heat. Add shallot and cook, stirring often, until soft (2 to 3 minutes). Stir in cream and lemon peel. Bring to a boil; then boil, stirring often, until sauce is slightly thickened (about 3 minutes).

4. Reduce heat to medium. Add drained pasta, the ½ cup reserved cooking water, asparagus, lemon juice, salmon, and chopped dill. Toss gently just until heated through (3 to 4 minutes); season to taste with salt and pepper. Divide pasta mixture between 2 warm dinner plates. Sprinkle with caviar, if desired; garnish with dill sprigs.

PER SERVING: 543 calories, 21 g total fat, 12 g saturated fat, 66 mg cholesterol, 651 mg sodium, 70 g carbohydrates, 3 g fiber, 20 g protein, 73 mg calcium, 4 mg iron

30-MINUTE LASAGNE

Pictured on page 155

PUTTING TOGETHER HOME-COOKED LASAGNE DOESN'T HAVE TO BE AN ALL-DAY PROJECT. BY RELYING ON READY-TO-USE INGREDIENTS SUCH AS PURCHASED MARINARA SAUCE, PACKAGED SHREDDED CHEESE, AND FRESH EGG ROLL WRAPPERS (WHICH DON'T REQUIRE PRECOOKING), YOU CAN ASSEMBLE AN OVEN-READY LASAGNE IN UNDER 15 MINUTES. IN KEEPING WITH THE TRADITIONAL RECIPE, THOUGH, WE STILL INCLUDE A CREAMY BÉCHAMEL SAUCE.

30 MINUTES

1½ tablespoons butter or margarine

1 tablespoon all-purpose flour

¾ cup milk

Ground nutmeg, salt, and freshly ground pepper

4 egg roll wrappers (*each* about 6 inches square)

1 cup prepared or homemade marinara, spaghetti, or other tomato-based pasta sauce

¾ cup shredded mozzarella cheese

2 tablespoons freshly grated Parmesan cheese

1. Melt butter in a 1- to 1½-quart pan over medium-high heat. Add flour and stir until bubbly. Remove pan from heat and gradually add milk, whisking until smooth. Return to heat and bring to a boil, stirring; then boil for 1 minute, stirring constantly. Season to taste with nutmeg, salt, and pepper. Remove from heat.

2. Choose a small baking dish (of any shape) in which egg roll wrappers will fit snugly. In dish, layer a fourth of the marinara sauce, one egg roll wrapper, a third of the béchamel sauce, a third of the mozzarella cheese, and a fourth of the Parmesan cheese. Repeat layers twice more, ending with marinara sauce, an egg roll wrapper, and Parmesan.

3. Bake in a 500° oven until lasagne is golden brown on top and sauce is bubbly around edges (about 15 minutes). Let stand for about 5 minutes before cutting.

PER SERVING: 615 calories, 30 g total fat, 15 g saturated fat, 80 mg cholesterol, 1,389 mg sodium, 65 g carbohydrates, 1 g fiber, 23 g protein, 48 mg calcium, 3 mg iron

ORZO WITH SHRIMP, FETA & ARTICHOKE HEARTS

INSPIRED BY MEDITERRANEAN FLAVORS, THIS HEALTHFUL DISH WOULD GO NICELY WITH A GREEK-STYLE SALAD OF ROMAINE LETTUCE, CUCUMBERS, SLICED TOMATOES, AND OLIVES IN A LOW-FAT DILL DRESSING. (OR TRY THE CUCUMBER AND TOMATO SALAD ON PAGE 30, LEAVING OUT THE FETA CHEESE.) ENJOY A WELL-CHILLED CHARDONNAY OR SAUVIGNON BLANC WITH THE MEAL.

15 MINUTES

1 cup dried orzo

½ cup frozen tiny peas

⅓ cup fat-free reduced-sodium chicken broth

2 tablespoons dry white wine

1½ teaspoons finely shredded lemon peel

Half of 1 (about 6-oz.) jar quartered marinated artichoke hearts, drained and thinly sliced

4 ounces cooked shelled, deveined shrimp (36 to 42 per lb.)

¼ cup crumbled feta cheese

1. In a 2- to 3-quart pan, bring about 1 quart water to a boil over high heat; stir in pasta and cook, uncovered, until just tender to bite (8 to 10 minutes). Or cook pasta according to package directions. Add peas to pasta and cook for 1 more minute; then drain peas and pasta well.

2. While pasta is cooking, combine broth, wine, and lemon peel in a 1- to 1½-quart pan. Cover and bring to a boil over high heat. Reduce heat and keep warm.

3. Return drained pasta and peas to cooking pan. Add broth mixture, artichokes, shrimp, and about half the cheese; mix well. Divide pasta mixture between 2 warm dinner plates and sprinkle with remaining cheese.

PER SERVING: 503 calories, 9 g total fat, 3 g saturated fat, 126 mg cholesterol, 706 mg sodium, 74 g carbohydrates, 6 g fiber, 29 g protein, 142 mg calcium, 6 mg iron

FETTUCCINE FONDUTA

A CROSS BETWEEN FONDUE AND CHEESE SAUCE, ITALIAN FONDUTA IS MADE WITH FONTINA CHEESE, SERVED OVER PASTA OR RISOTTO—AND TRADITIONALLY TOPPED WITH COSTLY WHITE TRUFFLES, WHICH PERFECTLY ACCENT THE FONTINA'S RICH, NUTTY FLAVOR. OUR RENDITION OF THE DISH IS A SIMPLIFIED ONE-PAN VERSION; DRIZZLE IT WITH LUXURIOUS WHITE TRUFFLE OIL, IF YOU LIKE, AND SERVE WITH A RADICCHIO SALAD, WARM BREAD, AND A LIGHT, SMOOTH RED WINE.

20 MINUTES

2 cups fat-free reduced-sodium chicken broth

6 ounces dried fettuccine

2 teaspoons cornstarch

⅔ cup milk

2 large eggs

1½ cups (about 6 oz.) shredded fontina cheese

Freshly ground pepper and freshly grated nutmeg

Salt

1 to 2 teaspoons white truffle oil (optional)

1. Bring broth to a boil in a wide frying pan over high heat. Break pasta strands in half and add to broth. Reduce heat and boil gently, uncovered, stirring often to prevent sticking, until pasta is just tender to bite (8 to 10 minutes).

2. Meanwhile, in a small bowl, smoothly blend cornstarch and milk. In another small bowl, beat eggs to blend.

3. When pasta is tender, stir cornstarch mixture into it; continue to stir until mixture comes to a boil. Then ladle 2 or 3 spoonfuls of the hot pasta-cooking liquid into beaten eggs, stirring constantly. Reduce heat to lowest setting and pour egg mixture into pan. Stirring with a wide spatula, cook just until a little of the egg thickens on bottom of pan. Remove from heat, sprinkle with cheese, and stir until cheese is melted. Mixture should be very creamy.

4. Ladle pasta mixture into 2 warm wide bowls and sprinkle generously with pepper and nutmeg. Season to taste with salt. If desired, drizzle ½ to 1 teaspoon truffle oil over each serving.

PER SERVING: 796 calories, 36 g total fat, 20 g saturated fat, 323 mg cholesterol, 1,410 mg sodium, 73 g carbohydrates, 2 g fiber, 45 g protein, 605 mg calcium, 4 mg iron

Gemelli with Tuna, Basil, Lemon & Crisp-fried Shallots

Fresh basil and lemon dress up canned tuna in a quick sauce for gemelli ("twins")— thin, twisted-together double pasta strands. To enjoy this dish at its best, try a gourmet Italian tuna packed in olive oil; the wonderful flavor is worth the extra cost. Crisp-fried sliced shallots add a crunchy finishing touch.

25 MINUTES

⅓ cup very thinly sliced shallots

All-purpose flour

6 ounces dried gemelli

2 tablespoons vegetable oil

Salt

1 can (about 6 oz.) oil-packed albacore tuna

1 large clove garlic, minced or pressed

1 teaspoon finely shredded lemon peel

About 2 teaspoons lemon juice

¼ cup slivered fresh basil

Basil sprigs

1. Place shallots in a small bowl; sprinkle with a little flour, then shake off excess.

2. In a covered 3- to 4-quart pan, bring about 2 quarts water to a boil over high heat; stir in pasta and cook, uncovered, until just tender to bite (8 to 10 minutes). Or cook pasta according to package directions.

3. Meanwhile, heat oil in a small frying pan over medium-high heat. Add shallots and stir until golden and crisp (1 to 1½ minutes). Remove shallots from pan with a slotted spoon and drain on paper towels. Sprinkle lightly with salt; set aside. Discard oil.

4. Drain tuna; pour about 1 tablespoon oil from can into pan used to fry shallots (discard remaining tuna oil). Add garlic; swirl pan over medium-high heat until garlic is fragrant (about 30 seconds). Add drained tuna, lemon peel, 2 teaspoons of the lemon juice, and slivered basil; stir often, using a fork to separate tuna into flakes, just until tuna is heated through (about 2 minutes).

5. Drain pasta well, then return to cooking pan. Top with tuna sauce and mix gently, using 2 forks. Add more lemon juice to taste, if desired. Divide pasta mixture between 2 warm plates. Sprinkle with fried shallots and garnish with basil sprigs.

PER SERVING: 630 calories, 22 g total fat, 3 g saturated fat, 25 mg cholesterol, 337 mg sodium, 73 g carbohydrates, 3 g fiber, 34 g protein, 52 mg calcium, 5 mg iron

Tagliarini with Pan-browned Scallops, Corn & Basil Beurre Blanc

Here's a memorable entrée for a formal dinner. Large, succulent sea scallops are quickly seared, then set atop a bed of tagliarini and bright vegetables tossed in a silky wine-and-butter reduction. To balance the richness of the main course, you might start the meal with baby greens in vinaigrette and conclude with lemon sorbet topped with shredded fresh mint.

30 MINUTES

Tagliarini with Pan-browned Scallops, Corn & Basil Beurre Blanc

3 tablespoons fat-free reduced-sodium chicken broth

3 tablespoons dry white wine

1 tablespoon white wine vinegar

1 tablespoon minced shallots

1 large clove garlic, minced or pressed

3 tablespoons whipping cream

2 tablespoons butter

6 ounces dried tagliarini

6 sea scallops (about 8 oz. *total*), *each* 1½ to 2 inches in diameter

Salt and freshly ground pepper

1 tablespoon olive oil

½ cup slivered red bell pepper

½ cup fresh or frozen yellow corn kernels

½ cup lightly packed tiny whole fresh basil leaves

1. To make beurre blanc, mix broth, wine, vinegar, shallots, and garlic in a 1½-quart pan. Bring to a boil over high heat; boil until reduced by half (about 5 minutes). Add cream; again boil until reduced by half (2 to 3 more minutes). Reduce heat to low; add butter (in a single chunk) and stir constantly until incorporated. Remove from heat and keep warm.

2. Meanwhile, in a covered 3- to 4-quart pan, bring about 2 quarts water to a boil over high heat; stir in pasta and cook, uncovered, until just tender to bite (6 to 8 minutes). Or cook pasta according to package directions.

3. While pasta is cooking, rinse scallops, pat dry, and sprinkle with salt and pepper. Heat oil in a wide nonstick frying pan over medium-high heat. Place scallops in pan, flat side down. Cook for 2 minutes. Then turn over with a spatula and cook until well browned on bottoms and just opaque but still moist in center; cut to test (about 2 more minutes). Transfer to a plate; cover and keep warm.

4. Add bell pepper and corn to pan; cook, stirring often, until pepper is just tender-crisp to bite (1 to 2 minutes).

5. Drain pasta well and return to cooking pan. Add beurre blanc, bell pepper mixture, half the basil leaves, and any scallop juices that have accumulated on plate. Mix gently, using 2 forks. Divide pasta mixture between 2 warm dinner plates. Arrange 3 scallops atop each serving; scatter with remaining basil leaves.

PER SERVING: 709 calories, 28 g total fat, 13 g saturated fat, 93 mg cholesterol, 382 mg sodium, 81 g carbohydrates, 6 g fiber, 34 g protein, 124 mg calcium, 5 mg iron

LINGUINE WITH CLAMS IN GARLIC & CHARDONNAY BROTH

TENDER PASTA STRANDS AND CANNED CLAMS ARE TOSSED WITH A WINE-AND-GARLIC BROTH GENEROUSLY SPECKLED WITH PARSLEY. FOR A SPLASH OF COLOR, SPRINKLE EACH SERVING WITH A CONFETTI OF DICED TOMATO. IF YOU PREFER FRESH PASTA, YOU CAN USE IT IN PLACE OF DRIED; IT WILL COOK IN ABOUT HALF THE TIME. ACCOMPANY WITH CRUSTY COUNTRY BREAD TO SOAK UP THE SAUCE.

15 MINUTES

6 ounces dried linguine

1 can (about 6½ oz.) chopped clams

1 tablespoon olive oil

2 cloves garlic, minced or pressed

2 tablespoons minced shallots

½ cup Chardonnay or other dry white wine

1 bottle (about 8 oz.) clam juice

1½ tablespoons minced parsley

⅛ teaspoon crushed red pepper flakes
Salt

1 small firm-ripe pear-shaped (Roma-type) tomato (about 3 oz.), diced

1. In a covered 3- to 4-quart pan, bring about 2 quarts water to a boil over high heat; stir in pasta and cook, uncovered, until just tender to bite (8 to 10 minutes). Or cook pasta according to package directions.

2. Meanwhile, drain clams, reserving liquid. Set clams and liquid aside. Heat oil in a wide frying pan over medium-high heat; add garlic and swirl pan until garlic is fragrant (about 30 seconds). Add shallots and cook, stirring often, until soft (2 to 3 minutes). Add wine, clam juice, and reserved clam liquid. Increase heat to high and bring to a boil; then boil until liquid is reduced by half (about 10 minutes). Stir in clams, parsley, and red pepper flakes.

3. Drain pasta well, add to clam sauce, and mix gently, using 2 forks. Season to taste with salt. Divide pasta mixture between 2 warm dinner plates and sprinkle with tomato.

PER SERVING: 469 calories, 9 g total fat, 1 g saturated fat, 32 mg cholesterol, 325 mg sodium, 70 g carbohydrates, 3 g fiber, 24 g protein, 100 mg calcium, 17 mg iron

SHELLFISH LINGUINE WITH DRIED TOMATOES & OLIVES IN SAFFRON BROTH

IF YOU'RE FOND OF SEAFOOD, YOU'LL ENJOY THIS HANDSOME ENTRÉE—A COMBINATION OF LINGUINE AND ASSORTED FRESH SHELLFISH IN A FLAVORFUL WINE BROTH THAT'S TINGED A TEMPTING GOLD FROM TOMATOES AND A PINCH OF SAFFRON. TO SAVOR EVERY DROP OF THE BROTH, SERVE THE DISH IN WIDE, SHALLOW BOWLS, AND DON'T FORGET TO OFFER PLENTY OF BREAD.

25 MINUTES

¼ cup oil-packed dried tomatoes

1 clove garlic, minced or pressed

1 small ripe tomato (about 4 oz.), diced

⅛ teaspoon ground saffron

⅓ cup Sauvignon Blanc or other dry white wine

1 cup fat-free reduced-sodium chicken broth

¼ cup oil-cured black ripe olives, pitted

6 ounces dried linguine

8 mussels in shells

8 raw shrimp (16 to 20 per lb.)

6 small hard-shell clams in shell, suitable for steaming

¼ cup lightly packed fresh basil leaves, slivered

Salt

Basil sprigs

1. Drain dried tomatoes, reserving 1 tablespoon of the oil; cut tomatoes into thin slivers and set aside. Heat tomato oil in a 2- to 3-quart pan over medium-high heat. Add garlic and swirl pan until garlic is fragrant (about 30 seconds). Stir in dried tomatoes, fresh tomato, saffron, wine, broth, and olives. Bring to a boil; then reduce heat and simmer, uncovered, for about 10 minutes to blend flavors.

2. Meanwhile, bring about 2 quarts water to a boil in a covered 3- to 4-quart pan over high heat; stir in pasta and cook, uncovered, until just tender to bite (8 to 10 minutes). Or cook pasta according to package directions. Drain well; keep warm.

3. While pasta and broth are cooking, prepare seafood: scrub mussels and pull off beards. Shell, devein, and rinse shrimp. Scrub clams.

4. Add mussels to broth. Cover and simmer for 2 minutes. Add shrimp and clams; continue to simmer until mussels and clams pop open (3 to 5 more minutes). Stir in slivered basil; season to taste with salt. Ladle shellfish and broth over pasta, discarding any unopened mussels and clams. Garnish with basil sprigs.

PER SERVING: 578 calories, 13 g total fat, 1 g saturated fat, 71 mg cholesterol, 1,147 mg sodium, 79 g carbohydrates, 5 g fiber, 30 g protein, 106 mg calcium, 13 mg iron

Shellfish Linguine with Dried Tomatoes & Olives in Saffron Broth

ANGEL HAIR WITH CRAB, ARUGULA & VERMOUTH

CRAB LOVERS WILL ADORE THIS LIGHT, SIMPLE SHOWCASE FOR THEIR FAVORITE SHELLFISH. DELICATE ANGEL HAIR PASTA IS TOPPED WITH A COMBINATION OF GREEN ONIONS, TINY CHERRY TOMATOES, WILTED ARUGULA, AND SWEET CRABMEAT, ALL FLAVORED WITH A TOUCH OF LEMON PEEL AND A SPLASH OF DRY VERMOUTH. YOU MIGHT SERVE THE DISH WITH ARTICHOKE & DRIED TOMATO MÉLANGE ON GREENS (PAGE 36).

15 TO 20 MINUTES

6 ounces dried angel hair pasta (capellini)

2 tablespoons butter or margarine

1 clove garlic, minced or pressed

½ cup thinly sliced green onions

1½ teaspoons finely shredded lemon peel

1 cup whole tiny cherry tomatoes; or 1 cup halved regular-size cherry tomatoes

⅓ cup dry vermouth

8 ounces cooked crabmeat

1 tablespoon lemon juice

2½ cups lightly packed arugula sprigs, cut into 2-inch-wide strips

Salt and freshly ground pepper

Lemon wedges

1. In a covered 3- to 4-quart pan, bring about 2 quarts water to a boil over high heat; stir in pasta and cook, uncovered, until just tender to bite (about 3 minutes). Or cook pasta according to package directions.

2. Meanwhile, melt 1 tablespoon of the butter in a wide frying pan over medium-high heat. Add garlic, onions, lemon peel, tomatoes, and vermouth. Bring to a boil, stirring often; then reduce heat and simmer, uncovered, until tomatoes are slightly softened (about 5 minutes).

3. To pan, add crab, lemon juice, arugula, and remaining 1 tablespoon butter. Stir gently just until crab is heated through and arugula is barely wilted (about 2 more minutes). Season to taste with salt and pepper.

4. Drain pasta well and return to cooking pan. Top with crab sauce and mix gently, using 2 forks. Divide between 2 warm dinner plates and garnish with lemon wedges.

PER SERVING: 606 calories, 15 g total fat, 8 g saturated fat, 144 mg cholesterol, 461 mg sodium, 71 g carbohydrates, 4 g fiber, 36 g protein, 226 mg calcium, 5 mg iron

Vegetarian Entrées

Mashed Parsnips with White Beans & Mesclun Mix (page 202)

VEGETARIAN MONTE CRISTO
THIS HEARTY SANDWICH IS A MEAL IN ITSELF; JUST ADD A SCOOP OF ORANGE SORBET FOR DESSERT. IF YOU BUY THE FRESH MINT AND CILANTRO AT THE MARKET, YOU'LL HAVE LEFTOVERS; USE THEM FOR HERB PESTO TO SPOON OVER PASTA OR MEAT FOR ANOTHER MEAL (YOU CAN FOLLOW A TRADITIONAL BASIL PESTO RECIPE).

30 MINUTES

2 tablespoons olive oil

1 small yellow bell pepper (about 5 oz.), seeded and diced

1 small zucchini (about 4 oz.), chopped

1 medium-size tomato (about 6 oz.), chopped

2 teaspoons minced cilantro

1 teaspoon minced fresh mint

Salt and freshly ground pepper

4 slices white or whole wheat bread (*each* about 1 inch thick)

4 ounces Gruyère cheese, thinly sliced

½ cup milk

1 large egg

4 cilantro sprigs

1. Heat 1 tablespoon of the oil in a wide frying pan over medium-high heat. Add bell pepper and zucchini; cook, stirring often, until vegetables just begin to brown (about 5 minutes). Add tomato, minced cilantro, and mint; stir until heated through. Season to taste with salt and pepper. Remove from heat.

2. Cover 2 slices of the bread with half the cheese; spread vegetable mixture over cheese, dividing equally. Top with remaining cheese, then with remaining 2 slices bread.

3. Rinse and dry pan used to cook vegetables. In a wide, shallow bowl or pie pan, whisk milk with egg to blend.

4. Heat remaining 1 tablespoon oil in frying pan over low heat. Dip sandwiches, one at a time, in egg mixture, turning to coat both sides. Gently press 2 of the cilantro sprigs atop each sandwich. Place sandwiches in oil, cilantro side down. Cover and cook until golden on bottom (about 4 minutes). Turn sandwiches over and continue to cook, covered, until golden on other side (about 3 more minutes). Cut sandwiches into halves to serve.

PER SERVING: 697 calories, 40 g total fat, 15 g saturated fat, 178 mg cholesterol, 721 mg sodium, 55 g carbohydrates, 4 g fiber, 31 g protein, 772 mg calcium, 4 mg iron

TRY TOFU FOR DINNER

Vegetarians and meat-eaters alike enjoy tofu (soybean curd) for a variety of reasons. It's rich in calcium and iron and low in calories, and it has a mild, light taste that's agreeable to all sorts of seasonings. The following five recipes look to tofu's Asian origins for their flavors and ingredients; if any of the foods called for is unavailable in your supermarket, look for it in a health food store or Asian market. These are all one-dish meals, needing only a beverage and dessert as accompaniments. Tropical fruits such as mangoes, litchis, or pineapple make a nice finishing touch, but if you want something fancier, try Thai Banana Split (page 222) or Sparkling Sorbet (page 234).

CRISPY TOFU STEAKS WITH TERIYAKI & SWEET POTATO

25 MINUTES

- 3 tablespoons sake
- 3 tablespoons mirin
- 6 slices peeled sweet potato (*each* 2½ to 3 inches in diameter and ¼ to ½ inch thick; about 5½ oz. *total*)
- 3 tablespoons soy sauce
- 3 tablespoons brown sugar
- 1 cup panko (coarse dry bread crumbs)
- 2 large eggs
- 10 to 12 ounces medium-firm tofu, rinsed and drained
- 4 teaspoons vegetable oil
- 8 ounces packaged triple-washed baby spinach

1. In a 2-quart pan, combine sake, mirin, and sweet potato slices. Bring to a boil over high heat; then reduce heat, cover, and simmer until potato is tender when pierced (8 to 10 minutes). Lift potato slices from pan with a slotted spoon and transfer to 2 warm dinner plates. Add soy sauce and sugar to pan and stir until sugar is dissolved (do not boil). Remove from heat and set aside.

2. While potatoes are cooking, sprinkle bread crumbs on a plate. In a pie pan, beat eggs to blend. Cut block of tofu in half crosswise; then cut each piece in half horizontally. Roll each piece of tofu in crumbs, then in egg, then in crumbs again (use a spatula to turn tofu if it begins to tear).

3. Place tofu in a broiler pan and drizzle with 2 teaspoons of the oil. Broil 2 inches below heat until browned (about 5 minutes). Turn pieces over, drizzle with remaining 2 teaspoons oil, and broil until browned on other side (about 4 more minutes). Arrange tofu on plates alongside sweet potatoes.

4. Shortly before tofu is done, combine spinach with 2 tablespoons water in a 3-quart pan. Cover and cook over low heat until spinach is wilted (about 5 minutes).

5. Lift spinach from pan; arrange on plates with tofu and sweet potatoes. Spoon soy mixture around tofu and over vegetables.

PER SERVING: 701 calories, 23 g total fat, 4 g saturated fat, 213 mg cholesterol, 1,935 mg sodium, 89 g carbohydrates, 12 g fiber, 28 g protein, 307 mg calcium, 15 mg iron

TOFU SALAD SANDWICHES

15 MINUTES

- 7 to 8 ounces firm tofu, rinsed and drained
- ¾ teaspoon curry powder
- ¼ teaspoon ground cumin
- ⅓ cup mayonnaise
- 3 tablespoons minced red onion
- 1 small clove garlic, minced
- 1½ tablespoons chopped cilantro
  Salt and freshly ground pepper
- 4 slices white or whole wheat bread
- 1 large tomato (about 8 oz.), sliced

1. In a medium-size bowl, mash tofu, curry powder, and cumin with a fork until largest pieces are the size of a pea. Mix in mayonnaise, onion, garlic, and cilantro. Season generously with salt and pepper.

2. Spread tofu mixture over 2 slices of the bread. Top with tomato, then remaining 2 slices bread. Cut into halves or quarters to serve.

PER SERVING: 583 calories, 40 g total fat, 6 g saturated fat, 22 mg cholesterol, 503 mg sodium, 38 g carbohydrates, 6 g fiber, 23 g protein, 805 mg calcium, 14 mg iron

SESAME TOFU WITH GREEN BEANS

20 MINUTES

- 2½ tablespoons soy sauce
- 2 teaspoons Dijon mustard
- 1½ teaspoons Asian sesame oil
- 1 tablespoon minced green onion
- 8 ounces firm tofu, rinsed and drained
- 4 ounces thin green beans (ends removed)
- 1 large egg
- 1½ tablespoons sesame seeds
- 1 tablespoon olive oil

1. In a bowl, stir together 1½ tablespoons of the soy sauce, mustard, sesame oil, and onion. Spoon half the sauce into center of 2 dinner plates; set remaining sauce aside.

2. Cut tofu into ¾- by ¾- by 4-inch logs; roll in remaining 1 tablespoon soy sauce to coat. Set aside.

3. In a covered 2-quart pan, bring about 1 inch of water to a boil over high heat. Drop beans into boiling water; return to a boil and cook, uncovered, until tender-crisp when pierced (3 to 5 minutes). Drain.

4. When you begin heating water for beans, beat egg to blend in a small bowl. Spread sesame seeds on a plate. Dip one side of each piece of tofu first in egg, then in seeds to coat. Heat olive oil in a wide frying pan over medium-high heat. Add tofu, seed side down. Cook until seeds are golden brown (about 5 minutes). Then turn pieces to cook remaining sides just until hot (about 1 minute per side). Mound tofu pieces in the circles of sauce on dinner plates.

5. Add remaining sauce to beans; mix gently. Sprinkle beans over tofu.

PER SERVING: 366 calories, 26 g total fat, 4 g saturated fat, 106 mg cholesterol, 1,458 mg sodium, 13 g carbohydrates, 4 g fiber, 24 g protein, 880 mg calcium, 14 mg iron

YUDOFU (SIMMERING TOFU)

20 MINUTES

- 1 piece (about 4 inches square) giant kelp (kombu)
- 6 ounces packaged triple-washed baby spinach
- 1 pound medium-firm tofu, rinsed and drained
- 2 teaspoons finely chopped green onion
- 2 teaspoons grated white radish (daikon)

- 2 teaspoons dried bonito flakes
- 1 teaspoon grated fresh ginger
  Dipping Sauce (below)

DIPPING SAUCE

- ½ cup water
- 3 tablespoons mirin
- 2 tablespoons soy sauce
- ½ teaspoon sugar
- ¼ cup dried bonito flakes

1. Cut square of kelp into quarters. Place kelp and spinach in a 3- to 4-quart pan. Cut tofu into 12 equal pieces; gently place atop kelp and spinach. Add enough water to cover tofu. Cover pan and bring water to a simmer over medium heat.

2. Meanwhile, place condiments—onion, radish, the 2 teaspoons bonito flakes, and ginger—in mounds on 2 small plates, dividing equally. Set one plate at each diner's place.

3. Prepare Dipping Sauce. Place one bowl of steaming sauce at each diner's place.

4. To serve, ladle hot water, tofu, kelp (if desired), and spinach equally into 2 warm large, deep soup bowls. Each diner mixes condiments into his or her dipping sauce, then lifts foods from water (using chopsticks or a fork) to dip into sauce.

DIPPING SAUCE

In a small pan, combine ½ cup water, mirin, soy sauce, and sugar. Bring to a simmer over medium-high heat (do not boil). Remove pan from heat and stir in the ¼ cup bonito flakes. Pour sauce through a fine wire strainer into 2 small bowls (about 1-cup size), dividing equally; discard bonito flakes.

PER SERVING: 292 calories, 11 g total fat, 2 g saturated fat, 2 mg cholesterol, 1,212 mg sodium, 25 g carbohydrates, 8 g fiber, 22 g protein, 306 mg calcium, 16 mg iron

THAI BASIL TOFU

25 MINUTES

- 8 ounces medium-firm tofu, rinsed and drained
- 1 small onion (about 4 oz.)
- 4 ounces asparagus
- 2 tablespoons vegetable oil
- 1 clove garlic, minced or pressed
- 2 teaspoons minced fresh ginger
- ⅓ cup canned coconut milk
- 1½ tablespoons soy sauce
- 1½ tablespoons unseasoned rice vinegar
- 2 teaspoons Asian fish sauce (*nuoc mam* or *nam pla*)
- ¼ to ½ teaspoon crushed red pepper flakes
- ½ cup lightly packed slivered fresh basil
  Basil sprigs

1. Cut tofu into 16 equal pieces. Set aside.

2. Cut onion into wedges about the same thickness as asparagus spears. Snap off and discard tough ends of asparagus, then cut spears diagonally to the same length as onion wedges.

3. Heat oil in a wide frying pan over medium-high heat. Add onion, asparagus, garlic, and ginger; cook, stirring often, until onion is light golden (about 5 minutes). Spoon asparagus mixture into a bowl and set aside.

4. To pan, add tofu, coconut milk, soy sauce, vinegar, fish sauce, and red pepper flakes. Bring to a boil over high heat; then boil, stirring, until liquid is reduced by a third (about 5 minutes). Return asparagus mixture to pan and stir to coat with sauce. Add slivered basil; stir to heat through. Garnish with basil sprigs.

PER SERVING: 347 calories, 28 g total fat, 10 g saturated fat, 0 mg cholesterol, 988 mg sodium, 15 g carbohydrates, 4 g fiber, 15 g protein, 204 mg calcium, 9 mg iron

COLLARD GREEN ROLLS

CANNED CORN SPEEDS UP THE ASSEMBLY OF THESE GRAIN- AND VEGETABLE-STUFFED GREENS, BUT USE FRESH KERNELS CUT FROM THE COB IF YOU PREFER. WARM ROASTED ALMONDS MAKE A CRISP, RICH COMPLEMENT TO THE COLLARD ROLLS. FOR DESSERT, OFFER CHOCOLATE OR PEANUT BUTTER ICE CREAM TOPPED WITH CRUSHED PRALINE OR NUT BRITTLE. IN PLACE OF COLLARDS, YOU CAN USE OTHER GREENS, SUCH AS CABBAGE OR CHARD; IF THE LEAVES ARE SMALL, OVERLAP THEM TO MAKE THE ROLLS.

30 MINUTES

4 ounces shiitake mushrooms

½ cup quinoa

1¼ cups regular-strength vegetable broth

Salt and freshly ground pepper

2 large collard green leaves

3 tablespoons olive oil

⅔ cup diced yellow summer squash

½ cup chopped onion

⅔ cup drained canned corn kernels

½ cup diced avocado

½ teaspoon white wine vinegar

Lemon wedges

1. Rinse mushrooms, then trim and discard bruised stem ends. Slice mushrooms and set aside.

2. Rinse quinoa in a strainer under running water. Drain, place in a 2- to 3-quart pan, and add 1 cup of the broth; bring to a boil over high heat. Reduce heat, cover, and simmer until broth has been absorbed and quinoa is tender to bite (10 to 12 minutes). Season to taste with salt and pepper; remove from heat and keep warm.

3. While quinoa is cooking, bring about ¾ inch of water to a boil in a wide frying pan over high heat. Cut stems from collard leaves; chop and reserve. Submerge leaves in boiling water and cook until a brighter green in color (about 2 minutes). With tongs, lift greens from water and place on paper or cloth towels to drain; pat dry and set aside.

4. Rinse and dry frying pan, then heat oil in pan over medium-high heat. Add mushrooms, squash, onion, and collard stems. Cook, stirring occasionally, until onion begins to brown and all vegetables are tender when pierced (about 5 minutes). Stir in corn and avocado; season to taste with salt and pepper. Stir ¾ cup of the vegetable mixture into quinoa. Set remaining vegetable mixture aside; keep warm.

5. Lay cooked collard greens out flat on a board. Cut out and discard tough stem bases from leaves. To stuff leaves, pull cut ends at leaf bases together to overlap. Place half the quinoa-vegetable mixture at base of each leaf. Starting at this end, roll up leaf, folding in sides as you go. Cut each roll in half diagonally; place on a warm dinner plate.

6. Stir vinegar and remaining ¼ cup broth into remaining vegetable mixture. Surround collard rolls with vegetable mixture. Offer lemon wedges and salt to season rolls to taste.

PER SERVING: 504 calories, 30 g total fat, 4 g saturated fat, 0 mg cholesterol, 783 mg sodium, 55 g carbohydrates, 11 g fiber, 10 g protein, 62 mg calcium, 6 mg iron

HERO SANDWICHES WITH ITALIAN BEAN PURÉE

HAVE PLENTY OF NAPKINS ON THE TABLE WHEN YOU SERVE THESE HEAVYWEIGHT SANDWICHES. THEY'RE REALLY BIG, THE SIZE THE DELI SERVES—YOU MIGHT WANT TO SAVE HALF FOR LATER. OFFER ORANGES OR TANGERINES TO PEEL FOR DESSERT.

30 MINUTES

2 crunchy-crusted sandwich rolls (*each* about 5 inches in diameter)

6 tablespoons olive oil

12 ounces portabella mushrooms, stems trimmed to ½ inch, caps thinly sliced

Salt and freshly ground pepper

⅔ cup rinsed, drained canned cannellini (white kidney beans)

1 clove garlic, minced or pressed

1 teaspoon lemon juice

2 canned or bottled whole roasted red peppers, drained

1 cup lightly packed fresh basil leaves

1 very large yellow tomato (about 12 oz.), sliced

½ small (about 4-oz.) red onion, thinly sliced and separated into rings

1. Cut each roll in half horizontally. With a serrated knife, carefully cut out the inside of each roll half (in a single piece, if possible), leaving a shell about ¼ inch thick. Set roll halves and removed bread aside.

2. Heat 3 tablespoons of the oil in a wide frying pan over medium-high heat. Add mushrooms and cook, stirring often, until soft (about 6 minutes). Sprinkle with salt and pepper, remove from pan, and set aside.

3. To make bean purée, pour beans into pan used for mushrooms. Add remaining 3 tablespoons oil, garlic, and lemon juice; mash with a fork. Season to taste with salt and pepper. Remove from heat.

4. Spread bean purée over bottom halves of rolls, dividing equally. Top with red peppers; sprinkle with salt and pepper, then with half the basil. Top with a layer of the bread removed from inside of roll halves, using half of it. Top with mushrooms, then remaining bread from inside of roll halves. Finally, layer on tomato and onion; sprinkle with salt, pepper, and remaining basil. Add top halves of rolls. To serve, cut sandwiches into halves with a serrated knife.

PER SERVING: 723 calories, 45 g total fat, 6 g saturated fat, 0 mg cholesterol, 568 mg sodium, 69 g carbohydrates, 13 g fiber, 18 g protein, 206 mg calcium, 7 mg iron

SPRING VEGETABLE PLATTER WITH MINT AÏOLI

PACKAGED BABY CARROTS ARE A BOON TO THE TIME-CONSCIOUS COOK. HERE, THEIR CRISPNESS OFFERS A PLEASANT CONTRAST TO THE SOFTER TEXTURES OF BOILED EGGS AND POTATOES. TO SAVE EVEN MORE TIME, YOU CAN SUBSTITUTE RINSED, CRISPED INNER ROMAINE LETTUCE LEAVES FOR THE ASPARAGUS. THINK OF CANDIED LACE BOWLS (PAGE 220) FILLED WITH CHOCOLATE ICE CREAM FOR DESSERT.

30 MINUTES

KOHLRABI FRITTERS

EASTERN EUROPEAN IN ORIGIN, THESE FRITTERS GO NICELY WITH SLICED CUCUMBERS AND WATERCRESS (MAKE A DOUBLE PORTION OF THE LEMON SAUCE AND USE HALF FOR DRESSING THE CUCUMBERS). SERVE BAKED APPLES WITH CHERRY SAUCE AND CREAM FOR DESSERT, OR SIMPLY OFFER A BOWL OF ICED CHERRIES—THEY'RE DELICIOUS WITH THE CHÈVRE.

30 MINUTES

8 ounces kohlrabi or zucchini

¼ cup all-purpose flour

1 large egg, beaten

1 tablespoon minced fresh dill

1 teaspoon grated lemon peel

Salt and freshly ground pepper

1 tablespoon olive oil

1 tablespoon lemon juice

1 teaspoon sugar

Soft fresh chèvre (such as Montrachet or Couturier) or sour cream

Dill sprigs (optional)

1. Break stems from kohlrabi. Cut stem bases from leaves and discard. Using a food processor, coarsely grate kohlrabi bulbs and finely chop leaves. Place in a bowl. Add flour, egg, minced dill, and lemon peel; mix well. Season to taste with salt and pepper.

2. Heat oil in a wide frying pan over medium heat. Spoon 3-tablespoon portions of kohlrabi mixture into hot oil; flatten each fritter to ½ inch thick. Cook fritters until golden on bottom (about 5 minutes); then turn over and continue to cook until golden on other side (2 to 3 more minutes).

3. Meanwhile, to prepare lemon sauce, stir together lemon juice, sugar, and ½ teaspoon salt in a small bowl until sugar and salt are dissolved.

4. To serve, divide fritters between 2 warm dinner plates. Serve with chèvre, lemon sauce, and additional pepper to grind over everything. Garnish with dill sprigs, if desired.

PER SERVING: 184 calories, 9 g total fat, 2 g saturated fat, 106 mg cholesterol, 627 mg sodium, 19 g carbohydrates, 1 g fiber, 6 g protein, 35 mg calcium, 1 mg iron

Kohlrabi Fritters

Bok Choy & Tofu with Spelt-Onion Pancakes

VEGETARIAN ENTRÉES

BOK CHOY & TOFU WITH SPELT-ONION PANCAKES

TEAR THESE CHINESE ONION PANCAKES INTO PIECES TO WRAP AROUND SAUTÉED BOK CHOY AND TOFU IN A SOY-BASED SAUCE; OR EAT THE PANCAKES ALONGSIDE THE FILLING. YOU CAN SUBSTITUTE BROCCOLI OR ASPARAGUS FOR BOK CHOY. YOU'LL FIND SPELT FLOUR IN HEALTH AND NATURAL FOOD STORES.

30 MINUTES

Spelt-Onion Pancakes (below)

8 ounces medium-firm tofu, rinsed and drained

2 teaspoons vegetable oil

8 ounces baby bok choy

2 tablespoons regular-strength vegetable broth

2 tablespoons soy sauce

1 tablespoon unseasoned rice vinegar

1½ teaspoons sugar

½ teaspoon Asian sesame oil

SPELT-ONION PANCAKES

1 large egg

½ cup regular-strength vegetable broth

⅓ cup spelt flour

⅓ cup all-purpose flour

¼ teaspoon baking powder

1 teaspoon Asian sesame oil
Salt

2 teaspoons vegetable oil

⅓ cup thinly sliced green onions

1. Prepare Spelt-Onion Pancakes. Wipe pan clean.

2. Cut tofu into 12 equal pieces. In frying pan used for pancakes, heat 2 teaspoons vegetable oil over medium-low heat. Add bok choy, cover, and cook for 5 minutes, stirring once. Push bok choy to one side of pan; add tofu to other side. Pour the 2 tablespoons broth over all, cover, and cook until tofu is heated through (about 4 minutes).

3. While bok choy and tofu are cooking, stir together soy sauce, vinegar, sugar, and the ½ teaspoon sesame oil in a small bowl.

4. Lift bok choy from pan and drain briefly; then place on 2 warm dinner plates, dividing equally. Pour soy mixture over tofu in pan; then, with a spatula, lift tofu from pan and divide between plates. Pour sauce from pan over tofu and bok choy. Serve with pancakes, tearing them into pieces to eat plain or to wrap around bok choy and tofu.

SPELT-ONION PANCAKES

1. In a small bowl, whisk together egg, the ½ cup broth, spelt flour, all-purpose flour, baking powder, and the 1 teaspoon sesame oil until smooth. Season to taste with salt.

2. Heat 1 teaspoon of the vegetable oil in a 9-inch frying pan over medium-high heat. Pour half the batter into pan and swirl to cover pan bottom; sprinkle with half the onions. Cook until pancake looks slightly dry on top (about 2 minutes); then turn over and cook on other side (about 1 more minute). Remove pancake to a warm plate. Repeat to cook second pancake, using remaining 1 teaspoon vegetable oil, remaining batter, and remaining onions. Cover pancakes with a pan lid to keep warm.

PER SERVING: 433 calories, 22 g total fat, 3 g saturated fat, 106 mg cholesterol, 1,518 mg sodium, 42 g carbohydrates, 5 g fiber, 20 g protein, 302 mg calcium, 10 mg iron

GOLDEN EGGS & ONIONS ON ITALIAN TOAST

THIS RECIPE'S SIMPLICITY AND SPEED OF PREPARATION ARE REMINDERS THAT FEW STAPLE INGREDIENTS ARE MORE USEFUL THAN EGGS FOR SPUR-OF-THE-MOMENT MEALS. FRESH PEARS AND SQUARES OF GOOD DARK OR MILK CHOCOLATE MAKE A PLEASING DESSERT.

20 TO 25 MINUTES

1 tablespoon butter or margarine

8 ounces onions, thinly sliced

½ cup regular-strength vegetable broth

2 tablespoons all-purpose flour

½ cup milk

3 hard-cooked large eggs, chopped
Salt

4 slices crusty Italian bread (*each about ¾ inch thick*), toasted
Minced parsley

1. Melt butter in a wide frying pan over medium-high heat. Add onions and cook, stirring often, until soft and lightly browned (7 to 10 minutes).

2. In a small bowl, mix a little of the broth with flour to make a smooth paste; then add this mixture to remaining broth, stir to blend, and mix into onion mixture. Add milk, increase heat to high, and stir until mixture boils; then boil and stir for 2 more minutes.

3. Stir eggs into sauce and season to taste with salt. Place 2 slices of toast on each warm dinner plate; spoon egg mixture over toast and sprinkle with parsley.

PER SERVING: 435 calories, 18 g total fat, 8 g saturated fat, 343 mg cholesterol, 766 mg sodium, 49 g carbohydrates, 4 g fiber, 19 g protein, 180 mg calcium, 3 mg iron

SCRAMBLED EGGS WITH KALE & PARMESAN

WITH OR WITHOUT THE CRISP, BUTTERY TOAST CUPS, THESE EGGS MAKE A NOURISHING MEAL AT ANY TIME OF DAY. ACCOMPANY WITH SALAD GREENS OR STEAMED FRESH ASPARAGUS. YOU'LL NEED JUST ONE KALE LEAF FOR THE EGGS; USE THE REST OF THE BUNCH IN ANY RECIPE CALLING FOR KALE, COLLARD OR BEET GREENS, SWISS CHARD, OR SPINACH. IF YOU SERVE THE DISH FOR LUNCH OR SUPPER, YOU MIGHT CONCLUDE THE MEAL WITH GINGERSNAP ICE CREAM SANDWICHES.

30 MINUTES

Scrambled Eggs with Kale & Parmesan

Toast Cups (below)

1 kale leaf

2 teaspoons butter or margarine

¼ cup chopped onion

Salt and freshly ground pepper

4 large eggs

1 tablespoon water

3 tablespoons freshly grated
Parmesan cheese

2 tablespoons chopped tomato

TOAST CUPS

2 slices soft white or whole wheat
bread (*each* about ¼ inch thick)

1 tablespoon butter or margarine,
melted

1. Prepare Toast Cups; place one on each warm dinner plate.

2. While cups are baking, cut out stem from kale leaf. Chop stem; cut leaf into thin strips.

3. Melt the 2 teaspoons butter in a wide frying pan over medium-high heat. Add chopped kale stem and onion; cook, stirring often, until onion is tender and kale stem is tender-crisp to bite (about 7 minutes). Add slivered kale leaf and stir until wilted (about 2 minutes). Season to taste with salt and pepper and remove from heat.

4. In a bowl, whisk together eggs and water to blend. Place pan with kale mixture over high heat and pour eggs over vegetables. Cook, lifting cooked portion to allow uncooked eggs to flow underneath, until about half the eggs are set. Sprinkle cheese over eggs and continue to cook and stir until eggs are almost set.

5. Spoon eggs into Toast Cups and sprinkle with tomato.

TOAST CUPS

Brush both sides of each slice of bread with the 1 tablespoon melted butter. Gently press each slice into a 2½-inch muffin cup, letting edges extend beyond top of cup. Bake in a 400° oven until bread is golden (8 to 10 minutes).

PER SERVING: 326 calories, 23 g total fat, 11 g saturated fat, 457 mg cholesterol, 450 mg sodium, 13 g carbohydrates, 1 g fiber, 18 g protein, 204 mg calcium, 2 mg iron

PILAF WITH BAKED EGGS
Eggs baked in a savory pilaf enriched with Swiss cheese make a satisfying lunch or supper. Accompany with arugula in a balsamic vinaigrette, and serve biscotti and espresso to end the meal.

30 MINUTES

1 tablespoon butter or margarine

⅓ cup finely chopped shallots

⅔ cup quick-cooking barley

1 cup regular-strength vegetable broth

¼ teaspoon dried marjoram

½ cup shredded Swiss cheese

Salt and freshly ground pepper

2 large eggs

1 small pear-shaped (Roma-type) tomato (about 3 oz.), cut into ¼-inch-thick slices

1. In an 8- to 10-inch frying pan with an ovenproof handle, melt butter over high heat. Add shallots and cook, stirring, until lightly browned (about 3 minutes). Add barley and stir until lightly toasted (about 2 minutes). Add broth and marjoram; bring to a boil, stirring. Then reduce heat, cover, and simmer, stirring occasionally, until barley is tender to bite (about 12 minutes). Stir about half the cheese into pilaf; season to taste with salt and pepper.

2. Using back of a spoon, make 2 deep wells in pilaf. Crack eggs, one at a time, into a small dish; slide one egg into each well. Arrange tomato around eggs.

3. Bake in a 400° oven until egg whites are set and yolks are as firm as you like (about 8 minutes for liquid yolks). About 3 minutes before eggs are done, sprinkle with remaining cheese. To serve, scoop onto plates with a wide spatula.

PER SERVING: 442 calories, 20 g total fat, 10 g saturated fat, 255 mg cholesterol, 703 mg sodium, 46 g carbohydrates, 6 g fiber, 21 g protein, 322 mg calcium, 2 mg iron

Pilaf with Baked Eggs

WINTER VEGETABLE HASH

THIS SWEET-TASTING HASH OF STURDY ROOT VEGETABLES—PARSNIP, YAM, CARROT, AND ONION—IS A FILLING MEAL WITH OR WITHOUT THE OPTIONAL POACHED EGGS. SERVE WITH BUTTERED TOAST, INNER ROMAINE LETTUCE LEAVES, AND PICKLED BEETS. OFFER YOUR FAVORITE FRUIT ICE FOR DESSERT.

20 MINUTES

3 tablespoons olive oil

¾ cup baby or baby-cut carrots

1 large onion (about 8 oz.), coarsely chopped

12 ounces parsnips (about 3 medium-size)

1 medium-size yam or sweet potato (about 8 oz.)

Poached Eggs (optional; below)

Salt and freshly ground pepper

Minced parsley

Capers or minced dill pickle

POACHED EGGS

1 tablespoon vinegar

2 large eggs

1. Heat oil in a wide frying pan over medium-high heat. Add carrots and onion; cook for 4 to 5 minutes, stirring occasionally to prevent scorching. Meanwhile, peel parsnips and yam and cut into ¾-inch cubes.

2. Add parsnips and yam to pan; cover and continue to cook until all vegetables are golden brown and yam mashes easily when pressed (about 10 minutes), stirring occasionally to prevent vegetables from sticking.

3. About 5 minutes before vegetables are done, prepare Poached Eggs, if desired.

4. To serve, season hash to taste with salt and pepper and spoon onto 2 warm dinner plates. Slide an egg onto each serving of hash, if desired. Garnish with parsley and capers.

POACHED EGGS

In a 2-quart pan, bring about 2 inches of water to a boil over high heat. Reduce heat to a simmer and add vinegar. Crack eggs, one at a time, into a small dish; then gently slide them into boiling water. Return to a simmer; then simmer, uncovered, until whites are set but yolks are still soft (about 3 minutes). Lift from water with a slotted spoon, draining off as much water as possible. Keep warm in a warm bowl, if needed.

PER SERVING WITHOUT EGGS: 454 calories, 21 g total fat, 3 g saturated fat, 0 mg cholesterol, 65 mg sodium, 63 g carbohydrates, 11 g fiber, 5 g protein, 116 mg calcium, 2 mg iron

MASHED PARSNIPS WITH
WHITE BEANS & MESCLUN MIX

Pictured on page 185

FRENCH MESCLUN MIX (OFTEN SOLD AS "SPRING MIX" OR "WINTER MIX") IS AVAILABLE LOOSE OR IN PACKAGES IN MOST WELL-STOCKED SUPERMARKETS. HERE, IT'S SERVED WITH SIMPLY SEASONED MASHED PARSNIPS AND CREAMY-TEXTURED WHITE BEANS. ACCOMPANY WITH WEDGES OF SOFT FLATBREAD OR PITA BREAD. OFFER MELON SLICES AND CANDIED GINGER TO FINISH.

20 MINUTES

12 ounces parsnips (about 3 medium-size)

5 tablespoons olive oil

Salt and freshly ground pepper

1 can (about 15 oz.) cannellini (white kidney beans) or other large white beans, rinsed and drained

3 tablespoons lemon juice

1 clove garlic, minced or pressed

¼ cup minced arugula

2 cups lightly packed mesclun mix, rinsed and crisped

1. Peel parsnips and slice ½ inch thick. Place in a 1- to 2-quart pan and add enough water to cover. Bring to a boil over high heat; then reduce heat, cover, and simmer until tender when pierced (about 5 minutes). Drain. Transfer to a food processor, add 1 tablespoon of the oil, and whirl until puréed. Season to taste with salt and pepper.

2. While parsnips are cooking, mix beans, remaining ¼ cup oil, lemon juice, garlic, and arugula in a small bowl. Season to taste with salt and pepper.

3. Spoon parsnip purée onto 2 warm dinner plates. Lift beans from dressing and spoon evenly atop purée. Add mesclun mix to dressing remaining in bowl and toss to mix; serve with parsnips and beans.

PER SERVING: 586 calories, 36 g total fat, 5 g saturated fat, 0 mg cholesterol, 292 mg sodium, 55 g carbohydrates, 16 g fiber, 14 g protein, 165 mg calcium, 4 mg iron

RED LENTIL & ESCAROLE STEW

RED LENTILS, GREEN ESCAROLE, AND BRIGHT FRESH TOMATO MAKE THIS WARMING STEW PRETTY TO LOOK AT. BE SURE YOU USE DECORTICATED (HULLED) RED LENTILS; THEY COOK TWICE AS FAST AS REGULAR BROWN ONES. IF YOU LIKE, REPLACE THE ESCAROLE WITH BEET GREENS, SWISS CHARD, OR KALE. STIRRING BUTTER IN AT THE END IS OPTIONAL, BUT IT GIVES THE DISH AN ALMOST SATINY TEXTURE. FOR DESSERT, NIBBLE ON DATES WITH HALVAH OR CHÈVRE.

30 MINUTES

Red Lentil & Escarole Stew

2 teaspoons butter or margarine

1 small onion (about 4 oz.), chopped

¼ cup chopped carrot

1 clove garlic, minced or pressed

¾ cup Red Chief or other red lentils

3 cups regular-strength vegetable broth

6 cups lightly packed escarole (cut crosswise into 1-inch strips)

1 large tomato (about 8 oz.), chopped

2 tablespoons dry sherry

½ teaspoon crumbled dried rosemary

1 tablespoon butter or margarine (optional)

Salt and freshly ground pepper

1. Melt the 2 teaspoons butter in a 3-quart pan over medium-high heat. Add onion, carrot, and garlic; stir often until vegetables begin to brown (5 to 7 minutes). Meanwhile, sort lentils and discard any debris; then rinse and drain.

2. Add lentils and broth to pan with vegetables. Bring to a boil; then reduce heat and simmer, uncovered, until lentils are almost tender to bite (about 10 minutes). Add escarole and stir until wilted (about 5 minutes).

3. Increase heat to high and bring stew to a boil. Add tomato, sherry, and rosemary. Return to a boil; add the 1 tablespoon butter, if desired, and stir until mixture looks creamy (about 2 minutes). Season to taste with salt and pepper.

PER SERVING: 419 calories, 7 g total fat, 3 g saturated fat, 10 mg cholesterol, 1,614 mg sodium, 66 g carbohydrates, 16 g fiber, 25 g protein, 183 mg calcium, 9 mg iron

POLENTA WITH EGGS & PESTO

PREPARED POLENTA ROLL COMES IN TWO WEIGHTS AND DIAMETERS; THE SLIMMER (ABOUT 2-INCH-WIDE) 1-POUND SIZE IS THE RIGHT ONE FOR THIS RECIPE. END THE MEAL WITH PEARS AND A WEDGE OF IMPORTED PARMESAN CHEESE.

20 MINUTES

Pesto Sauce (below)

2 teaspoons olive oil

4 slices prepared plain polenta roll (*each* about ¾ inch thick)

1 or 2 canned or bottled whole roasted red peppers, torn into halves or thirds

2 tablespoons white wine vinegar

4 large eggs

4 canned anchovy fillets, drained well

2 teaspoons drained capers

PESTO SAUCE

½ cup lightly packed fresh basil leaves

¼ cup grated Parmesan cheese

3 tablespoons olive oil

1 small clove garlic, minced or pressed

Salt and freshly ground pepper

1. Prepare Pesto Sauce and set aside.

2. In a 2- to 3-quart pan, bring about 2 inches of water to a boil over high heat; reduce heat, cover, and keep at a simmer until needed.

3. Heat the 2 teaspoons oil in a wide frying pan over medium-high heat. Add polenta slices and cook, turning once, until browned and crusty on both sides (7 to 10 minutes). Add red peppers to pan and stir gently just until warm.

4. When polenta is almost ready, add vinegar to simmering water. Crack eggs, one at a time, into a small dish and gently slide them into water. Return water to a simmer; then simmer, uncovered, until whites are set but yolks are still soft (about 3 minutes). Lift eggs from water with a slotted spoon, draining off as much water as possible. Keep warm in a warm bowl, if needed.

5. Place 2 polenta slices on each warm dinner plate. Spoon Pesto Sauce over polenta and drape with red peppers; then top each serving with 2 poached eggs. Garnish with anchovies and capers.

PESTO SAUCE

In a food processor, combine basil, cheese, the 3 tablespoons oil, and garlic. Whirl until basil is finely chopped; season to taste with salt and pepper.

PER SERVING: 549 calories, 39 g total fat, 9 g saturated fat, 439 mg cholesterol, 1,059 mg sodium, 25 g carbohydrates, 4 g fiber, 23 g protein, 286 mg calcium, 4 mg iron

YELLOW SQUASH & CORN PUDDING

FROZEN CORN KERNELS ARE A TIME-SAVER WHEN YOU MAKE THIS PUDDING. SERVE IT WITH A CRISP SALAD OR TOP WITH WILTED GREENS. WHILE THE PUDDING BAKES, MAKE THE MOST OF THE OVEN BY BAKING CORED APPLES WITH MAPLE SYRUP FOR DESSERT (TOP THEM WITH ICE CREAM OR HEAVY CREAM).

30 MINUTES

2 tablespoons butter or margarine

1 large onion (about 8 oz.), sliced

8 ounces yellow summer squash, diced

½ teaspoon dried thyme

Salt

½ cup whole milk or whipping cream

1 cup frozen corn kernels

1 large egg

2 tablespoons all-purpose flour

½ cup grated Parmesan cheese

1. Melt butter in a wide frying pan over medium-high heat. Add onion, squash, thyme, and a pinch of salt; cook, stirring occasionally to keep vegetables from sticking, until onion and squash are tender to bite (10 to 15 minutes).

2. When vegetables are almost tender, heat milk and corn in a small pan over high heat (or in a bowl in the microwave) until steaming. In a medium-size bowl, whisk egg and flour until smooth. Slowly blend in milk and corn, whisking constantly. Then stir in onion mixture and ⅓ cup of the cheese; season to taste with salt.

3. Evenly spoon batter into 2 buttered individual gratin dishes (about 2-cup size) or a 4- to 5-cup casserole. Sprinkle with remaining cheese. Bake in a 400° oven until firm to the touch (about 15 minutes). If baked in individual dishes, serve from the dish; if baked in a casserole, cut into wedges to serve.

PER SERVING: 467 calories, 27 g total fat, 16 g saturated fat, 172 mg cholesterol, 598 mg sodium, 41 g carbohydrates, 5 g fiber, 19 g protein, 422 mg calcium, 3 mg iron

PASILLA CHILES STUFFED WITH TWO CHEESES

MEXICAN DAIRY PRODUCTS ARE EASY TO FIND IN LATINO MARKETS, BUT YOU CAN MAKE SUBSTITUTIONS. USE PARMESAN IN PLACE OF CRUMBLY COTIJA CHEESE, SOUR CREAM FOR RICH CREMA, AND LONGHORN CHEDDAR FOR ASADERO. TOSS SALAD GREENS WITH A SHERRY VINAIGRETTE TO SERVE ALONGSIDE. IF YOU'RE USING CREMA, USE IT AGAIN IN GUAVA PASTE WITH CREMA & FIGS (PAGE 228) FOR DESSERT.

30 MINUTES

2 fresh pasilla chiles (about 4 oz. *each*)

2 teaspoons butter or margarine

1 small onion (about 4 oz.), diced

1 cup frozen corn kernels

⅓ cup crumbled cotija cheese

2 tablespoons crema

4 ounces asadero cheese

Crema (optional)

1. Cut chiles in half lengthwise. Pull out and discard seeds. Set chiles aside.

2. Melt butter in a wide frying pan over medium-high heat. Add onion and cook, stirring often, until soft (5 to 7 minutes). Add corn and stir until heated through. Remove pan from heat; stir in cotija cheese and the 2 tablespoons crema. Fill chiles equally with corn mixture and arrange, filled side up, in a baking pan (any size as long as chiles don't fit too snugly).

3. Cut asadero cheese into 4 strips, each about ½ by 1 by 3 inches. Stuff one strip into each chile. Bake in a 450° oven, uncovered, until chiles are soft and tinged with brown (about 15 minutes). If desired, offer crema to spoon over chiles.

PER SERVING: 417 calories, 25 g total fat, 16 g saturated fat, 77 mg cholesterol, 687 mg sodium, 31 g carbohydrates, 4 g fiber, 23 g protein, 542 mg calcium, 2 mg iron

SWISS MACARONI & CHEESE WITH STEWED APPLES

BITTER GREENS SUCH AS ENDIVE, DANDELION, AND ROMAINE—SERVED CHILLED AND CRISP OR WARM AND WILTED—CONTRAST PLEASANTLY WITH SWEET APPLES AND BUTTERY CHEESE IN THIS ENTRÉE. END WITH BOWLS OF SWEETENED CHESTNUT SPREAD AND CRÈME FRAICHE (SEE PAGE 226) OR PEARS AND SQUARES OF CHOCOLATE. (LOOK FOR SPELT MACARONI IN A HEALTH FOOD STORE.)

25 MINUTES

2 medium-size full-flavored, quick-cooking apples, such as Gala (about 12 oz. *total*)

3 tablespoons butter or margarine

1 large onion (about 8 oz.), thinly sliced

6 ounces small dried spelt macaroni or other elbow macaroni

1 cup (about 4 oz.) shredded Gruyère cheese

Salt and freshly ground pepper

Green onion slivers or chopped parsley

1. Peel, core, and slice apples. Place in a 1- to 2-quart pan, add 1 tablespoon water, cover, and cook over low heat until apples are soft (about 15 minutes).

2. Meanwhile, melt 1½ tablespoons of the butter in a wide frying pan over medium-high heat. Add sliced onion and cook, stirring occasionally, until some pieces are turning brown and crisp and most are soft (about 10 minutes).

3. Also while apples are cooking, bring about 1½ quarts water to a boil in a 3- to 4-quart pan over high heat. Stir in macaroni and cook, uncovered, until just tender to bite (about 10 minutes); or cook according to package directions. Drain well; return to pan and mix in remaining 1½ tablespoons butter and cheese. Season to taste with salt and pepper.

4. Spoon macaroni onto 2 warm dinner plates. Top with fried onion and green onion. Spoon stewed apples alongside.

PER SERVING: 818 calories, 37 g total fat, 22 g saturated fat, 109 mg cholesterol, 375 mg sodium, 93 g carbohydrates, 6 g fiber, 29 g protein, 621 mg calcium, 4 mg iron

Butternut Squash with Sage & Gruyère

ACCOMPANY THIS SIMPLE DISH WITH RYE TOAST TRIANGLES TO SCOOP UP THE SAGE-SEASONED SQUASH AND MELTED CHEESE. A GREEN SALAD ROUNDS OUT THE MEAL. BLACKBERRIES WITH BROWN SUGAR ARE A REFRESHING CONCLUSION.

30 MINUTES

1 tablespoon olive oil

1 very small butternut squash (1½ to 1¾ lbs.), peeled, seeded, and cut into ¾-inch chunks

1 medium-size onion (about 6 oz.), coarsely chopped

1 clove garlic, minced or pressed

1 teaspoon minced fresh sage or ½ teaspoon dried sage

Salt and freshly ground pepper

1 cup (about 4 oz.) shredded Gruyère cheese

4 fresh sage leaves (optional)

1. Heat oil in a wide frying pan over low heat. Add squash, onion, garlic, and minced sage; sprinkle lightly with salt and pepper. Cover and cook until squash is tender when pierced (about 15 minutes), stirring once. Scatter cheese over squash, cover pan, and heat until cheese is melted (about 30 seconds).

2. Lift squash mixture to 2 warm dinner plates or gratin dishes; garnish with sage leaves, if desired.

PER SERVING: 458 calories, 26 g total fat, 12 g saturated fat, 62 mg cholesterol, 205 mg sodium, 42 g carbohydrates, 7 g fiber, 21 g protein, 733 mg calcium, 2 mg iron

Swiss Chard Pizza

SHARP-FLAVORED, DEEP GREEN SWISS CHARD, SWEET CURRANTS, AND NUTTY GRUYÈRE CHEESE TOP THIS "EAT YOUR GREENS" PIZZA. IF YOU PREFER, USE BEET GREENS, ESCAROLE, KALE, OR ROMAINE LETTUCE IN PLACE OF CHARD, ADJUSTING THE COOKING TIME AS NEEDED TO WILT THE GREENS. ESPRESSO ICE CREAM SPRINKLED WITH CRUSHED PRALINE OR NUT BRITTLE MAKES A SATISFYING DESSERT.

25 MINUTES

6 ounces Swiss chard

2 teaspoons olive oil

¼ cup thin wedges of red onion

2 tablespoons currants

1½ teaspoons balsamic vinegar

2 packaged small baked pizza crusts, *each* about 6 inches in diameter (or 1 large crust, about 11 inches in diameter)

½ cup grated Gruyère cheese

⅛ teaspoon ground nutmeg

1 tablespoon sliced almonds

1. Trim and discard discolored ends of chard stems. Rinse and drain chard; then slice stems and coarsely chop leaves. Set chard aside, keeping stems and leaves separate.

2. Heat oil in a wide frying pan over medium-high heat. Add onion and chard stems; stir often until onion begins to brown (5 to 7 minutes). Add chard leaves, currants, and vinegar; cook until leaves are wilted (2 to 3 minutes). Set aside.

3. Place pizza crusts on a baking sheet. Reserve 1 tablespoon of the cheese; sprinkle half the remaining cheese over each crust, covering crust to within 1 inch of the edge. Sprinkle nutmeg over cheese, then top evenly with chard mixture. Sprinkle with reserved 1 tablespoon cheese, then with almonds. Bake in a 450° oven until cheese is melted (about 7 minutes).

PER SERVING: 603 calories, 25 g total fat, 8 g saturated fat, 31 mg cholesterol, 522 mg sodium, 76 g carbohydrates, 8 g fiber, 17 g protein, 425 mg calcium, 4 mg iron

CAMBOZOLA & SAGE PIZZA WITH WILTED SPINACH SALAD

YOU'LL FIND PUNGENT FRESH SAGE LEAVES BOTH ATOP AND BENEATH THE CHEESE IN THIS SIMPLE PIZZA. ACCOMPANY IT WITH A GARLICKY WILTED SPINACH SALAD AND GLASSES OF RED WINE OR VERY TART SPARKLING LEMONADE.

15 MINUTES

---

2 packaged small baked pizza crusts, *each* about 6 inches in diameter (or 1 large crust, about 11 inches in diameter)

12 fresh sage leaves

3 ounces cambozola cheese, sliced

2 thin slices red onion, separated into rings

4 ounces packaged triple-washed baby spinach

¼ cup thinly sliced red onion

1 clove garlic, minced or pressed

1 tablespoon sherry vinegar

4 to 6 calamata olives

2 tablespoons olive oil

Salt and freshly ground pepper

1. Place pizza crusts on a baking sheet. Scatter 3 of the sage leaves over each crust. Arrange cheese over crusts, covering them to within 1 inch of the edge; top with remaining 6 sage leaves and onion rings, dividing equally. Bake in a 450° oven until cheese is bubbly (about 8 minutes).

2. Meanwhile, in a serving bowl, mix spinach, the ¼ cup onion, garlic, vinegar, and olives.

3. When pizzas are almost done, heat oil in a small frying pan over high heat until hot but not smoking (about 30 seconds). Pour oil over salad, turning greens with tongs so hot oil wilts as many leaves as possible. Season salad to taste with salt and pepper; serve alongside pizzas.

PER SERVING: 719 calories, 38 g total fat, 12 g saturated fat, 32 mg cholesterol, 1,152 mg sodium, 76 g carbohydrates, 10 g fiber, 17 g protein, 359 mg calcium, 5 mg iron

Cambozola & Sage Pizza with Wilted Spinach Salad

POTATOES & CHANTERELLES

This rich, earthy dish is best accompanied by a salad of bitter winter greens. For dessert, offer chilled crisp apples—or, for a fancier conclusion, Ice Cream with Cognac & Caramelized Walnuts (page 224).

30 MINUTES

6 ounces fresh chanterelles or shiitake mushrooms

1 tablespoon butter or margarine

1 clove garlic, minced or pressed

½ teaspoon dried thyme

12 ounces thin-skinned potatoes, scrubbed

Salt and freshly ground pepper

¾ cup whipping cream or regular-strength vegetable broth

1. Place mushrooms in a plastic food bag. Fill bag with water; then seal bag and shake to wash mushrooms. Drain mushrooms well; if they are still gritty, repeat rinsing. Trim and discard bruised stem ends; cut mushrooms lengthwise into ¼-inch-thick slices.

2. In a wide frying pan with an ovenproof handle, melt butter over medium heat. Add mushrooms, garlic, and ¼ teaspoon of the thyme; cook, stirring often, until mushrooms are soft (about 5 minutes). Meanwhile, cut potatoes crosswise into ¼-inch-thick slices.

3. Season mushrooms to taste with salt and pepper. Arrange potato slices over mushrooms, overlapping them to fit. Pour cream over top; sprinkle with remaining ¼ teaspoon thyme, salt, and pepper. Increase heat to high and bring cream to a boil; then reduce heat, cover, and simmer until potatoes are tender when pierced (about 20 minutes).

4. Uncover pan. Broil about 4 inches below heat until cream begins to brown (about 3 minutes).

PER SERVING: 471 calories, 34 g total fat, 21 g saturated fat, 115 mg cholesterol, 103 mg sodium, 37 g carbohydrates, 4 g fiber, 7 g protein, 73 mg calcium, 3 mg iron

RACLETTE

Pungent in aroma but mild in flavor, raclette cheese is the star of this famous Swiss fireside dinner. Warm the cheese beside the fire; then scrape the melted portions onto dinner plates, top with a grind or two of black pepper, and eat with new potatoes, warm walnuts in the shell, and cornichons. Juicy apples or pears make a nice dessert (or serve them with the meal for a pleasant contrast in textures and flavors). Hot dinner plates keep the cheese flowing; handle them with thick napkins or place them in plate liners or wicker plate holders. Any leftover cheese (you'll probably have at least 4 ounces) can be melted in omelets for breakfast.

30 MINUTES

Raclette

6 to 8 small red thin-skinned
   potatoes (*each* about 1½ inches
   in diameter), scrubbed
1 wedge (¾ to 1 lb.) raclette cheese
   Freshly ground black pepper
6 to 8 walnuts in the shells
¼ cup cornichons

1. Place potatoes in a 2- to 3-quart pan and add enough water to cover. Cover and bring to a boil over high heat; then reduce heat and simmer, covered, until potatoes are tender when pierced (10 to 15 minutes). Drain well and place in a shallow basket to serve.

2. While potatoes are cooking, heat 2 ovenproof dinner plates in a 200° oven until very hot (about 10 minutes).

3. Place cheese on a board or heatproof platter. Position board at an angle near the glowing coals of a fireplace (prop it in the right position by placing a brick beneath it). When cheese melts readily, scrape some onto hot dinner plates. Grind pepper over cheese. Eat with potatoes, walnuts to crack open, and cornichons. (You can also melt cheese in a 500° oven. Bake on a heatproof platter until oozing, 10 to 15 minutes; watch carefully. As cheese hardens, return it to oven as needed.)

PER SERVING: 651 calories, 43 g total fat, 19 g saturated fat, 100 mg cholesterol, 1,050 mg sodium, 33 g carbohydrates, 4 g fiber, 34 g protein, 816 mg calcium, 2 mg iron

TOMATO BASIL SANDWICHES

THICK, JUICY RIPE TOMATO SLICES AND FRAGRANT BASIL LEAVES MAKE A PLAIN BUT PERFECT SANDWICH FILLING. SIP A MINT ITALIAN SODA WITH THIS SUMMERTIME MEAL; END WITH CHOCOLATE-GLAZED ICE CREAM BARS (PAGE 216).

15 MINUTES

1 small red onion (about 4 oz.), thinly sliced

⅓ cup mayonnaise

4 slices soft whole-grain bread (*each* about ⅓ inch thick)

Salt and freshly ground pepper

1 large ripe tomato (about 8 oz.), thickly sliced

1⅓ cups lightly packed fresh basil leaves

2 tablespoons minced fresh basil (optional)

2 tablespoons minced parsley (optional)

1. Separate onion slices into rings. Submerge onion rings in a bowl of ice and water and let stand for 10 minutes. Drain well and pat dry.

2. Spread mayonnaise over one side of each slice of bread. Lay half the onion slices over 2 slices of bread; sprinkle generously with salt and pepper. Top with tomato, then basil leaves, then remaining onion; season with salt and pepper again. Top with remaining 2 slices of bread.

3. With a serrated knife, trim crusts from sandwiches, if desired; then cut each sandwich into 4 triangles. If desired, mix minced basil and parsley on a small plate and dip one edge of each triangle into minced herbs. Serve triangles standing side by side, points up and herbs facing out.

PER SERVING: 441 calories, 31 g total fat, 5 g saturated fat, 21 mg cholesterol, 472 mg sodium, 36 g carbohydrates, 7 g fiber, 8 g protein, 104 mg calcium, 3 mg iron

Tomato Basil Sandwiches

Quinoa & Two-bean Salad

Try this grain-and-bean salad in a tart herb dressing for a warm-weather lunch or supper, perhaps with a bowl of vegetable broth dotted with minced vegetables or tiny pasta shapes. Cherry tomatoes and chocolate-dipped orange wedges complete the menu.

30 MINUTES

---

1 cup quinoa

4 ounces thin green beans
(ends removed)

4 ounces thin wax beans
(ends removed)

¾ cup chopped kohlrabi or
frozen corn kernels

Green Dressing (below)

1 cup lightly packed mesclun mix,
rinsed and crisped

GREEN DRESSING

¼ cup olive oil

¼ cup lemon juice

3 tablespoons minced parsley

1 tablespoon minced fresh tarragon

Salt and freshly ground pepper

1. Rinse quinoa in a strainer under running water. Drain, place in a 2-quart pan, and add 1½ cups water. Bring to a boil over high heat; then reduce heat, cover, and simmer until water has been absorbed and quinoa is tender to bite (10 to 12 minutes). Spoon grain from pan and spread over bottom and up sides of a large bowl to cool.

2. While quinoa is cooking, bring about 1 inch of water to a boil in a covered wide frying pan over high heat. Drop green beans, wax beans, and kohlrabi into boiling water; return to a simmer and cook, uncovered, until all vegetables are tender when pierced (about 7 minutes). Drain, rinse with cold water until cool, and drain again. Place in a medium-size bowl.

3. Also while quinoa is cooking, prepare Green Dressing.

4. Pour three-fourths of the dressing over quinoa; pour remaining dressing over vegetables. Toss to mix. Divide quinoa between 2 dinner plates; top with vegetables and garnish with mesclun mix.

GREEN DRESSING

In a small bowl, stir together oil, lemon juice, parsley, and tarragon; season to taste with salt and pepper.

PER SERVING: 620 calories, 32 g total fat, 4 g saturated fat, 0 mg cholesterol, 85 mg sodium, 73 g carbohydrates, 14 g fiber, 15 g protein, 131 mg calcium, 10 mg iron

DESSERTS

Fig Blossoms (page 234)

CHOCOLATE-GLAZED ICE CREAM BARS THE KEY TO

SUCCESS IN ASSEMBLING THESE OLD-FASHIONED TREATS IS TO USE VERY
COLD ICE CREAM AND CHOCOLATE THAT'S WARM AND MELTED, BUT NOT
HOT; THAT WAY, NOT MUCH ICE CREAM WILL MELT AWAY WHEN YOU POUR
ON THE COATING. SERVE THE BARS ON DESSERT PLATES, PERHAPS
GARNISHED WITH A FEW FRESH BERRIES.

30 MINUTES

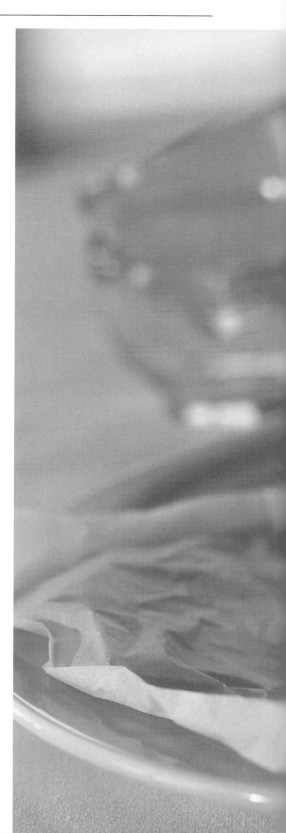

2 (1-inch-thick) slices espresso or
   caramel ice cream, cut from a
   cylindrical 1-pint carton of ice
   cream (see Note below)
⅓ pound bittersweet chocolate,
   chopped

1. Place ice cream slices on a wire rack set over a dinner plate
or baking pan. Place in freezer.

2. Place two-thirds of the chocolate in a 1- to 2-quart pan. Set
over lowest heat and stir constantly until almost completely
melted. Remove from heat, add remaining chocolate, and continue to stir until all chocolate is melted and smooth (about 1
minute).

3. Remove plate with ice cream slices from freezer. Spoon about
1 tablespoon of the chocolate evenly over top of each ice cream
slice. Return to freezer until chocolate is hard (about 5 minutes).
Meanwhile, divide remaining chocolate evenly between two ½-
cup dry measuring cups.

4. With a spatula, flip ice cream slices over on rack so chocolate
side is down. Then, working quickly, pour ½ cup more chocolate over each slice; with a knife, spread chocolate smoothly over
slices. Excess chocolate will flow over edges (chocolate that has
dripped onto plate may be used in chocolate chip cookies or
remelted to use as a dip for fresh fruit). Return coated slices, still
on rack and plate, to freezer until chocolate is hard (15 to 20
minutes). To serve, transfer each bar to a dessert plate with a spatula; eat with knife and fork.

Note: To slice ice cream, use scissors to cut ice cream carton
lengthwise to base. Cut or tear carton from base so it lies flat.
Using a hot knife, cut ice cream horizontally to make round
slices (hot knife will slide through ice cream more easily, pre-
venting a flattened side). Place any unused ice cream in an airtight container and return to freezer.

PER SERVING: 593 calories, 39 g total fat, 22 g saturated fat, 50 mg cholesterol, 90 mg sodium, 68 g carbohydrates, 2 g fiber, 9 g protein, 179 mg
calcium, 3 mg iron

Baked Alaska for Two

BAKED ALASKA FOR TWO

YOUR FAVORITE SORBET OR ICE CREAM HIDES UNDER BILLOWY BAKED MERINGUE. IF YOU LIKE, USE TWO FLAVORS; COMBINE MANGO WITH PURPLE BERRY OR RASPBERRY SORBET, OR TRY CHOCOLATE WITH ESPRESSO, CARAMEL, OR HAZELNUT ICE CREAM. IF YOU'RE CONCERNED ABOUT EGG SAFETY, USE A MERINGUE MIX, OFTEN SOLD IN SUPERMARKETS NEAR THE CAKE-DECORATING SUPPLIES. BE SURE TO PREHEAT THE OVEN BEFORE BEGINNING THIS RECIPE.

25 MINUTES

1 pint sorbet or ice cream (use all one flavor or ½ pint *each* of 2 flavors; see suggestions in recipe introduction above)

2 large egg whites

¼ teaspoon cream of tartar

⅓ cup granulated sugar or firmly packed brown sugar

1. Preheat oven to 500°.

2. Use scissors to cut sorbet carton lengthwise to base. Cut or tear carton from base so it lies flat. (If using 2 flavors of sorbet, remove cartons from two 1-pint containers of sorbet; use a hot knife to cut each 1-pint cylinder in half crosswise, then reassemble cylinders so each is half one flavor, half the other. Freeze one 2-tone cylinder for other uses.) Place sorbet cylinder, wide end down, in a baking pan.

3. In a large bowl, beat egg whites and cream of tartar with an electric mixer on high speed until foamy. Add sugar, 1 tablespoon at a time, beating until meringue is stiff and glossy. Cover sorbet with meringue, sealing it to pan.

4. Bake on lowest rack of oven until meringue is light brown (3 to 5 minutes). Transfer baked Alaska to a serving plate and serve at once. To serve, cut in half vertically.

PER SERVING: 365 calories, 0 g total fat, 0 g saturated fat, 0 mg cholesterol, 78 mg sodium, 89 g carbohydrates, 0 g fiber, 5 g protein, 18 mg calcium, 1 mg iron

CANDIED LACE BOWLS

UNPEELED ORANGES ARE CONVENIENT MOLDS FOR EDIBLE BOWLS MADE FROM LACY CARAMELIZED SUGAR. FILL THE CRISP CANDY CUPS WITH ICE CREAM, PERHAPS WITH A TOPPING OF COGNAC AND CARAMELIZED WALNUTS (PAGE 224). ONCE THE BOWLS ARE COOL, TRY TO SERVE THEM WITHIN AN HOUR.

20 MINUTES

2 oranges (*each* at least 3 inches in diameter)
Vegetable oil
½ cup sugar

1. Push a metal skewer or tapered chopstick (narrower end first) crosswise through each orange. Using your fingers or a paper towel, thoroughly oil half of the outside of each orange, making sure oil gets into all creases, especially around end of fruit.

2. Place sugar in a 1- to 2-quart pan. Heat over medium-high heat, tilting pan to mix sugar as it melts and begins to caramelize. When all sugar is melted (5 to 6 minutes), remove pan from heat.

3. Hold one orange over pan of caramel syrup to catch drips; spoon syrup in a thin stream over oiled half of orange to make a lacy pattern. Then hang skewered orange in a bowl to cool by resting skewer ends on rim of bowl (candy bowl will take 3 to 5 minutes to cool). Repeat with second orange.

4. Gently cup the candy-covered side of one orange in your hand and ease candy bowl from orange with a gentle wiggling motion, taking care not to bump caramel against skewer (bowl will break). Serve within 1 hour; or, to hold for up to 2 days, place in an airtight container and store at room temperature.

PER CANDY BOWL: 203 calories, 1 g total fat, 0 g saturated fat, 0 mg cholesterol, 1 mg sodium, 50 g carbohydrates, 0 g fiber, 0 g protein, 1 mg calcium, 0 mg iron

PAINTED CHOCOLATE CUPS

"HURRY UP AND WAIT" DESCRIBES THE PROCESS INVOLVED IN MAKING THESE DRAMATIC DESSERT CUPS. YOU WORK FAST SO THEY HAVE PLENTY OF TIME TO REST IN THE FREEZER: THE LONGER THEY CHILL, THE EASIER IT IS TO REMOVE THE FOIL WITHOUT BREAKING THE FRAGILE BITTERSWEET SHELL. FILL THE CUPS WITH ICE CREAM AND SPOON FRESH BERRIES, BROKEN NUTS, OR CRUSHED NUT BRITTLE ON TOP.

30 MINUTES

About 6 ounces bittersweet chocolate, chopped

1. Place chocolate in a 1- to 2-quart pan. Set over lowest heat and stir frequently until melted and smooth (about 3 minutes); remove from heat.

2. While chocolate is melting, place one foil cupcake liner in each of two 2½-inch muffin cups. Or, for more dramatic chocolate cups, cut two 6-inch squares of foil. Press center of each square into a muffin cup; then press foil against sides of cup, folding it as needed to make as smooth a lining as possible.

3. Using a ½-inch-wide, soft-bristled paintbrush and working quickly, paint melted chocolate over inside of one foil-lined cup, coating all surfaces as thickly as you can. When one cup is painted, place in freezer until chocolate is no longer shiny (about 5 minutes); meanwhile, paint remaining cup. When second cup is painted, set it in freezer until chocolate is no longer shiny; meanwhile, touch up any thin areas in first cup. Return first cup to freezer; touch up second cup and return to freezer. Freeze cups until all chocolate is no longer shiny (at least 5 minutes).

4. Remove one cup from freezer, using foil liner to lift it from muffin pan. Holding cup at base, peel foil off chocolate, working quickly so warmth of your hand does not melt chocolate. Place cup and any broken pieces on a dessert plate or in a wide, shallow bowl. Repeat with second cup. (Broken pieces look attractive on plate; you can also use them as garnish for ice cream in cup.) Hold at room temperature for up to 3 hours; or cover airtight and refrigerate for up to 2 weeks.

PER CHOCOLATE CUP: 415 calories, 30 g total fat, 16 g saturated fat, 0 mg cholesterol, 0 mg sodium, 47 g carbohydrates, 2 g fiber, 6 g protein, 40 mg calcium, 3 mg iron

Painted Chocolate Cups

THAI BANANA SPLIT

FAVORITE SOUTHEAST ASIAN INGREDIENTS—COCONUT, BANANAS, AND PEANUTS—MARRY HAPPILY IN THIS SIMPLE VERSION OF AN AMERICAN FAVORITE. YOU COAT SLICED BANANAS IN CARAMELIZED SUGAR, THEN SPOON THE FRUIT OVER COCONUT ICE CREAM AND SPRINKLE WITH PEANUTS AND MILK CHOCOLATE. (COCONUT ICE CREAM CAN BE PURCHASED FOR TAKEOUT IN MANY SOUTHEAST ASIAN RESTAURANTS.)

20 MINUTES

About 2 ounces milk chocolate (in a single chunk), at room temperature

2 bananas

1 tablespoon roasted salted peanuts

⅓ cup sugar

¼ cup whipping cream

1 cup coconut ice cream

1. Set chocolate on a cutting board. Pull a vegetable peeler firmly over surface of chocolate to shave it into shreds; set aside. Peel bananas and cut diagonally into 2-inch lengths; set aside. Finely chop peanuts; set aside.

2. Place sugar in a 1- to 2-quart pan. Heat over medium-high heat, tilting pan to mix sugar as it melts and begins to caramelize. When all sugar is melted (4 to 5 minutes), reduce heat to low and add bananas. With a wide metal spatula, roll bananas in caramel syrup until smoothly coated. Working quickly, lift bananas from syrup, letting any excess syrup drip back into pan; divide bananas between 2 dessert dishes.

3. To caramel syrup left in pan, add cream and stir to blend. Then remove from heat and stir constantly until sauce is smooth (about 8 minutes).

4. Scoop ice cream equally into dessert dishes alongside bananas. Drizzle caramel sauce over ice cream; sprinkle peanuts and shaved chocolate over all.

PER SERVING: 635 calories, 29 g total fat, 17 g saturated fat, 68 mg cholesterol, 94 mg sodium, 95 g carbohydrates, 3 g fiber, 7 g protein, 171 mg calcium, 1 mg iron

AMARETTI PROFITEROLES
HERE'S AN EASY TWIST ON ELEGANT PROFITEROLES, WITH CRISP AMARETTI STANDING IN FOR THE TRADITIONAL CREAM PUFFS. YOU SANDWICH THE COOKIES TOGETHER WITH ICE CREAM, THEN SERVE THEM AS YOU WOULD PROFITEROLES—DRIZZLED WITH CHOCOLATE SAUCE AND RESTING IN A POOL OF THE SAME.

20 MINUTES

1 cup coffee or chocolate ice cream

8 amaretti (crunchy Italian almond macaroons)

¼ cup chopped bittersweet chocolate

¼ cup whipping cream

1. Scoop ¼ cup of the ice cream onto flat side of each of 4 cookies. Top with remaining cookies, flat side down. Freeze while you prepare chocolate sauce.

2. In a 1- to 2-quart pan, stir chocolate and cream over lowest heat until chocolate is melted and mixture is smoothly blended.

3. Remove profiteroles from freezer. Dip a spoon or tines of a fork into melted chocolate; streak chocolate over exposed ice cream and ends of cookies on one side of each profiterole.

4. Pour remaining chocolate mixture onto centers of 2 dinner or dessert plates. Set 2 profiteroles, chocolate-streaked side up, in chocolate sauce on each plate.

PER SERVING: 426 calories, 26 g total fat, 14 g saturated fat, 56 mg cholesterol, 70 mg sodium, 48 g carbohydrates, 0 g fiber, 6 g protein, 102 mg calcium, 1 mg iron

ICE CREAM WITH COGNAC & CARAMELIZED WALNUTS
SMOOTH CARAMEL ICE CREAM IS A PERFECT SWEET, CREAMY FOIL FOR BRANDY, BRINGING OUT THE LIQUOR'S FLAVOR WHILE SOFTENING ITS BITTERNESS. KEEP IN MIND THAT A LITTLE BRANDY GOES A LONG WAY HERE—ONE TINY SPLASH MAKES FOR AN EXQUISITE DESSERT, BUT ADD ANOTHER TINY SPLASH AND YOU'LL OVERWHELM THE FLAVORS OF TOASTED WALNUTS AND ICE CREAM.

15 MINUTES

¼ cup walnut halves

2 tablespoons sugar

About 1 cup caramel or vanilla ice cream

2 teaspoons cognac

1. Place walnuts and sugar in a 1- to 2-quart pan. Heat over medium-high heat, tilting pan to mix sugar as it melts and begins to caramelize. When sugar begins to melt, stir nuts so they don't burn. When all sugar is melted (about 3 minutes), pour mixture onto foil or parchment paper. Working fast, use 2 forks to separate nuts. Let cool (7 to 8 minutes).

2. Scoop ice cream into 2 dessert bowls. Pour 1 teaspoon of the cognac over each serving; top evenly with caramelized walnuts.

PER SERVING: 273 calories, 15 g total fat, 5 g saturated fat, 29 mg cholesterol, 54 mg sodium, 30 g carbohydrates, 1 g fiber, 4 g protein, 96 mg calcium, 0 mg iron

Cardamom-glazed Pears

CARDAMOM-GLAZED PEARS
THESE PEARS ARE SO QUICK TO PREPARE, YOU CAN EASILY MAKE THEM WHILE BAKING A BATCH OF BAR COOKIES TO SERVE ALONGSIDE. TRY SHORTBREAD STUDDED WITH TOASTED ALMONDS—AND ADD A SCOOP OF ICE CREAM TOO, IF YOU LIKE.

15 MINUTES

⅛ teaspoon ground cardamom or
  2 cardamom pods

2 medium-size Bartlett pears
  (about 6 oz. *each*)

1 tablespoon butter or margarine

2 tablespoons maple syrup

1. If using cardamom pods, cut them open and pull out seeds; crush seeds with a knife or with mortar and pestle. Set aside.

2. Peel, halve, and core pears. Melt butter in a small to medium-size frying pan over medium-high heat. When butter sizzles, arrange pears in pan, cut sides down; cook without stirring until pears begin to brown (about 4 minutes). Add syrup and cardamom; continue to cook, turning pears once, until syrup is warm (about 1 more minute). Remove from heat at once.

3. Spoon pears and syrup equally onto 2 dessert plates.

PER SERVING: 195 calories, 6 g total fat, 4 g saturated fat, 16 mg cholesterol, 60 mg sodium, 37 g carbohydrates, 4 g fiber, 1 g protein, 33 mg calcium, 1 mg iron

SIMPLE DESSERTS

SOME OF THE MOST ELEGANT DESSERTS ARE STRIKINGLY SIMPLE: A FEW JUICY ORANGE SEGMENTS DRIZZLED WITH CHOCOLATE, A BOWL OF GLOSSY BLACK CHERRIES ON ICE. UNDERSTATED YET BEAUTIFUL, THESE ARE IDEAL ENDINGS FOR AN IMPECCABLE MENU OF "PERFECT" DISHES: THEY ARE LOVELY COMPLEMENTS TO A WONDERFUL MEAL, NOT ATTENTION-GETTING GRAND FINALES. OF COURSE, SIMPLE DESSERTS CAN BE COMFORTABLY HOMEY, TOO. ICE CREAM SANDWICHES, WARM FRUIT SHORTCAKES, OR TALL ICE CREAM SODAS ARE JUST RIGHT AFTER A QUICK SUPPER OF GRILLED HAMBURGERS OR A CRISP CHEF'S SALAD. ON THESE PAGES, YOU'LL FIND OVER TWO DOZEN SIMPLE SWEETS—SOME ELEGANT ENOUGH TO CONCLUDE THE MOST REFINED REPAST, SOME MORE RELAXED, BUT ALL EASY TO ASSEMBLE IN MOMENTS.

DATES, CHÈVRE & PORT

Between November and January, well-supplied produce markets occasionally offer **fresh dates** on the stem (they look like clusters of grapes). If you see them, buy them! The sugars haven't hardened yet, and the soft, luscious flesh almost melts on your tongue. Offer the dates with **chèvre** and a **high-quality port**.

SWEETENED CHESTNUT SPREAD

For each serving, spoon about ¼ cup **canned sweetened chestnut spread** into a wide, shallow bowl. Stir **crème fraîche** or sour cream to soften and spoon about ¼ cup atop chestnut spread in each bowl; swirl crème fraîche with tip of a knife. Sprinkle with **shaved chocolate** or unsweetened cocoa.

PERSIMMON WEDGES & LIME

Cut **crisp (Fuyu-type) persimmons** into ½-inch-thick wedges and fan out on dessert plates; offer **lime wedges** to squeeze over fruit.

PEARS & CHOCOLATE

Arrange **dried candied pear halves** or cored fresh pear wedges on a platter. Fill one small bowl with pieces of good **dark or milk chocolate,** another with warm toasted **walnuts;** serve with pears.

COMICE PEARS & GRUYÈRE

Choose firm (not hard), fragrant **Comice pears**. Core and cut into ½-inch-thick slices; fan out on dessert plates and present with wedges of **Gruyère cheese** and, if you like, warm toasted **walnuts**.

CONFETTI FRUIT SALAD

Dice your choice of **fresh fruit**. Try kiwi, oranges, and strawberries; bananas, quartered purple grapes, and kiwi; or mangoes, litchis, and fresh raspberries. Mound fruit on dessert plates without mixing the different types (keeping the fruits separate makes for a more striking presentation).

ICED BLACK CHERRIES

Present **black cherries** mixed with **crushed ice** in a lovely glass bowl; or just serve chilled black cherries without the ice.

CHERRIES WITH CHÈVRE OR SHEEP'S CHEESE

Offer a ceramic bowl of **cherries** at room temperature; accompany with a selection of **chèvre or sheep's cheeses** arranged on a woven tray.

PEACHES, BERRIES & LATE-HARVEST WINE

Assemble a compote by combining peeled, sliced **peaches** and **fresh berries** in a beautiful bowl; pour a **late-harvest wine** over fruit. Serve at once or chill to draw the fruit juices out into the wine.

BERRIES & BROWN SUGAR

Layer **fresh berries** of your choice (strawberries need to be sliced) with **brown sugar** and serve with a drift of **crème fraîche** or sour cream.

CHOCOLATE-DIPPED ORANGES

Peel and section an **orange**, removing all white membrane and strings. Dip a third of each segment in melted **bittersweet chocolate**. Dip tines of a fork in melted **white chocolate**; drizzle white chocolate over dark chocolate, moving fork back and forth to make thin lines.

HALVAH-STUFFED DATES

Slit open **dates** and remove pits. Push a chunk of **plain or marbled halvah** into each date; halvah chunks should be large enough to leave a wide "ribbon" exposed. If desired, caramelize granulated sugar (see page 222) and drizzle from tines of a fork over dates.

MELON & CANDIED GINGER

These two are natural complements. Cut slightly chilled (not cold) **melon** into wedges and offer with a plate of **candied ginger**.

WATERMELON RASPBERRY SLUSH

In a food processor or blender, purée **watermelon** with **fresh or frozen raspberries,** using about twice as much melon as berries. (Seed the melon if using a blender, since it will grind the seeds up. A processor leaves seeds whole, giving the slush a decorative look.) Pour purée into a metal pan and freeze, stirring occasionally, until slushy. Scoop into dessert bowls; garnish with **fresh mint leaves**.

GREEN GRAPES WITH AMARETTI

Serve chilled small bunches of juicy **green grapes** with brittle **amaretti** (crunchy Italian almond macaroons).

LITCHIS & SYRUP WITH CRUSHED ICE

Canned litchis are as fragrant and luscious as the fresh fruit—and much simpler to prepare. Pour **litchis** and their syrup into a pretty glass bowl filled with an equal quantity of **crushed ice**. Garnish with **rose petals**, fresh berries, or small fresh mint or basil leaves.

QUICK SHORTCAKES

Split purchased **scones** (warmed, if desired) and fill with **ice cream** and **fruit**. Try ginger scones with sliced peaches and peach ice cream, berry scones with berries and vanilla ice cream.

PEACH SODA

Fill tall glasses with alternate layers of sliced **fresh peaches** or apricots and **peach or vanilla ice cream**. Pour a small amount of **peach or apricot nectar** over the top; top off with **sparkling water**.

CHOCOLATE SODA

Fill tall glasses with **chocolate ice cream**; top with **chocolate syrup** and **sparkling water**.

VANILLA ICE CREAM WITH HONEY & PISTACHIOS

Scoop **vanilla ice cream** into bowls; drizzle with **honey** and sprinkle with minced **pistachios**.

MUD BALLS

Roll **chocolate ice cream** into 3-inch balls; roll balls in finely chopped **chocolate** to coat. Pour a pool of **hot fudge sauce** on each dessert plate; settle one mud ball into sauce on each plate.

CHOCOLATE ICE CREAM SANDWICHES

Split a **brownie** in half horizontally to make 2 layers. Sandwich brownie layers together with your favorite **ice cream**.

GINGER ICE CREAM SANDWICHES

Sandwich 2 **thin ginger cookies** together with **peach or pumpkin ice cream**.

VALENTINE ICE CREAM HEARTS

Pack **ice cream** or sorbet into heart-shaped cookie cutters; push out onto dessert plates. Or use other shapes, such as stars or bells.

CRUSHED NUT BRITTLE OVER ICE CREAM

Place **nut brittle** in a plastic bag; seal bag, then crush brittle with a rolling pin. Sprinkle crushed brittle over scoops of **almond, coffee, or chocolate ice cream**.

LEMON SORBET WITH MINT

Scoop **lemon sorbet** into dessert bowls; sprinkle with slivered **fresh mint**.

PEACH SORBET WITH RASPBERRIES

Onto each dessert plate, pour a pool of **raspberry sauce** (purchased or homemade; see page 234). Top with a scoop of **peach sorbet** and sprinkle with **fresh raspberries**.

TRIO OF SORBETS

Using a small oval ice cream scoop, arrange 3 scoops of **sorbet** (in 3 different flavors) on each dessert plate.

CARAMELIZED MACADAMIAS WITH CHOCOLATE

MILK CHOCOLATE SURROUNDS WHOLE MACADAMIAS COATED WITH CRUNCHY CARAMELIZED SUGAR IN THESE ENTICING SWEETMEATS. SERVE WITH TINY CUPS OF ESPRESSO AFTER A MEAL; OR OFFER LATER IN THE EVENING WITH A GLASS OF PORT.

30 MINUTES

⅓ cup whole macadamia nuts

3 tablespoons sugar

2 ounces milk chocolate (in a single chunk), ½ to ¾ inch thick

1. Place macadamias and sugar in a small pan. Heat over medium-high heat, tilting pan to mix sugar as it melts and begins to caramelize. When sugar begins to melt, stir nuts so they don't burn. When all sugar is melted (3 minutes), pour mixture onto foil or parchment, separating it into 2 mounds. Flatten each mound with back of a spoon; let cool (7 to 8 minutes).

2. While nuts are cooling, cut chocolate into 2 chunks. Line a wide frying pan with parchment paper; place chocolate chunks on paper, spacing them 3 inches apart. Place pan over lowest heat, cover, and heat for 3 minutes. Turn off heat and let stand until centers of chocolate chunks are barely soft when touched with a wooden pick (about 3 more minutes). Remove from heat.

3. Push one round of caramel-coated nuts into center of each softened chocolate chunk. Set pan in a wide frying pan filled with 1 to 2 inches of ice and water; reposition pan occasionally to keep ice under and surrounding pan. When chocolate is firm (about 15 minutes), peel paper from candies and serve.

PER SERVING: 379 calories, 25 g total fat, 8 g saturated fat, 6 mg cholesterol, 25 mg sodium, 39 g carbohydrates, 1 g fiber, 4 g protein, 72 mg calcium, 1 mg iron

GUAVA PASTE WITH CREMA & FIGS

POPULAR IN LATIN AMERICA, THIS SIMPLE CONFECTION IS MEANT TO BE SAVORED ONE TINY BITE AT A TIME. (THE FRENCH FAVOR A SIMILAR DESSERT, A COMBINATION OF SWEETENED CHESTNUT SPREAD AND CRÈME FRAÎCHE; SEE PAGE 226.) BOTH GUAVA PASTE—SOLD IN ROUND, FLAT TINS—AND CREMA (SOUR CREAM) ARE AVAILABLE IN LATINO MARKETS.

15 MINUTES

⅓ cup guava paste

¼ cup crema

2 tablespoons diced fresh figs

1. In a food processor or blender, whirl guava paste until light and fluffy. Spoon off-center into 2 wide, shallow soup bowls.

2. Stir crema, then spoon it into centers of bowls, covering a portion of the guava paste and making attractive swirls with the spoon. Garnish with figs.

PER SERVING: 207 calories, 6 g total fat, 4 g saturated fat, 13 mg cholesterol, 24 mg sodium, 38 g carbohydrates, 2 g fiber, 1 g protein, 35 mg calcium, 1 mg iron

GINGERBREAD CHOCOLATE CAKE

THIS DESSERT ISN'T A SOUF-FLÉ (IT'S EGGLESS), BUT IT ACTS LIKE ONE—BILLOWING UP AS IT BAKES, THEN SLOWLY SETTLING AFTER IT'S REMOVED FROM THE OVEN. EAT IT HOT, WITH ICE CREAM AND A SPRINKLING OF CINNAMON.

30 MINUTES

¼ cup firmly packed brown sugar
3 tablespoons butter or margarine
2 tablespoons molasses
½ teaspoon ground ginger
½ teaspoon ground cinnamon
⅛ teaspoon ground cloves
½ cup all-purpose flour
½ teaspoon baking soda
¼ cup chopped bittersweet chocolate
    Vanilla ice cream
    Ground cinnamon

1. In a small bowl, beat brown sugar, butter, molasses, ginger, the ½ teaspoon cinnamon, and cloves with an electric mixer on medium speed until blended. On low speed, beat in flour and baking soda until blended. Stir in chocolate.

2. Press dough equally into bottoms of two 1-cup soufflé dishes or two 2½-inch muffin cups. Bake in a 350° oven until cakes spring back when lightly pressed (about 13 minutes).

3. Cakes baked in soufflé dishes can be served in dishes. If you used a muffin pan, run a knife around edges of cakes to loosen; then invert pan onto a large plate and lift off. With a spatula, lift cakes and set right side up on 2 dinner or dessert plates.

4. Serve cakes warm, topped with ice cream and a dusting of cinnamon.

PER SERVING: 530 calories, 25 g total fat, 15 g saturated fat, 47 mg cholesterol, 508 mg sodium, 77 g carbohydrates, 1 g fiber, 5 g protein, 93 mg calcium, 4 mg iron

INDIVIDUAL BERRY CRISPS

HOMEY AND OLD-FASHIONED, THIS SUMMER DESSERT IS QUICK TO PUT TOGETHER. SERVE THE CRUMB-TOPPED BERRIES WITH VANILLA ICE CREAM FOR DESSERT, WITH LIGHTLY SWEETENED CREAM FOR BREAKFAST.

30 MINUTES

2 cups fresh blackberries
2 to 3 tablespoons granulated sugar
2 teaspoons all-purpose flour
⅛ teaspoon ground cinnamon
    Crumb Topping (below)

CRUMB TOPPING

¼ cup all-purpose flour
3 tablespoons firmly packed brown sugar
⅛ teaspoon ground cinnamon
⅛ teaspoon ground nutmeg
    Pinch of salt
2 tablespoons butter or margarine

1. In a medium-size bowl, gently mix berries, granulated sugar, the 2 teaspoons flour, and ⅛ teaspoon cinnamon (adjust amount of sugar depending on sweetness of berries). Divide mixture equally between 2 individual ramekins (at least 1-cup size).

2. Prepare Crumb Topping and crumble it evenly over berries. Bake in a 375° oven until topping is lightly browned and juices are bubbly around edges (about 20 minutes).

CRUMB TOPPING

In a small bowl, stir together the ¼ cup flour, brown sugar, ⅛ teaspoon cinnamon, nutmeg, and salt. With your fingers, work in butter until mixture resembles coarse crumbs.

PER SERVING: 382 calories, 12 g total fat, 7 g saturated fat, 31 mg cholesterol, 126 mg sodium, 68 g carbohydrates, 7 g fiber, 3 g protein, 74 mg calcium, 2 mg iron

CAKE WITH MELTED FRUIT UNDER MARSALA CREAM

WARMED FRESH BERRIES AND FIGS ARE SPOONED OVER ANGEL FOOD CAKE AND TOPPED WITH SOFT, MARSALA-SPIKED CREAM FOR A LUXURIOUS DESSERT. THE RECIPE CALLS FOR JUST 2 SLICES OF CAKE; WRAP THE REMAINING CAKE AIRTIGHT AND FREEZE FOR LATER USE. (YOU MIGHT SERVE SLICES ON A POOL OF FRESH STRAWBERRY SAUCE OR LEMON CREAM, WITH WHOLE STRAWBERRIES FOR GARNISH.)

20 MINUTES

1 cup mixed fresh berries (any combination of raspberries, blackberries, blueberries, and quartered strawberries)

2 fresh ripe black figs, quartered

6 tablespoons sugar

2 (1-inch-thick) slices purchased angel food cake, cut into 1-inch cubes

3 tablespoons marsala

¾ cup whipping cream

½ teaspoon unsweetened cocoa

¼ teaspoon ground cinnamon

1. In a 1½- to 2-quart pan, combine berries, figs, and 3 tablespoons of the sugar. Warm over low heat, stirring occasionally, just until fruit begins to release its juices (about 3 minutes). Meanwhile, divide cake equally between 2 dinner plates.

2. Spoon fruit and juices equally over cake. Set aside.

3. In pan used to warm fruit, stir together remaining 3 tablespoons sugar and marsala. Bring to a simmer over medium heat, stirring occasionally. Remove from heat and let cool.

4. In a large bowl, whip cream with an electric mixer until it has the consistency of a thick sauce; it should not mound or hold peaks. Fold marsala mixture into cream; then pour cream over cake and berries. To garnish, rub cocoa and cinnamon through a fine wire sieve held over cream.

PER SERVING: 589 calories, 28 g total fat, 17 g saturated fat, 100 mg cholesterol, 248 mg sodium, 78 g carbohydrates, 4 g fiber, 5 g protein, 134 mg calcium, 1 mg iron

Cake with Melted Fruit under Marsala Cream

STRAWBERRIES WITH BOURBON & SUGAR

STRAWBERRIES DIPPED IN SOUR CREAM AND BROWN SUGAR ARE A CLASSIC CHOICE FOR DESSERT AFTER A RICH MEAL. IN THIS EQUALLY SIMPLE AND ELEGANT PRESENTATION, THE JUICY RED BERRIES ARE DIPPED INTO TINY GLASSES OF BOURBON AND GRANULATED SUGAR.

5 MINUTES

---

14 ripe strawberries (leave hulls and any stems on, if desired)

3 to 4 tablespoons bourbon

3 to 4 tablespoons sugar

1. Mound half the strawberries on each of 2 dessert plates.

2. Pour bourbon equally into 2 small glasses, such as liqueur glasses; also divide sugar equally between 2 small glasses. Set one glass each of bourbon and sugar alongside berries on each plate.

3. To eat, dip berries first into bourbon, then into sugar.

PER SERVING: 154 calories, 0 g total fat, 0 g saturated fat, 0 mg cholesterol, 1 mg sodium, 24 g carbohydrates, 1 g fiber, 0 g protein, 4 mg calcium, 0 mg iron

CHOCOLATE MARRONS

CANDIED CHESTNUTS (MARRONS) CLOAKED IN CHOCOLATE AND CREAM AND ROLLED IN CHOPPED BITTERSWEET CHOCOLATE ARE LUSCIOUS CONFECTIONS. IN FRANCE, YOU MIGHT BE OFFERED ONE OF THESE TINY SWEETS WITH A CUP OF STRONG COFFEE AT THE END OF A MEAL.

20 MINUTES

⅓ cup chopped bittersweet or semisweet chocolate

4 teaspoons whipping cream

2 tablespoons finely chopped bittersweet chocolate or unsweetened cocoa

6 canned or bottled marrons in syrup (candied chestnuts), drained

1. In a small pan, combine the ⅓ cup chocolate and cream. Set over lowest heat (if heat is too high, chocolate becomes granular) and stir constantly until chocolate is melted and mixture is smoothly blended. Set pan in a larger pan filled with about 2 inches of ice and water and let stand until chocolate mixture is firm enough to hold its shape (about 2 minutes); as chocolate hardens, stir up firmer portions with a spoon and work them into softer chocolate. Remove pan from ice bath.

2. Spread the 2 tablespoons chopped chocolate on a small plate. Using your fingers, quickly shape a sixth of the chocolate-cream mixture around each chestnut, then roll in chopped chocolate to coat completely. Hold at room temperature for up to 3 hours; or cover airtight and refrigerate for up to 1 week (bring to room temperature before serving).

PER MARRON: 108 calories, 5 g total fat, 3 g saturated fat, 3 mg cholesterol, 11 mg sodium, 16 g carbohydrates, 1 g fiber, 1 g protein, 58 mg calcium, 0 mg iron

FIG BLOSSOMS

Pictured on page 215

20 MINUTES

THIS LOVELY DESSERT IS JUST AS GOOD AS A LATE-NIGHT AFTER-THEATER SNACK OR A LIGHT BUT DRESSY BREAKFAST. TO OFFER IT IN THE LATTER TWO ROLES, SPRINKLE THE FRUIT WITH PROSCIUTTO SLIVERS (ABOUT 2 TABLESPOONS PER SERVING).

Raspberry Sauce (below)

6 medium-size to large fresh ripe black figs

¼ cup crème fraîche or ricotta cheese

2 tablespoons fresh raspberries

Small fresh mint leaves or sprigs

RASPBERRY SAUCE

¾ cup fresh raspberries

3 tablespoons sugar

1 tablespoon framboise (optional)

2 teaspoons lemon juice

1. Prepare Raspberry Sauce; set aside.

2. Trim stems from figs. Starting from top of fruit, slice each fig lengthwise into quarters, cutting about three-fourths of the way through to bottom. Gently spread open "petals"; fill each fig with a sixth of the crème fraîche. Set aside.

3. With a spoon, swirl raspberry sauce in a decorative pattern over centers of 2 wide-rimmed dinner plates. Arrange 3 figs on each plate. Garnish with the 2 tablespoons raspberries and mint leaves.

RASPBERRY SAUCE

In a food processor, whirl the ¾ cup raspberries, sugar, framboise (if used), and lemon juice until smooth. Remove seeds from purée by rubbing it through a fine wire sieve set over a bowl; stir purée with a spoon or spatula to push it through.

PER SERVING: 322 calories, 12 g total fat, 7 g saturated fat, 25 mg cholesterol, 24 mg sodium, 55 g carbohydrates, 8 g fiber, 3 g protein, 131 mg calcium, 1 mg iron

SPARKLING SORBET

15 MINUTES

SIMPLE AND REFRESHING, THIS DESSERT GOES TOGETHER AT A MOMENT'S NOTICE. SCOOP PART OF A CARTON OF LEMON SORBET INTO INDIVIDUAL BOWLS; WHIP SPARKLING WINE INTO THE REST AND SERVE IT AS A FROSTY SAUCE. GRAPEFRUIT SORBET IS DELICIOUS PREPARED THIS WAY, TOO.

---

1 pint lemon sorbet

½ cup dry sparkling wine

½ cup fresh raspberries

10 small fresh basil or mint leaves

1. Scoop two-thirds of the sorbet (about 1⅓ cups) into 2 wide, shallow soup bowls, dividing equally.

2. In a food processor, whirl remaining sorbet until just soft enough to stir. Pour softened sorbet into a small bowl, add wine, and whip with a wire whisk just until blended. Pour sauce around sorbet in bowls, dividing equally. Sprinkle with raspberries and basil leaves.

PER SERVING: 276 calories, 0 g total fat, 0 g saturated fat, 0 mg cholesterol, 25 mg sodium, 60 g carbohydrates, 2 g fiber, 1 g protein, 32 mg calcium, 1 mg iron

MAPLE RUM PLUMS

FRESH PLUMS POACHED IN SPICED RUM AND MAPLE SYRUP MAY REMIND YOU OF AUTUMN IN NEW ENGLAND. SERVE THEM FOR DESSERT, ACCOMPANIED BY SHORTBREAD ROUNDS OR OTHER CRISP COOKIES; OR OFFER AT BREAKFAST, TOPPED WITH A LITTLE THICK CREAM.

25 MINUTES

4 ripe plums (any color), *each* **2 to 3 inches in diameter**

⅓ cup dark rum

⅓ cup maple syrup

1 or 2 cinnamon sticks (*each* **2½ to 3 inches long)**

1 teaspoon whole black or Sichuan peppercorns

½ teaspoon vanilla

1. Arrange plums in a single layer in a 2- to 3-quart pan. Add rum, syrup, cinnamon sticks, and peppercorns; then pour in enough water to cover plums. Cover and bring to a boil over high heat. Then uncover, reduce heat to a simmer, and simmer until fruit is tender when pierced (about 7 minutes).

2. Lift plums from pan and place 2 in each of 2 dessert bowls. Set aside. Bring cooking liquid to a boil over high heat; boil, stirring occasionally, until reduced to ½ cup (about 7 minutes).

3. Place pan of syrup in a larger pan filled with 2 to 3 inches of ice and water. Stir occasionally until syrup is chilled (about 2 minutes). Stir in vanilla.

4. Spoon syrup over plums; discard cinnamon sticks or use as a garnish. Serve plums warm or cool.

PER SERVING: 301 calories, 1 g total fat, 0 g saturated fat, 0 mg cholesterol, 6 mg sodium, 53 g carbohydrates, 3 g fiber, 1 g protein, 52 mg calcium, 1 mg iron

Maple Rum Plums

LEMON & ROSE POACHED PEACHES

FLAVORED WITH LEMON PEEL AND ROSE WATER, THIS DAINTY, FLORAL-SCENTED DESSERT IS GOOD FRESHLY MADE AND EVEN BETTER CHILLED. TO BEST APPRECIATE THE DELICATE FLAVOR, SERVE IT WITHOUT ACCOMPANIMENTS—EXCEPT, PERHAPS, A CUP OF SUITABLY FRAGRANT TEA (TRY DARJEELING, LIGHTLY STEEPED).

30 MINUTES

---

2 large peaches (about 1 lb. *total*)

⅔ cup water

¼ cup sugar

2 strips lemon peel (colored part only), *each* ½ by 1 inch

1 tablespoon orange-flavored liqueur

1 teaspoon rose water

Rose petals

6 to 12 fresh raspberries or blueberries

1. Place peaches side by side in a 2-quart pan. Add water, sugar, and lemon peel. Cover and bring to a boil over high heat. Then reduce heat to a simmer; simmer, covered, basting occasionally with cooking liquid, until fruit is tender when pierced (about 15 minutes).

2. Place pan of fruit and syrup in a large bowl filled with 3 to 4 inches of ice and water. Let stand, stirring occasionally, until syrup is cool and fruit is warm (about 10 minutes). Depending on size of bowl, you may need to replenish ice as it melts.

3. Lift peaches from syrup and place one peach in each of 2 large stemmed glasses or wide, shallow soup bowls. Stir liqueur and rose water into syrup; pour syrup over peaches. Sprinkle with rose petals and raspberries.

PER SERVING: 195 calories, 0 g total fat, 0 g saturated fat, 0 mg cholesterol, 0 mg sodium, 47 g carbohydrates, 3 g fiber, 1 g protein, 12 mg calcium, 0 mg iron

Lemon & Rose Poached Peaches

Index